BATTLE of the BOOKS

literary censorship in the public schools, 1950-1985

by
LEE BURRESS

The Scarecrow Press, Inc.
Metuchen, N.J., & London
1989

FRONTISPIECE: Citizens' Group burning 40 textbooks removed from Warsaw, Indiana, schools by school board. The textbook was *Values Clarification*. A report that the books were burned was in the *Warsaw Times-Union*, December 15, 1977. Photo by Michael Myers, *Warsaw Times-Union*, Warsaw, Indiana.

Permissions credits are listed in Acknowledgments

British Library Cataloguing-in-Publication data available.

Library of Congress Cataloging-in-Publication Data

Burress, Lee.
    Battle of the books : literary censorship in the public schools,
1950–1985 / by Lee Burress.
        p.   cm.
    Bibliography: p.
    Includes index.
    ISBN 0-8108-2151-6
    1. Censorship—United States—History—20th century.
2. Children's literature—Censorship—United States.   3. Young adult
literature—Censorship—United States.   4. School libraries—
Censorship—United States.   5. Public schools—Censorship—United
States.   6. Children—United States—Books and reading.   7. High
school students—United States—Books and reading.   I. Title.
Z658.U5B87   1989
098'.12'0973—dc19

                                                              88-30775

ACKNOWLEDGMENTS

Acknowledgment of permission to reprint passages from copyrighted material is made to the following persons and organizations. I am grateful to the persons and organizations below for permission to reprint their material.

Ellen Last for permission to quote from *Textbook Selection or Censorship: An Analysis of the Complaints Filed in Relation to Three Major Literature Series Proposed for Adoption in Texas in 1978*. Ph.D. dissertation, University of Texas, 1984. (Available from University Microfilms International, Ann Arbor, Michigan.)

Dorothy Thompson Weathersby for permission to quote from *Censorship of Literature Textbooks in Tennessee; A Study of the Commission, Publishers, Teachers, and Textbooks*. D.Ed. dissertation, University of Tennessee, 1975.

Kenneth L. Donelson and The Arizona Council of Teachers of English for permission to quote from the Arizona Survey of Censorship Problems, 1967.

James E. Davis for permission to quote from the Ohio Survey of Censorship Problems, 1982.

Limiting What Students Shall Read; A Report of a Study, sponsored by the Association of American Publishers, the American Library Association, and the Association for Supervision and Curriculum Development, 1981; reprinted by permission of the AAP, ALA, and ASCD.

The Philosophical Library, Inc., for permission to quote the definition of *sect* by E. Troeltsch in their *Encyclopedia of Religion*, 1945.

Richard Beach for permission to quote from his essay "Issues of Censorship and Research on Effects of and Response to Reading" from *Dealing with Censorship*, National Council of Teachers of English, 1979.

The University of California Press for permission to reproduce the chart from Marjorie Fiske's *Book Selection and Censorship*, 1959.

Lester Asheim and the *Wilson Library Bulletin* for permission to quote from an article titled, "Not Censorship but Selection," September 1953; © 1953 by the H. W. Wilson Company.

Ginn and Company for permission to quote a passage by Lionel Trilling from *American Literature* of the Ginn Literature Series by Edward J. Gordon and others. © Copyright 1964, by Ginn and Company (Xerox Corporation). Used by permission.

Barbara Parker and People for the American Way for permission to quote from the 1983–1984 survey and the New York regional office survey of 1980–1983 of school censorship problems.

Joseph E. Bryson and Elizabeth W. Detty for permission to quote from *Censorship of Public School Library and Instructional Material*, 1982.

Leanne Katz and the National Coalition Against Censorship for permission to quote from the July 1983 *Report on Censorship Litigation* and *Books on Trial*, January 1985.

Kirby Sprouls and the *Warsaw Times-Union* for permission to reprint the photograph in the frontispiece.

Nancy Larrick for permission to reprint the poem "City to a Young Girl" by Jody Caravaglia, taken from *Male and Female Under 18: Frank Comments from Young People About Their Sex Roles Today*, edited and with comments by Nancy Larrick and Eve Merriam. Published 1973 by Avon Books.

Excerpts from *Book Burning* by Cal Thomas. Copyright © 1983, pp. 14–15. Used by permission of Good News Publishers/Crossway Books, Westchester, Illinois 60153.

Excerpts from *The American Puritans* by Perry Miller. Copyright © 1956 by Perry Miller. Reprinted by permission of Doubleday & Company, Inc.

Ruth Charnes and The Council on Interracial Books for Children, Inc., for permission to reprint a portion of an editorial from the Council's *Bulletin*, Vol. 9, no. 2, 1978, p. 3.

Emily Dickinson's "The Robin's My Criterion for Tune," reprinted by permission of the publishers from *The Complete Poems of Emily Dickinson*, edited by Thomas H. Johnson, copyright 1951, 1955, 1979, 1983 by the President and Fellows of Harvard College. Also by permission of Little, Brown and Company from *The Complete Poems of Emily Dickinson*, edited by Thomas H. Johnson. Copyright 1929 by Martha Dickinson Bianchi; copyright © renewed 1957 by Mary L. Hampson.

TABLE OF CONTENTS

THE BATTLE OF THE BOOKS

This was but a prelude;
where books are burnt
human-beings will be burnt
in the end.
(Heinrich Heine, 1820)

INTRODUCTION

I BECAME INVOLVED in the problem of censorship in the 1950s while teaching at the College of Emporia (Kansas).

Congressman Ed Rees represented the Fourth Congressional District of Kansas at the time. He lived in Emporia and had been in public office all of his life. He is best known for legislation changing Armistice Day to Veterans' Day. During the 1950s he was a member of the Gathings Committee, which was established because of the belief that the cheap paperback books which had become available were a serious moral threat to the Republic. McCarthyism also no doubt contributed to the atmosphere of those years, with its belief that communism was subverting education.

The Gathings committee included several eminent persons: Emanuel Celler, Francis Walter, George P. Miller, Reva Beck Bosone, Louis E. Graham, Katherine St. George, Carroll D. Kearns, along with Edward Rees. E. C. Gathings was the chair of the committee. In 1952, the committee issued a majority report which advocated censorship. Emanuel Celler and Francis Walter issued a minority report disagreeing. George Miller abstained from an indication of approval or disapproval.

Ultimately the committee proposed legislation which would have established a federal censorship board. No book could move across state lines without approval of this board. Severe fines or imprisonment would have been imposed on anyone violating decisions of the board. The bill seemed clearly unconstitutional, and did not become law. But that a committee of the Congress would propose such a bill was astonishing to me.

The report of the Gathings committee struck several themes that have remained constant in the decades since. The con-

1

gressmen were unable to distinguish between books of considerable literary stature and books of little or no value. They severely
criticized, indiscriminately, such books as Caldwell's *God's Little
Acre*, *The Harem* by Louis Charles Royer, *Twilight Men—The
Story of a Homosexual* by Andre Tellier, *Strange Fruit* by Lillian
Smith, *She Made it Pay* by Les Scott, as well as *The Wayward
Bus* by John Steinbeck, *The Amboy Dukes* by Irving Shulman,
and *Don't Touch Me* by MacKinlay Kantor. One witness to the
committee said: ". . . since Hemingway and that group came
into vogue . . . colleges have quit teaching the young writers
how to write the stuff that the good clean magazines want. . . ."[1]

The report also emphasized the belief that reading allegedly
pornographic pocket books or comic books would lead to delinquency. *The Amboy Dukes* was a particular target, and several
law enforcement officials, school officials and psychiatrists, including Dr. Frederic Wertheim, criticized the book as contribut-
ing to delinquency. The book was the subject of much attempted
censorship in the 1950s by police and other officials, perhaps as a
result of its being mentioned in the Gathings report. But no court
ever held the book to be obscene. It is a serious and sad account
of boys growing up in the slums of a big city, left to themselves
while both parents worked in the defense factories of World War
II. The book deals with gang life in an explanatory fashion, and
criticizes a society in which adolescents are harassed by the police
and in the schools. It is a highly credible book; to blame it for the
delinquency of unsupervised poor young people in large cities is a
classic example of blaming the messenger for the message. While
the book is not great literature, it is a serious work of fiction that
merits reading. The situation described by the book remains current and is reflected week by week in the daily newspapers of New
York, Chicago, and Milwaukee. Since it presents the lives of
teenagers in a sympathetic way, it is not surprising that it was
popular among high school students; the book anticipated to
some degree the juvenile novel of later decades.

The Gathings report also charged that such books as *The
Amboy Dukes* were written for crassly commercial motives, that
decisions favoring freedom of the press by the eminent judge
Curtis Bok were influenced by his having relatives who owned
stock in publishing companies, including Bantam Books. The
charge that so-called pornographic materials are written and dis-

tributed out of profit motives continues to play a part in protests against those materials disliked by various critics, and they continue to give undocumented and probably vastly exaggerated estimates of the pornography industry as involving many billions of dollars.

Several clergymen testified against the alleged flood of pornographic paperback books. A representative of the Catholic National Organization for Decent Literature spoke of the "incalculable harm that is being done to the American society by the deliberate publication, widespread distribution, and open sale in food markets, drug stores, newsstands and many other retail outlets of literature that appeals to the lowest instincts of man." Another clergyman who testified against the "unconscionable purveyors of this profit-motivated slush" was the executive secretary of the Board of Temperance of the Methodist Church. Several other eminent clergymen testified—Presbyterian, Baptist, and other denominations. In the decades after the 1950s, representatives of these mainstream churches have begun to have more concern for freedom of the press.

The suspicion of paperback or pocket books has diminished somewhat since the 1950s, but at least one school system, in Anaheim, California, at one point forbade the use of any paperback book in the school system.

The Gathings committee chose not to reprint the testimony of representatives of the American Civil Liberties Union. The ACLU appeal for freedom of the press was merely briefly summarized. On the other hand, the committee chose to print in detail a letter which suggested that the influence of paperback books was so great that it was responsible for an epidemic of VD in the armed forces. The letter asserted: "The damage done to the youth of our nation and particularly the Armed Forces by the current literature is to me appalling. . . . I need only to remind you that the VD rate in Japan was 282 per thousand last month."[2] That books lead to VD has also been charged in recent years by Mel Gabler of Education Research Analysts. He has said repeatedly that "Until textbooks are changed, there is no possibility that crime, violence, VD, and abortion rates will do anything but continue to climb."[3]

The committee also struck a note that has been repeated in the intervening years, claiming that obscenity is a big business which floods the country with allegedly pornographic literature. Representative St. George said in the hearings of the committee: "Now the thing that has appalled me is that this stuff is very big business, that it is going out in millions, and that, as I see the picture, it has changed mores and morals of the country because after all, people can be judged by what they read."[4] The only evidence supplied to the committee to support the belief that "this stuff," meaning alleged obscenity, was a big business was testimony that some 300 million pocket books were sold each year. No testimony appeared that any significant fraction of the 300 million pocket books was in danger of being tried in the courts on obscenity charges. In fact, the committee report contained less than one hundred titles that were allegedly obscene. Even that was an absurd charge, and one that testimony by publishers contradicted.

Another feature of the charges of the committee, against comic books especially, was that pornography might well be a communist plot; there were also charges that comic books contained such other unpatriotic features as pacifism. As Bryson and Detty point out, objections to pacifism also appeared elsewhere in the 1950s.[5] In 1953 Mrs. Thomas J. White, a member of the Indiana textbook commission, believed the Tales of Robin Hood were communistic, as were references to the Quaker religion. Since Quakers did not believe in fighting, they helped communism. She was not successful in getting these materials removed. That she tried says something about the climate of opinion in the 1950s.

The committee also wrestled in an unsatisfactory way with the concept of obscenity. H. Ralph Burton, counsel for the committee, described the problem of defining obscenity in words which are still accurate, in spite of several Supreme Court decisions since that time, though the committee ignored his discussion:

> The common problem confronting the courts, and enforcement officers, in applying various statutes, whether it be a Federal, State, or local statute or ordinance, is the fact that while they, almost without exception, render it a crime to sell, distribute, exchange, exhibit, transport, publish, or possess obscene materials, the statute contains no definition or standard by which

the "obscenity" of a particular material may be determined. Usually, in an attempt at definition, the statute will contain a group of synonyms such as "lewd, lascivious, salacious, immoral, unchaste, or filthy." The courts have observed, time and again, that there is no possible objective standard by which "obscenity" may be determined, and it has been commonly held that the question of the obscenity of a particular material is a question of fact depending upon the facts and circumstances of each case. The briefest search of the court decisions with respect to "obscene" materials will indicate that there is no consistency in the decisions with respect to the same type of material from one period to another, or from one locale to another.[6]

In short, the report of the Gathings committee laid out the agenda for the attacks on books and other material in the public libraries and schools during the postwar decades. It also brought on stage a number of the actors in the book battles of the late twentieth century—ambitious politicians, well meaning clergymen, well meaning citizens (some of whom believe books cause VD), police and other law enforcement officials, some school officials, and a few representatives of defenders of intellectual freedom such as the American Civil Liberties Union. To have read the Gathings report was to be prepared for the conflicts of ensuing years over the nature and functions of books and their role in society.

I wrote a letter to the *Emporia Gazette*, pointing out how the bill proposed by the committee seemed to violate both the spirit and the letter of the First Amendment. When the *Gazette*, then managed by William Allen White's son, Bill White, did not run the letter, I inquired at the *Gazette* office and was told that they were waiting for a reply by Congressman Rees. Both letters finally appeared. As a result of my letter, telephone calls came to Luther Sharpe, the president of the college and a Presbyterian minister, urging that I be fired. Sharpe did not tell me of those telephone calls until I resigned from the college to take a position in Wisconsin. I was pleased at his defense of my right as a citizen to express my views in letters to the paper. Not all teachers in high schools or colleges have been so well treated.

Shortly after I came to the school which is now the University of Wisconsin, Stevens Point, a recent graduate returned to the campus during Christmas vacation to report that she had been instructed by her principal, in a Madison public high school, to remove *The Catcher in the Rye* from a reading list she had prepared for her students, because one parent had complained about it. Other teachers in the school system were allowed to retain the title on their reading lists.

Because I wondered how often teachers had such experiences, I asked The Wisconsin Council of Teachers of English to sponsor a study of censorship in the public schools of Wisconsin.

A questionnaire went to 1640 administrators and English teachers in Wisconsin; 600, or about 40 percent of the questionnaires, were returned. The resulting material was published by the Wisconsin Council as Special Bulletin No. 8: "How Censorship Affects the School."

There were a number of interesting results. Two doctoral dissertations were produced almost immediately, partially stimulated by the Wisconsin report.[7] A joint committee was formed by the National Council of Teachers of English with the American Association of School Librarians to survey a national sample of school librarians and English department chairmen. I wrote a report summarizing the returned questionnaires. The report was not published, in part because the AASL board found that its recommendations did not grow out of the survey, especially the recommendation that school staff members try to include a feature in union contracts ensuring academic freedom in the schools. The report, however, became available in the office of the National Council of Teachers of English and in the library at the University of Wisconsin, Stevens Point. It was used by later investigators of school censorship problems.

In 1973 I carried out a national survey of censorship pressures, sponsored by the Wisconsin Council of Teachers of English. The results were published as Special Bulletin No. 31 by the council. By 1977, the National Council of Teachers of English established another censorship committee with Professor Edward Jenkinson of Indiana University as chair. I was a member of the committee, and carried out a third national survey of censorship pressures, sponsored by the NCTE committee. The results of that survey were published as the second chapter in a book entitled *Dealing With Censorship*,[8] which was produced by the committee.

In 1982, I carried out a fourth national survey of censorship pressures, co-sponsored by the NCTE Committee Against Censorship and the Wisconsin Council of Teachers of English. While a full report of this fourth survey has not been published, much material from it has been used in various articles; that report has been drawn upon extensively for this book.

The activities of the National Council of Teachers of English in defense of intellectual freedom have been manifold. A partial summary of those activities is as follows:

1/ Formation of an ad hoc censorship committee, 1965–1968, along with the American Association of School Librarians, with Lee Burress and Georgia Cole as joint chairs.

2/ Formation of a standing committee against censorship, 1977—1st chair, E. Jenkinson; 2nd chair, Diane Shugert; 3rd chair, Lee Burress.

3/ Publications—Obscenity; the Law and the English Teacher, John P. Frank and Robert F. Hogan, 1966; Meeting Censorship in the School; A Series of Case Studies, John Hove, 1967; The Open Letter Taken from the Student's Right to Read, 1972; Student Press Rights, Robert Trager, 1974; Censorship: Don't Let It Become an Issue in Your Schools, 1978; Dealing with Censorship, James E. Davis, editor, 1979; Censorship and Guidelines, 12 authors, 1980; How to Deal with the Moral Majority, Lee Burress, Sheila Schwartz, and Geneva T. Van Horn, 1981; Censorship and Professional Guidelines, 1982; The Students' Right to Know, Lee Burress and Edward Jenkinson, 1982; The Students' Right to Read, 1982. In addition NCTE has published many articles on censorship and materials selection policies in its journals. Various regional affiliates of NCTE have also published articles and occasionally, as in Arizona, Wisconsin, Missouri, and Connecticut, devoted entire issues of affiliate journals to censorship.

4/ Conferences—Beginning at least as early as 1963 NCTE or its affiliates have planned entire conferences or sectional meetings of annual conferences on censorship. Many such meetings have been held.

5/ NCTE filed an amicus brief in the Supreme Court case originating in Island Trees, New York, and raised some money for that case. It is likely that NCTE might cooperate in the future in a similar way with key cases.

6/ NCTE belongs to the National Coalition Against Censorship. It has helped initiate regional coalitions against censorship in Wisconsin, Minnesota, and elsewhere.

7/ NCTE members have been actively engaged in testifying with regard to legislation before state book selection agencies, as Ed Jenkinson did in Texas in 1983, as Diane Shugart does in Connecticut, Lee Burress in Wisconsin, Ken Donelson in Arizona, Paul Slayton in Virginia, Ruth Lysne in Minnesota, as well as several other members in other states.

8/ NCTE has provided assistance to individual teachers who have called the organization in Urbana, IL. Affiliates have provided help in the various states.

9/ NCTE or its affiliates have sponsored several surveys of the frequency of censorship in the schools since 1963. Results have been published in several places.

10/ Many activities of the council are positive in nature and support intellectual freedom generally in the schools and in our society. An examination of the 56-page catalog of *Professional Publications for the Teacher of English and the Language Arts* will show the many contributions of NCTE toward intellectual freedom, not the least of which are substantial bibliographies of recommended books such as *Books for You: A Booklist for Senior High Students*, Robert C. Small, editor; *Guide to World Literature*, Warren Carrier and Kenneth Oliver; *Literature by and about the American Indian*, Anna Lee Stensland; *Black Literature for High School Students*, Barbara Dodds Stanford and Karima Amin. Many other titles might be cited.

There is an interesting sidelight on the name of the NCTE Committee. It was originally named the Censorship Committee. However, in 1978 a dairy farmer from Ohio telephoned me to state that he understood that I was an authority on censorship. There was, he said, a very bad book by Judy Blume in the local school, and he wondered if I would help him get rid of it. I asked him what was wrong with the book. He didn't really know specifically, but caught on that I was not very enthusiastic about getting rid of books by Judy Blume. He said, "Well, I guess I'm talking to the wrong guy." So the committee became the Committee Against Censorship.

The term "censorship," like the term "obscenity," is hard to define. Two somewhat differing definitions appear in the literature. Both agree that the operative element is the prevention of a communication. The definitions disagree, however, as to what further elements should be included. Should the term refer only to official agencies, the state or federal government? A lawyer, Howard N. Meyer, speaks of the "standard definition . . . as . . . interference by government agencies."[9] Meyer asserted that those citizens who urged that *Little Black Sambo* or *The Adventures of Huckleberry Finn* be removed from school libraries as racist books should not be called censors since they are not state officials.

As Jenkinson observed: ". . . most people who attempted to have books banned dislike being called censors. They maintain as parents or concerned citizens that they cannot be censors, since they lack the authority to remove books from the classroom or library shelves." As Jenkinson points out, they frequently cite the dictionary definition of censor as "an official who examines books, plays, etc. for the purpose of suppressing parts deemed objectionable on moral, political, military, or other grounds."[10] Mel and Norma Gabler insist they are not censors.

There is however a broader definition of censorship which includes any effort to prevent the fulfillment of a communication. Several contemporary scholars have used this broader definition. Typical of the broader definition is the one used by Bryson and Detty in their discussion of legal cases involving school censorship:

> Censorship—A process which limits access to books and materials based on value judgements or prejudices of individuals or groups. The act of censorship may be accomplished by (1) suppression of use, (2) removal of books or materials from the library or classroom, or (3) limiting access to library and instructional materials. Censorship withholds or limits the students' right to read, to learn, and to be informed and the teachers' right to academic freedom.[11]

Similar definitions may be found in the work of numerous other writers. Carolyn Peterson wrote: "Censorship is the attempt to influence teacher decisions on the selection and use of literature and other pertinent print material using other than purely professional criteria."[12] Peterson used the term "books" because she limited her study to works of literature. However, her definition is equally appropriate for audiovisual materials used in the schools.

One of the most frequently quoted broad definitions of censorship comes from an article written by Lester Asheim in 1953. Asheim distinguished between censorship and selection as follows:

> Selection . . . begins with a presumption in favor of liberty of thought; censorship, with a presumption in favor of thought control. Selection's approach to the book is positive, seeking its value in the book as a book and in the book as a whole. Censorship's approach is negative, seeking vulnerable characteristics wherever they can be found—anywhere within the book, or even outside it. Selection seeks to protect the right of the reader to read; censorship seeks to protect—not the right—but the reader himself from fancied effects of his reading. The selector has faith in the intelligence of the reader; the censor has faith only in his own.
>
> In other words, selection is democratic while censorship is authoritarian, and in our democracy we have traditionally tended to put our trust in the selector rather than in the censor.[13]

Professional methods of choosing the material for school or library differ significantly from the methods used by censors. Censors are primarily negative in their approach to learning resources. They wish to prevent the dissemination of particular information, or the circulation of particular books or films. Edwin Castagna defined censorship as ". . . any action by officials of government, church, or other organizations, or by private individuals, which, by legal actions, coercion, threat, or persuasion, prevents expression or communication."[14] Moreover, censors wish to make the result of their actions permanent. That is why book burning is so powerful a symbol of censorship, a burned book is permanently destroyed.

Book burning illustrates the profoundly negative nature of

censorship. It has actually occurred in the U.S.: *Slaughterhouse-Five* was burned at Drake, North Dakota, in 1974; *Of Mice and Men* at Oil City, Pennsylvania, August 1977; and *Values Clarification* at Warsaw, Indiana, December 1977. In January 1981 at Omaha, Nebraska, a pile of books was burned, including the *National Geographic, Daffy Duck* comic books, and *Fifty True Tales of Terror.* Copies of *The Living Bible* were burned in May 1981 at Gastonia, North Carolina, along with other materials.[15] People who burn books are insensitive, to say the least, to the frightening associations in many minds with the massive book burnings by the Nazis in Germany in May, 1933. The Germans forgot or ignored the words of the poet Heinrich Heine, who wrote in 1820: ". . . where books are burnt, human beings will be burnt in the end." With the German precedent of 1933 before us, we Americans forget Heine's words at our own peril.

In contrast to censorship, book selection is positive in its approach to learning resources. Librarians or teachers, acting professionally, choose from available books for the purpose of having the books read; they do not single out some title in an effort to prevent it from being read. They act, in short, in positive ways, not in negative ways. For example, a teacher in a junior-senior English novel class chose the novel *To Kill a Mockingbird* with its heroic lawyer and also chose *The Magician*, which presents a corrupt lawyer. Both novels offer realistic pictures of our society and contrast integrity and the lack of integrity in professional life. Both books use contemporary language and vividly concrete detail. They are attractive to young adults and well-suited to the purpose for which they were chosen, but both books have been attacked by critics who have apparently paid little or no attention to the relationship of these books to their educational purposes.

The librarian does not attempt to impose on readers a single standard of literary excellence, of scientific correctness, of good taste in language or political orthodoxy. Librarians attempt to choose books that will meet a broad range of reading interests and needs. Thus a good library should span from Hitler's *Mein Kampf* on the one hand to Marx's *Das Kapital* on the other, with an assortment of other political writers in between. The librarian's own political views are irrelevant.

There was a conflict in the Madison, Wisconsin public

library over *Calories Don't Count*. Certain dietitians at the University of Wisconsin argued, probably correctly, that the book was not scientifically accurate. But the effort to remove the book was resisted on the grounds that readers have a right to decide for themselves. The book *Manhood Ceremony* was challenged at Wisconsin Rapids, Wisconsin on the grounds, correctly, that it lacked literary excellence and contained much offensive language. The book was retained, as a popular book, and, as one reviewer said, a good example of its literary type—unfortunately a popular American type—the novel of horror and suspense.

Censorship is contrary to the practices of this democratic republic. It is a kind of vigilantism, an attempt to bypass the normal procedures of our society for the establishment of the curriculum and the selection of learning materials. The constitutions and legislatures of the various states determine the procedures and policies for selection of the state superintendent of instruction, the election of the school board, and guidelines for the curriculum. The citizens, by constitutional procedures, choose the members of the state legislature and the school board, and delegate to these officials the authority to control the curriculum and the book selection processes. But the censors frequently wish to bypass these procedures, and use pressure group tactics to eliminate the books or courses to which they object.

Not only is the process undemocratic, but the intent seems undemocratic, since its purpose is to withhold information from the reader. When access to information is restricted, it is less possible for informed citizens to make proper choices. If citizens do not have accurate information about the status of minority group persons, as described in such books as *Black Like Me* or *Down These Mean Streets*, how can they make reasonable decisions when they vote? Censors have attempted to withhold information about migrants (as in *The Grapes of Wrath*), information about drugs, about human reproduction, about theories of evolution, about sociology and anthropology, and about views of American history that the censors regard as unorthodox. This effort to withhold information is undemocratic since it prevents students from becoming fully informed members of this society, able to decide for themselves how to vote, and able to decide for themselves what is right. The ultimate purpose of withholding information is to limit the freedom of choice of the reader or student by controlling access to information.

There is a tendency among censors to conceal the fact that they are withholding information. Books were removed from the library at Island Trees, New York, after the librarian had left the school for the day.

In contrast to the secrecy with which censors frequently act is the public method by which professional persons evaluate and publicize their evaluations of literature in the selection aids and professional journals of the various disciplines of learning. Openness in action is an important characteristic of our democratic republic. The sunshine laws passed in most states ensure that committees that prepare the curriculum and select materials follow open and public methods of action.

The censor acts in nonprofessional ways. Censors do not consider the value or meaning of a work as a whole; they make arbitrary decisions about a book based on some single aspect of it—its language, for example, or a single episode, as in the recent case of the book *Foster Child*, by Marion Bauer, which was attacked because it describes, with decorous concreteness of detail, the sexual abuse of a foster child by a foster father. Professional reviews of this book spoke highly of the book's presentation of the life of a foster child in today's world.

The censors may attack a book because of the associations or life of the author. *The Grapes of Wrath* has been attacked on the false grounds that Steinbeck was a communist. The censors have ignored the great weight of scholarly opinions about the value of this book. Censors often have not read the entire book, but concentrate on some feature they regard as objectionable. Reviews are now being distributed nationally that list specific pages censors find objectionable, thus making it possible to object to the book without examining it as a whole.[16]

In contrast to these nonprofessional ways of dealing with books is the effort of the librarian or teacher to apply the principles of book selection that are part of their professional training.

There is a certain irrationality in some censorship activity. Some censors seem to think that use of a taboo word, or a reference to an unpleasant or tragic aspect of life, will automatically produce it in reality. As in the folk tale the phrase "Open sesame"

caused a wall to open on a great treasure, some persons think that
to say "flat tire," or "cancer," "tuberculosis," or "syphilis" will
produce those repellent aspects of life. In fact, saying those words
doesn't produce the reality, nor does avoiding such words protect
us from those unpleasant realities. The English speaking world
found the word "graveyard" very unpleasant; it substituted the
word "cemetery," but the experience of taking a loved one to the
cemetery is just as heartbreaking as taking a loved one to a graveyard. And adopting the contemporary euphemism "Memorial
Park" does not offer the heart much balm.

Finally, some censorship is caused by fear. Marjorie Fiske
pointed this out in her study of censorship in California. In a
country where teachers are dismissed for using some of the greatest literature of the twentieth century, such fear is understandable. On the whole, however, contrary to the image of the teacher or librarian as a timid, self-deprecatory person, it is quite clear
from the studies of the actual holdings of school libraries that
many librarians and teachers select the best of books without fear
of would-be censors. And in many schools, those selections are
upheld by the administration and the school board.

Julia T. Bradley, a lawyer, wrote a detailed analysis of the
differences between censorship and selection and concluded
there were significant differences between the two. She defined
censorship as "an act whereby one group imposes its value judgement upon another. . . ."[17] Bradley emphasized the desire of the
censor to make permanent and absolute decisions. The censor
wants permanently to end the opportunity of others to judge
books for themselves. In contrast, says Bradley, selection is a
process in which a series of relative choices are made. The only
limitations are budgetary. The selection process always involves
the question, is this the most useful book for a given purpose? If a
book is not chosen at one time, it is not destroyed; it is still
available for use later. Bradley's discussion is well worth reading.
It is significant that a lawyer believes that a legally defensible
distinction may be made between censorship and selection.

In this book a broad definition of censorship will be used.
Censorship is described as those activities whose goal is the removal of books, periodicals, films, or other materials from classroom use, from the school library, or from lists of recommended
titles, for the non-professional reasons described above.

The views expressed in this book are mine; the various professional groups or persons cited above contributed greatly to my education. I owe much to them, but they should not be held responsible for errors or limitations in this study.

1 MONTELLO, WISCONSIN: A CASE STUDY IN CENSORSHIP

MONTELLO, WISCONSIN, is a small town about fifty miles north of Madison. The town is north of the best farming region in the state, but there are prosperous dairy farms in the vicinity, along with Christmas tree plantations, some tourist resorts and a considerable number of homes of retired persons who have built on nearby lakes or in the pleasant pine woods.

During the 1979–80 school year a student checked out four books by Judy Blume, including *Then Again, Maybe I Won't*; *Are You There God? It's Me, Margaret*; and *Deenie*. Apparently because of a decision by the student's parent, the books were not returned. The school superintendent, Ronald Ertner, asked the district attorney for assistance in retrieving the books. When the district attorney was informed that the value of the books was about ten dollars apiece, he refused to take action and advised the school superintendent to seek redress in small claims court. Understandably, no further action was taken.

In the 1980–81 school year, a challenge was filed against the book *The Magician* by Sol Stein, which was used in an English class. The English teacher had taken the precaution of sending home with each student in the class a brief description of the book and a parental permission slip. Of the twenty-five students, twenty returned signed permission slips; the teacher made an alternate assignment for the students whose parents refused permission to read the book, along with class time to discuss the alternate assignment. However, these precautions did not prevent a challenge from being filed.

Excerpts of *The Magician* considered most objectionable were distributed in the Montello community by unknown persons. These excerpts, taken out of context, completely misrepresented the book. As a protest against the excerpting process by which the book was attacked, Gene Conrad, a local newspaper editor, then distributed excerpts from the Bible, showing how that book could be similarly misrepresented by such an irrational process. He also announced that if *The Magician* were removed from use, he would file a formal challenge against the Bible.

The actions of the person who challenged the book and the defense of freedom of thought by Gene Conrad produced an outpouring of letters to the Marquette County, Wisconsin, *Tribune*; the Portage, Wisconsin, *Register*; and to some degree also to Milwaukee and Madison newspapers. There were more than 100 newspaper stories or letters as well as a two-hour radio debate by persons involved in the episode.

The protesting letters referred to the book as trash, filth, un-American, unchristian, filled with obscenity, and pornographic. A somewhat typical letter in the *Tribune* for February 12, 1981, is as follows:

Dear Editor,

After reading various letters to the Editor defending the anti-Christ pornographer Sol Stein's *The Magician*, foisted upon the public school children—it makes me wonder just how much lower morality can slide to be like unto Sodom and Gomorrah!

As Moses stated, ". . . Their foot shall slide in due time" (Deut. 32:35). If only those do-gooders were so ready to defend prayer in our schools and the Pledge of Allegiance to Our Flag instead of a smutty book like *The Magician* authored by an anti-Christ "Whose mouths must be stopped, who subvert whole houses, teaching things which they ought not, for filthy lucre's sake. . . . Wherefore rebuke them sharply, that they may be sound in faith; not giving heed to Jewish fables, and the commandments of men, that turn from the truth" (Titus 1:11,13 and 14).

This is another prime example where an unassumable [sic] minority foists immorality common to their ilk upon an impressionable majority. Jesus warned of them, "It were better for Him that a milestone were hanged about his neck and He cast into the sea, than that He should offend one of these little ones" (Luke 17:2). As it now appears—there will be a shortage of milestones—and standing room only at the bottom of the sea.

Not all letters struck an anti-semitic note in attacking the book. A more common theme was objection to the book's so-called bad language and supposed sexual frankness. There was also objection to the book because of its criticism of the American legal system and because of its supposed negativism.

The school had in existence a carefully thought out review procedure, because of the efforts of the school superintendent. A majority of the review committee were local citizens, not staff members of the school, appointed by the school board after recommendation by the school superintendent. The committee was in existence before the challenge was filed. It was chaired by the local Methodist minister.

After reviewing the book, the committee recommended by a vote of 5–2 that the book be retained in use, and the school board accepted the recommendation after what was reported in the press as a somewhat contentious public meeting. One news report stated that the discussion lasted "nearly ninety minutes and was punctuated by shouting, catcalls, and scripture reading from the Bible."[1]

In February 1981, shortly after the decision was made to retain *The Magician,* ten persons came to the school libraries and checked out 33 books.[2] They reportedly had a list from which they searched for titles in the school libraries. They were unwilling to explain the source of the list. The school district had at that time no policy concerning the use of books by citizens, and the adults were allowed to check the books out.

A perhaps atypical feature of the Montello affair was that one member of the school staff telephoned a member of the Wisconsin Intellectual Freedom Coalition. The staff member, a teacher, reported that the books had been checked out and that there were allegations that they would not be returned. The 33 books were:

MONTELLO HIGH SCHOOL, 2/16/81

Abortion Rap—Diane Schulder
The Diary of a Young Girl—Anne Frank
The Baby Broker—Lynne McTaggart
Catch-22—Joseph Heller
The Catcher in the Rye—J.D. Salinger

The Great Gatsby—F. Scott Fitzgerald
Growing Up Absurd—Paul Goodman
Hard Feelings—Don Bredes
Jamie—Jack Bennett
Legislated Learning—Arthur E. Wise
No Bed of Roses—Joan Fontaine
Nobody Knows My Name—James Baldwin
The Outsiders—S.E. Hinton
Rape: The Bait and the Trap—Jean Scott MacKeller
Richie—Thomas Thompson
The Rights of Students—Alan H. Levine and Eve Cary
Runaway Teens—Arnold Madison
Shockwave Rider—John Brunner
The Teenage Body Book—Charles Wibbelsman
To Hell with the Kids—Gruhlke
When the Legends Die—Hal Borland

MONTELLO'S FOREST LANE ELEMENTARY SCHOOL, 2/16/81

Adam's Daughter—Gertrude Samuels
The Diary of a Young Girl—Anne Frank
Dave's Song—Robert McKay
Diary of a Frantic Kid Sister—Hila Colman
Mother's Guide to Young Years Library—Thomas
My First Love and Other Disasters—Pascal
The Outsiders—S.E. Hinton
Run, Shelley, Run—Gertrude Samuels
Starring Sally J. Freedman as Herself—Judy Blume
Who Wants to be Alone?—John Craig

Coincidentally, the Wisconsin Intellectual Freedom Coalition was holding a meeting of its executive committee the next day, at Madison, Wisconsin. At that meeting, a short resolution was adopted opposing the withdrawal of the books. The resolution was telephoned to most of the important Wisconsin media, including newspapers in Madison and Milwaukee, the Associated Press, the state radio network news bureau, and several of the major TV stations in the state. At least twelve news agencies were informed of the Montello event. CBS, NBC, and other national media ultimately reported on this event.

While the WIFC did not know the names of the persons who checked out the books, the press soon found out. In a short time some of those persons, greatly to their surprise, found themselves being asked by TV and print news reporters why they had taken the books and whether they intended to return them or to keep them, as some reports indicated.

The publicity seemed to have been quite surprising to the ten persons involved in the incident, and not welcome. An important role in this event was played by Gene Conrad, the editor of the local weekly paper, the Marquette County *Tribune*. Conrad ran a series of editorials condemning the action of the persons who had checked out the books.

Perhaps as a result of the publicity, the book challengers, who called themselves the Concerned Citizens, announced that they would return the books and would use the school system's formal method of filing challenges against the books. Ultimately they did file challenges against ten of the books.

The book controversy preceded a school board election, which was scheduled for April 7, 1981. Before the election, on March 7, 1981, the state radio station at Madison, Wisconsin scheduled a debate on the Montello situation for the weekly Saturday morning two-hour public forum.

The librarian of the high school, in her first year out of college, and the writer of this report were on the program, along with Bea Weiss, a member of the school board, and Charles Solterman, a candidate for a seat on the school board.

In the course of the two-hour discussion over station WHA, Bea Weiss allegedly charged a biology teacher in the high school with advocating the use of marijuana. There is only one biology teacher in the Montello High School, and he brought suit over this allegation, with the aid of the Wisconsin Education Association Council, the local union to which most of the teachers belonged. He won the suit.

According to an article in the Milwaukee *Journal*, which appeared some time after the events described above, a local citizen became quite concerned about this conflict and was instrumental in getting candidates to run for the school board whom he believed to be well-qualified and who would support the school's procedure for book selection.

At the election, the two pro–censorship candidates, Bea

Weiss and Charles Solterman, were defeated. They received about 400 votes. Two persons who campaigned on anti-censorship positions received 1200 votes.

The challenged books were referred to a review committee composed of some school staff members and some citizens of the local community, with the local Methodist minister as chair. The committee recommended that *The Magician* continue in use.

An interesting feature of the conflict over *The Magician* was the role played by the publisher and author. The teacher who used the book telephoned the publisher, Dell, to ask for legal assistance. She was never able to talk to any person in authority. Therefore, I tried to phone Dell. No lawyer or person of managerial status would talk to me. I was finally, after several telephone calls, referred to Doubleday and Company, which, I was informed, now owned Dell and would make any decisions.

After repeated calls, I talked to an apparently very young and insecure lawyer at Doubleday; I told him about the conflict at Montello, that the book *The Magician*, published by Dell, was widely being charged with being obscene, and that excerpts out of context were being distributed in the community. I suggested that the company ought to assist the teacher who had selected the book and now needed support. The Doubleday lawyer reported that his superiors could offer no help. Apparently teachers who select books from Dell or Doubleday are not likely to get help from these publishers in censorship situations.

When Sol Stein, the author of *The Magician*, learned of the attack on his book, he offered to send one paperback copy of the book to any household in the school district. One of the things that frequently happens when a book is challenged is that copies of the book get very hard to find. Many libraries have only one or two copies of a given title. The review committee, frequently composed of seven to ten persons, probably gets all the available copies for their use. It is therefore difficult for the book to get wide distribution. It is not unusual for all the available copies of challenged books to sell out in a given region, as several reports have shown.[3] Sol Stein's willingness to undertake distribution was very useful and quite amusing.

One of the results of the distribution was illustrated on a national TV program devoted to the Montello case. A local housewife who was interviewed said that when she saw the excerpts from the book, she thought it was terrible that such a book was in use in the schools. But when she got a copy and read the whole book she changed her mind and saw that the excerpts in their context in the whole book were not objectionable. The book, taken as a whole (to quote Chief Justice Burger), was quite worthwhile, she asserted, and quite appropriate for classroom use.

There was some concern, before the school board meeting at which the review committee was to report, that there might be violence at that meeting. One reason for this fear was the possibility that a Wisconsin group called the Posse Comitatus might be involved in the book controversy. In the course of the WHA forum discussion of the Montello conflict, the moderator asked Charles Solterman if he was a member of the Posse Comitatus. He said that he was not.

However, an ad was placed in the Oxford, Wisconsin *Shopper's Newsletter* by a local citizen advocating the views of the Posse. That was the same person who wrote the letter cited above attacking the books and advocating their removal. A number of citizens in Montello believe that the Posse generally supported the removal of the challenged books.

The Posse Comitatus (a Latin phrase meaning "the power of the county") is a Wisconsin group somewhat similar to the Ku Klux Klan. Representatives of the Posse deny connection with the Klan, but persons allegedly representing the Klan have been reported in Wisconsin newspapers as seeking connection with the Posse.

The Posse ad (which appeared in the Oxford, Wisconsin, *Shopper's Newsletter* for February 7, 1981) is clearly anti-Semitic. It refers to Eisenhower as a Jew and to "Jew controlled news and traitors in all levels of government." It refers to the "Jew international banker," to the "Jewish master plan to destroy Christian America," and includes a host of other anti-Semitic details.

Another Posse ad appeared in the Oxford *Shopper's Newsletter* for February 25, 1981. A copy of it is included here (see pp. 23–25). Few teachers or librarians would agree that this cartoon describes what in fact is happening in the public school. It is clear, however, that the ad's criticism of the schools is intended for national distribution.

America's schools are no longer public schools for educating children. They have instead become "Government Centers for Indoctrination." These government "schools" surreptitiously introduce your children into drugs, sexual immorality, rebellion against parents, humanism, marxism, and communism. Unbelievable? Not at all. The evidence is all about you. Do you want to save your children or your grandchildren from destruction? These three books will tell you how. Order one or all today from: **America's Promise, Box 5334, Phoenix, Arizona 85010.**

#1. **Change Agents in the Schools**, by Barbara M. Morris, 280 pages $8.00
#2. **The Hate Factory** (schools), by Erica Carle, 74 pages   3.00
#3. **Vaccination, the Silent Killer**, by Honorof & McBean, 124 pages   3.00
    Order any at the above prices or all three for $12, postage paid to you

NAME................................ ADDRESS ....

CITY, STATE, ZIP ....

CIRCLE ORDER: #1 #2 #3 DATE .... AMOUNT ENCLOSED $ ....

BY LAW OF

Posse Comitatus

United States Citizens for Constitutional Rights

REDEEM THE REPUBLIC!

"If My people (Israelites), which are called by My name (Christians), shall humble themselves, and pray, and seek My face, and turn from their wicked ways, then will I hear from heaven, and will forgive their sin, and will heal their land."
II Chronicles 7:14

James P. Wickstrom

NATIONAL DIRECTOR OF COUNTER INSURGENCY OF POSSE'S OF AMERICA

In GOD We Trust

Posse Comitatus
Post Office Box 31
Evansville, Wi 53536

U.S. CONSTITUTION

One disturbing feature of Posse thought and action is the threat of guns to defend Posse ideas and principles. Many Posse members are reported to have well-supplied bunkers with guns and ammunition. There have been several conflicts between the police in Wisconsin and members of the Posse.

For these reasons, there was fear that Posse members would come armed to the school board meeting. There were therefore several policemen in the audience when the report was made. While the meeting was very tense, no guns were displayed. At least one school board member went to the police station after the meeting to request an escort home. Other school board members reported that they were followed home by strange cars, down dark and lonely rural Wisconsin roads. There was, however, no overt violence.

The thirty-three books were finally returned, although ten were returned not to the school library but to the board members on the grounds that they were too objectionable to be in the school library.

One book was finally disapproved by the review committee: *Hard Feelings* by Don Bredes; two books, *Happy Endings Are All Alike* by Sandra Scoppetone, and *Rape: The Bait and the Trap* by Jean S. MacKeller, were put on a shelf for restricted use until they could be replaced with presumably better books on the same subject.

Some persons argue that parental objection to a book, periodical, or film used in the schools is not in itself censorship. The challenges do constitute pressure which, in some schools at least, erodes the willingness of the school to provide the best learning materials for students. A confidential respondent reported to me that after the Montello episode, a nearby school quietly removed *The Magician* and several other books from the school library. The removal was made by the superintendent and the librarian. How many of those occurrences there were cannot positively be known, but it has been obvious for several years that when a book is attacked in one school, newspaper publicity makes the title well-known, and the book is then challenged or quietly removed in a number of other places. Undoubtedly, that has happened to *The Catcher in the Rye*, to *Go Ask Alice*, and to many other books.

Other public controversies have occurred at Drake, North

Dakota in 1973; at Neillsville, Wisconsin in 1974; in Tell City, Indiana in 1981; in St. David's, Arizona in 1982; and in several other places. Perhaps the most dramatic confrontation over school books occurred in Kanawha County, West Virginia, in 1974. Five rural elementary schools were dynamited, as was the office building of the Board of Education. School buses were accompanied to school by state patrolmen because of rifle fire; a car owned by parents who continued to send their children to school was fire-bombed. Telephone threats harassed other parents and tried to intimidate them into boycotting the schools. Several businesses were picketed, including the public transit facilities, a Union Carbide plant, and a department store owned by a school board member. Coal miners struck the mines briefly as a protest against materials used in the schools; one of the clergymen who led the protests went to jail for conspiring to bomb the schools. At a school board meeting on December 12, 1974 several citizens at the meeting carried placards announcing, "We are KKK members." At the end of the meeting the superintendent, assistant superintendent and two school board members were physically attacked by protesters. The superintendent was maced by a woman in the audience. A deputy superintendent suffered permanent loss of hearing as a result of the attack.

Several national organizations became involved in the controversy. Robert Doran, actor and leader of a California anti-pornography group, Citizens for Decency Through Law, acted as leader of the protest movement for some time. The Gablers also participated in the struggle. NEA held a public hearing, which resulted in a clear and sensitive report concerning the conflict.[4]

On the whole, these public controversies are relatively infrequent, compared with the increasingly common requests by individuals that a book be removed from use in the classroom, from the library, or from a list of recommended titles. These requests are usually made quietly, and dealt with quietly. Indeed, one librarian wrote: "We have no problems with censorship, we simply remove the book quietly."

Carolyn Peterson studied 308 publicly reported controversies over book use that occurred between 1968 and 1975.[5] She demonstrated that there were many times more quiet efforts to remove books than publicly reported ones. She believed that the public controversies had a more severe effect on education than the quiet day-by-day censorship pressures that are increasingly experienced by school staff members. That belief would be hard to test empirically, though undoubtedly the immediate effect on public education in Kanawha County, West Virginia was quite traumatic, as many observers have pointed out. There is no doubt a continuum between many quiet events and those that receive maximum publicity, as in Kanawha County, West Virginia, or in Montello, Wisconsin. Both ends of the continuum present severe impediments to the continued development of an effective American school system.

In addition to the quiet removal of books as a result of publicity, a significant number of books are challenged and removed through the schools' reconsideration processes.[6] As a result of those challenges, many good or relevant or great books are removed from use in schools. If censorship is defined as removing a title from a recommended list, removing a book from classroom use, or removing a book from a library, it is clear that much of it occurs in today's school systems.

2 A SURVEY OF THE CENSORSHIP SITUATION: SOURCES, OBJECTIONS, INCREASES IN CENSORSHIP ACTIVITY

AS THE PAPERBACK REVOLUTION brought into the public schools a wide variety of the realistic literature of the twentieth century, objections of the sort that occurred at Montello began to develop. In addition to the ready availability of the more contemporary literature, several other forces began to play upon the public schools.

The increasing number of complaints from some sections of the public were immediately noticed by staff members in the schools—teachers and librarians as well as administrators. Many school people attempted at first to meet the complaints quietly and silently, in the belief that publicity would only increase the difficulties experienced by the schools. The National Education Association for several years in the 1950s and 1960s conducted an informal poll of complaints experienced by school administrators, but this information was not published. On one occasion, I was given an opportunity to examine the file of information in the Washington office of the NEA about complaints concerning books, but I was asked not to publicize this information. The NEA office, and many persons involved in education, believed that to publicize efforts to censor school books would result in additional censorship pressures on whatever titles were mentioned.

Some librarians still believe that the best strategy for dealing with censorship attempts is to give such efforts minimum publicity. They are therefore unwilling to report the names of challenged titles or the frequency with which challenges occur in their institutions. Generally, however, as the Office for Intellectual Freedom of the American Library Association and the NEA office for teacher rights currently demonstrate, most agencies concerned with intellectual freedom now attempt to use the maximum of publicity.[1]

It is true that a censorship episode concerning a given title in one community sometimes results in the same title being removed from schools in neighboring communities. Nevertheless, unless the general public knows what is going on, the censors will win the day. On the whole, the widest publicity seems most protective for intellectual freedom.

Several approaches have been used to gather information about censorship problems in the schools. Most common has been a questionnaire addressed to English departments or to school librarians. Some investigators have used interviews. One investigator studied reports in the American Library Association's *Newsletter on Intellectual Freedom*.[2] Another studied holdings in a selected sample of Colorado school libraries.[3] While most have examined the school library or the texts used in the schools, one investigation concentrated on the most frequently attacked book in the postwar years, *The Catcher in the Rye*.[4] Many of these investigations were carried out as doctoral studies. Two very interesting dissertations took a somewhat different approach. Dorothy Thompson Weathersby examined several literary anthologies selected for use in Tennessee, and compared the poems, plays, or works of fiction included in the anthologies with the original texts. Much censorship was revealed by this study.[5] Another dissertation, by Ellen Last, examined the objections of the several critics in Texas, including Mel and Norma Gabler, to the literary anthologies proposed for adoption in Texas in 1978.[6] A list of other graduate dissertations and theses may be found in the appendix.

These many sources of information provide reasonably well-demonstrated answers to the following questions:

1/   What are the sources of the censorship pressures? That is, who are the would-be censors?
2/   What are the objections that cause censors to wish some

work of literature removed? What kind of literature is
attacked?
3/ Are the censorship pressures increasing?
4/ Are there regional differences in the frequency of censorship?
5/ Do race, class, and cultural differences play a role in censorship pressures?
6/ What is the result of the censorship pressure?

In this and following chapters an effort will be made to answer
these questions.

1/ *What are the sources of the censorship pressures? Who are the
censors?*

The immediate sources today of the censorship pressures on
teachers and librarians are the parents of the students in the
schools. Supporting the parents may be a local group; beyond the
local group may be a national organization, such as the John
Birch Society, the Educational Research Analysts, Inc. of Longview Texas (the organization managed by Mel and Norma
Gabler), or the Moral Majority, Inc. The various organizations
communicate via a national hot line, by newsletters, or other
publications. The Educational Research Analysts, Inc. was reported in 1979 to have a mailing list of 10,000 names.[7]
    Usually the complaining parent does not report an affilia-
tion with either a local group or a national organization. When
there was a complaint about Studs Terkel's book *Working* at the
Kettle Moraine public schools in Wisconsin, teachers there believed that a local group initiated the action. When members of
that group came to the board meetings that dealt with this issue,
they were careful to sit in different parts of the meeting room,
according to the observation of the teachers in that school system.
No one in challenging the use of *Working* mentioned an
organization.
    When Judith Schroeder of DePere, Wisconsin wrote a let-
ter asking that the eight school boards in Brown County, Wisconsin reconsider four books by Judy Blume, the address on the
letterhead was that of a group named Parents Aiding Education.

Schroeder disclaimed any relationship to a national group, however.

National surveys in the 1960s listed relatively few reports linking organizations with complaints. The Ahrens study of 1965 reported nine local organizations and four national organizations (two reports of DAR, one of Ku Klux Klan, and one from an Eastern States Evaluation Organization) as sources of objections.[8] The NCTE study of 1966 elicited only one report of an organization as the source of a complaint. However, by the time of a 1982 survey, 17 percent of the questionnaires returned indicated an organizational source of the censorship pressure. In 1985 organizations are much more willing to indicate their stand publicly than earlier in the postwar years.

Nevertheless, the person whom the English teacher or librarian finds complaining about a book is most likely to identify herself or himself simply as a parent, and is unlikely to refer to an organizational affiliation. The arguments offered for removing the book may well be the identical arguments offered nationally by the Moral Majority, for example in the book *Book Burning* by Cal Thomas, a national officer of the Moral Majority. But no reference may be made by the complaining parent to the ultimate source of the arguments. Undoubtedly there are many parents who find themselves disturbed by some book used in the school, and who act quite independently on their feelings. Many of these people, as will be noted later, are quite amenable to reasonable explanations for the use of material that seems new or startling to them as parents.

Since parents have direct access to the books used by the students in the schools it is not surprising that they are the persons most likely to confront a teacher or librarian with a request that a book be removed from use in the library. Because parents have less access to periodicals, to films and to school newspapers, they are less likely to complain about these materials. Exceptions to this principle—complaints about the film *The Lottery* or the periodical *Ms.*—are probably the result of information from newsletters or other publications of national organizations.

As a number of incidents make clear, quite frequently a single complaint by a parent results in a book being censored. Where the school has a policy and has established procedures for dealing with complaints about learning materials, the outcome may be different. But it is unpleasant testimony to the lack of bravery of some school administrators that they are willing to remove material on the basis of a single complaint.[9]

The various studies of this subject suggest that across the decades the proportion of parents who are the source of complaints has increased and the proportion of complaints from within the school has declined. Nevertheless, the second most frequent source of censorship in the schools remains members of the school staff—administrators, teachers or librarians. However, the schools have become more resistant to censorship pressures, so that the pressures increasingly come from outside the schools, rather than from within. The 1982 survey that I carried out showed the following distribution of complaints:

TABLE 1

Source	No. of Objections		Percent of Objections	
	1982	1966	1982	1966
Parent	328	102	65.3	48.6
The School				
librarian	28	16	5.5	7.6
teacher	42	35	8.3	16.7
English Dept. Chair	1	4	.2	1.9
administrator	13	32	2.6	15.2
board of education	11	1	2.2	.5
Total	95	88	18.8	41.9
Clergy	17	9	3.3	4.3
Student	22	9	4.3	4.3
Local Organization	4	1	.7	.5
Other, not listed	35	1	7.0	.5
	78	20	15.3	9.6
Total	501	210	99.4	100.1

In 1957 sociologist Marjorie Fiske interviewed 204 librarians and administrators in 46 senior high schools and 48 public libraries in 26 communities in California. The Fiske report has since become a classic concerning censorship problems in libraries. A major feature of this report was the evidence of much censorship by librarians, teachers, and administrators. Note the chart beneath of the sources of complaint in the school libraries of the Fiske Study.[10]

Objectors:

Within the school			
Administrators	23		
Librarians	42		
Teachers	8		
Total	73	or	73%
Outside the school			
Parents	18		
Others	3		
Total	21	or	21%
Students	6		
Total	6	or	6%
Total objectors	*100*	*or 100%*	

Members of the school staff became much less likely to use censorship pressures as they became better informed. Several professional organizations developed programs designed to enhance intellectual freedom in the schools. The American Library Association organized the Office for Intellectual Freedom and began to publish its *Newsletter*. Organizations of school administrators began to have sessions on school censorship problems at their annual meetings; such sessions were unknown in the earlier years of the postwar period. Moreover, a number of administrators have joined such groups as the Wisconsin Intellectual Freedom Coalition, or similar groups in Minnesota, Oregon, Illinois or Connecticut. In the 1980s two major organizations of college and university teachers, MLA and AAUP, began to pay attention to this issue, in sharp contrast to those groups' traditional lack of concern for high school instruction in the past.

Organizations of English teachers and librarians have become the most vigorous defenders of intellectual freedom in the United States, though this does not prevent some individual teachers or librarians from removing books as a result of pressure from complaining parents. A librarian removed the book *Deenie* from a school in Brown County, Wisconsin in 1981 as a result of the letter to the eight Brown County, Wisconsin Public School systems asking them to reconsider four novels by Judy Blume— *Deenie, Forever, Are You There God? It's Me Margaret,* and *Then Again, Maybe I Won't.* The librarian who removed *Deenie* said that it was not appropriate for a middle school, and therefore removed the book. This is an atypical reaction by a librarian to a complaint; more often, librarians defend a challenged book and it remains in the school library.

English teachers also on occasion object to books or other materials. As Carolyn Peterson noted, when teachers object to books, they are likely to be successful in having the books removed. Her study of 308 publicly reported events indicated that teacher objections in those events resulted in 100 percent success in having material removed or restricted from use.[11] Librarians are also in a position to be quite successful in banning books when they so choose.

Several cases have been reported of teachers or administrators stealing books in order to assure their removal.[12] In fact, taking books without checking them out and then not returning them is fairly common. Administrators have frequently used this method of dealing with a complaint. The administrator takes the book from the library and simply does not return it. In many school systems, there is little that the teachers or librarian can do about it. As in the Montello case, described earlier, parents also sometimes take books and do not return them. The morality of stealing books does not concern the censor.

It is useful to complement the information from surveys with information from other sources, as Carolyn Peterson suggested. Her study indicated that a few incidents have occurred in which law officers have intervened to object to a book. Slightly over 4 percent of the events she studied concerned law officers.[13] One case has been reported in Wisconsin of a policeman asking that a book be removed. It is not the function of the police to determine what books are used in the schools, and the failure of some schools to resist such pressures is disturbing. Peterson reported that, in the group of events she studied, the law officers succeeded slightly less than half the time in having a book censored. That police interference is rare may be suggested by the fact that no respondent reported the police as a source of objection on the four national surveys carried out by this writer. There was, however, an egregious case in Michigan in the early 1960s in which a teacher spent a few days in jail for having assigned a chapter of *The Stranger* by Camus to a sixth grade class. While that might have been a poor assignment, it certainly did not justify imprisonment, for even a few days. Peterson also reports a case in which a teacher was arrested for distributing obscene material, because he assigned *Slaughterhouse-Five*.[14]

Relatively few clergymen are reported on questionnaires as the initiators of complaints about school learning materials. However, in several very publicized events clergymen have led protests against school materials. An illustration is the case of Tell City, Indiana.[15] A fundamentalist clergyman, who lived, incidentally, in Kentucky across the Ohio River from Tell City, in the winter of 1981 filed a petition containing 60 names objecting to *Of Mice and Men*, which along with "other books" was asserted to be "evil and contained suggestive remarks." In a column for the local newspaper, the minister asserted that the schools taught "humanism," which he identified with "atheism." Another fundamentalist minister from Tell City joined in criticizing the public schools; he scheduled a public meeting in February at which Mel Gabler spoke. About 300 persons, many of whom came to support the public schools, are reported to have attended the rally. At the March meeting of the school board a strong statement by the board supported the teachers and the textbook materials, and the controversy died down, though not without a traumatic and divisive effect on the community.

Fundamentalist clergymen led protests against school materials in a number of other places, including Kanawha County, West Virginia, Neillsville and Amherst, both in Wisconsin. Campaigns of this sort, which go beyond an objection to a single book, give the clergymen who lead them much publicity and have a variety of effects on the schools. However, samples of protests about learning materials suggest that on the whole local clergymen play a fairly small role in the censorship pressures experienced today by most teachers or librarians, though an individual event such as occurred at Tell City, Amherst, Neillsville, or Kanawha County, may be very disruptive for the school staff involved and for the local community. The TV evangelists, such as Falwell and LaHaye, have played a major role in the wave of criticism of the public schools.

In considering the question "Who are the censors?" it quickly becomes obvious that many people are willing to censor something. Very few persons agree with former Supreme Court Justices Black and Douglas that the First Amendment should be literally interpreted to mean that there should be no restraints of any sort on speech or other forms of communication. Critics of almost every political position are likely to assert that some perfectly legal materials should not be in the public schools or the public libraries.

The willingness to censor is related to the intensity of belief in an evil which is the primary focus of concern for the would-be censor. Some feminists are willing to censor sexist language or erotic realism; some liberals are willing to censor racist material; some Birch society members are willing to censor communist material; some members of the Moral Majority are willing to censor pornography. In each case the desire to prevent access to the evil material is more pressing than the somewhat abstract ideals of the First Amendment.

2/ What are the objections that cause censors to wish some works of literature removed? What kind of literature is attacked?

As Nyla Ahrens pointed out in 1965, the objectors focus their attacks primarily on the realistic literature of the twentieth century, especially literature written by Americans.[16] All the later studies confirm this judgment. It is clear that the nature of the literature in school libraries has changed since 1950, and continues to change. In contrast to a few books shelved in the rear of a study hall, many school libraries today are attractive complexes with a wide variety of materials—books in the thousands, many periodicals, along with all the contemporary audio-visual equipment and materials. The 1977 NCTE survey indicated that responding libraries averaged between 9,000 and 10,000 volumes that circulated.[17] In 1982 the figure had increased to between 13,000 and 14,000 volumes.[18] In each year, some libraries reported as many as 35,000 volumes. Such libraries are increasingly attractive to students and significantly increase library use.

The 1982 survey elicited 304 titles of books, 57 different periodicals, and 45 films as the object of challenges. The complete lists may be found in Appendix A. In addition to challenged books, periodicals and films, there were 64 reports of challenges to the school newspapers. In all, the 1982 survey contained the highest proportion of respondents indicating a challenge to one medium or another—slightly over 50 percent. As is detailed later in this report, it is highly likely that the growth in library size is an important factor in growth in censorship pressures. The library holdings have become broadly representative of twentieth-century selections, and have greater emphasis not only on writers from the United States but on so-called minority group writers— women, along with Black writers, Hispanic writers, and writers from various other groups including American Indian and Asiatic. Unquestionably the representation of writers other than white Anglo-Saxon male is still less than the available material, but there has been a substantial increase in the proportion of such writers in school libraries since 1950.

School libraries today contain a much more realistic body of material than was previously the case. It is inconceivable that such titles as *Our Bodies, Ourselves* or *The Teenage Survival Book* would have been in a high school library before 1950, for several reasons, not the least of which would have been the nonexistence of the materials. The most vigorous change in the school library, along with material that deals with sex, has been the inclusion of a new genre of literature, the so-called junior level or adolescent novel. Novels written specifically for teenagers did not exist before 1950.

Since then *The Catcher in the Rye, The Red Car, Forever, Deenie, My Darling, My Hamburger,* and many hundreds of other titles have come into libraries. These books are usually quite realistic concerning courtship, sex, marriage, divorce, death, and other aspects of the life of teenagers in this society. Donelson pointed out that adolescent literature pictures the "life that a twentieth century teenager experiences each day, a life usually quite different from that of his parents—hence, the rise in attempts to shelter young people from it."[19] There are so many of these titles and so much interest in this kind of literature that a special section of English teachers in the National Council of Teachers of English has been organized, a group entitled the

Assembly on Adolescent Literature. This group has annual meetings, with reports on various aspects of this new literary genre.

In addition to the growth in numbers and the change in the nature of the books in the school library has come a broadening of the function of the library. While school libraries have always to some degree fulfilled the same function that public libraries do—providing a wide range of materials for the reading interests of those who use the library—this function has come to be much more important than in the past. Many books added to the libraries are sometimes rather pejoratively referred to as "leisure reading material." This area of the growth of the school library makes available to students much material that seems offensive to some people in this society, and therefore generates censorship pressures. Few people object to encyclopedias, reference works or dictionaries (except in Texas and a few other places).

That the realistic, twentieth-century literature, written by United States authors is most likely to generate censorship is quite well documented by the various studies. An examination of the nine hundred titles listed in Appendix B of this book establishes the correctness of this conclusion. One of the many ironies is the fact that much censorship comes from groups that identify themselves as patriotic and American, yet they concentrate their activities against some of the best writers that this nation has produced.

Of the 30 books most frequently attacked since 1965,[20] based on six studies of censorship pressures on the public schools, 25 were written by authors from the United States. Of those 30 books, only two were written before 1900—*The Adventures of Huckleberry Finn* and *The Scarlet Letter*. With the probable exception of *The Scarlet Letter*, the books may be described as realistic in dialog, in sexual frankness, and in the treatment of class and race differences.

Five of the books are junior novels: *The Catcher in the Rye, The Chocolate War, Forever, It's Okay If You Don't Love Me,* and *My Darling, My Hamburger.*

Eleven of the books deal with non-Anglo-Saxon whites: *The Adventures of Huckleberry Finn, Anne Frank: The Diary of a Young Girl, Black Like Me, The Good Earth, A Hero Ain't Nothin' But a Sandwich, If Beale Street Could Talk, I Know Why the Caged Bird Sings, The Learning Tree, Manchild in the Prom-*

ised Land, One Day in the Life of Ivan Denisovich, and *One Flew Over the Cuckoo's Nest.*

There is general agreement in the several studies mentioned above that the major objections to books used in the public schools concern allegedly obscene or bad language, along with sexual references. As the chart on pages 42–43 shows, based on the 1982 survey, well over half of 502 objections listed by the respondents dealt with obscene or bad language and with sexual references. Classifying the objections presents difficulty since some objectors use such emotional epithets as "Trash" or "Filth." Examples of such evaluations may be found in Appendix B. The dissertation by Ellen Last, dealing with objections by the Gablers to literary anthologies proposed for Texas in 1978, notes the frequency with which the Gablers rely on such terms to indicate their disapproval of various authors.

Many objections, however, are quite clear. A parent who objected to *Brave New World* asserted that the book contained objectionable profanity and explicit sexual discussions. Another parent said that the book encouraged drug use. The frequent objections to *The Adventures of Huckleberry Finn* reiterate that the book contains "bad language," e.g., the word "nigger," or contains racial references, which in some eyes make any book suspect. *The Catcher in the Rye* has been the object of a nationally published attack, which lists the number of occurrences of each so-called profane word. If one were interested in such data, it would be possible to learn exactly how many times each epithet appeared in the book.

The term "bad language" is ambiguous. It sometimes refers to so-called bad grammar, and sometimes to profanity. Some critics have a clear link in their minds joining non-middle-class language with immorality. Almost as soon as *The Adventures of Huckleberry Finn* was published there were objections to encouraging young people to read a book with such so-called bad grammar. The Concord, Massachusetts library banned the book shortly after publication; the Brooklyn Public Library excluded both *Huckleberry Finn* and *Tom Sawyer,* in 1905.[21]

The literary value in a realistic presentation of the lives of working class people who do not use middle-class language seems difficult for some parents to understand. Ma Joad in *The Grapes of Wrath* is as nearly a saint as any figure in twentieth-century

American literature, in spite of her substandard language. But her saintly qualities do not redeem the book for those persons who expect every book to contain only impeccably correct, middle-class language, and who see in *The Grapes of Wrath* only "bad grammar" and alleged obscenities.

The clearest objections to so-called bad language per se are illustrated by pressures against several standard dictionaries by the textbook committee of a prominent patriotic organization of women in Texas and by a feminist group there. As a result of the objections, five dictionaries were removed from the state adoption list in Texas: *The American Heritage Dictionary of the English Language,* High School Edition; *The Doubleday Dictionary; The Random House College Dictionary,* Revised Edition; *Webster's New World Dictionary of the American Language,* College Edition; and *Webster's Seventh New Collegiate Dictionary.* [22]

Dictionaries have been attacked in Anchorage, Alaska; Cedar Lake, Indiana; and Eldon, Missouri. The objectors list various words including, for example, "bed," which has as one of its meanings to have sexual intercourse. In Texas, 26 objectionable words were listed. In Missouri, 39 objectionable words were listed.

The Dictionary of American Slang has been attacked throughout the postwar period. In 1963 the state superintendent of public instruction in California, Max Rafferty, orchestrated an attack which led to that book's removal from libraries in Costa Mesa and Newport Beach. Since then the book has been attacked in Arizona, North Carolina, and several other states.

Of the other 220 objections to challenged books in the 1982 survey, 85 were not explained by the objectors. They stated either that the book was not appropriate, without explaining why, or they gave no reason at all. This leaves 129 objections that dealt with the content of the book.

This distribution reflects what is probably true of our society. There is substantial acceptance of the belief that obscenity does not merit protection by the First Amendment, as the Supreme Court has said. There is also much acceptance of the belief that the libraries should provide a wide range of material, as the Library Bill of Rights of the American Library Association asserts. Thus the objectors perceive and act on the belief that the

OBJECTORS AND OBJECTIONS TO 304 BOOKS
(1982 SURVEY)

	Parents	Librarian	Administrative Assistant	Teacher	English Chair	Administrators	Board of Education	Clergy	Students	Not Listed	Local Group	
Obscene, Bad Language	142	9	1	7		2	3	3	7	9	4	183
Sexual References	65	6		9	1	7	1		4	2		99
Not Appropriate	18	5		1		3	1	1	2			31
Obscene Pics, Nudity	3	3		5		1		1	1	1		15
Violence	10	1		1				1				13
Moral Values	7	1		1								9
Drugs	6								1			7
Religious Ideas	6			1				4	3			14
Racial Ideas	12								1			13
Trash	3			2								5
Distorted View of Life	3											3
Witches, Occult	7			3				1	1			12

												Total
Marriage & Family	2											2
Not Accurate	2	1		2			1					6
Anti-War	1											1
Political Ideas	1					4						5
Humanism	1							2				3
Vulgar				1								1
Critical of Parents				1								1
Subject Matter	12	1		4		1		1				19
No Reason	25	1		3		1		1		23		54
Corrupts Young/Con-dones Bad Behavior	1							1				2
Evolution								2				2
Too Realistic View of Vietnam War				1								1
Author's Lifestyle	1											1
Total	328	28	1	42	1	13	11	17	22	35	4	502

charge of obscenity or bad language will gather public support as the basis for removing books or other materials from libraries. On the other hand, if there is substantial support for providing a wide range of materials, then charges restricting the intellectual content of a book, its racial, religious, or political ideas, are less likely to receive much public support, and so the frequency of such charges diminishes.

The frequency with which books are charged with being obscene presents libraries with very real problems. The Miller decision of the Supreme Court, which announced that community standards might be used to determine obscenity, exacerbates the situation, since it leads some critics of the schools to believe that any charge of obscenity should be taken seriously as grounds for removal of, for example, *The Grapes of Wrath*, removed from the American Literature class in Kanawha, Iowa, or such other books as *Deenie*, attacked in many places. *Andersonville*, *The Big Sky*, *Black Like Me*, *The Catcher in the Rye*, and many other titles have had obscenity as the principal charge against them.

As of this writing, no book used in the public schools has been found to be obscene by a court in the United States. Nevertheless, there is a widespread belief by some sections of the public that any charge of obscenity should result in the almost immediate removal of the book from the school library or the classroom. Some school officials are willing to act on that belief, unfortunately.

It is interesting to note that the 1982 survey produced only three occurrences of the charge of secular humanism as the basis for challenging the use of a book in the public schools. The efforts of various groups to remove *The Learning Tree* from the school system in Mead, Washington, which has thus far failed in two court tests, were based on the assertion that the book teaches secular humanism. That charge has not apparently as yet caught on for substantial sections of the general public.

The tendency of the general public to use obscenity or bad language as the basis for urging the removal of books from the schools may hide other objections which the critics may feel are politically not prudent. The existence of hidden motives behind the charges of obscenity seems well established, as several observers have noted. L.B. Woods suggested that ". . . many objections that are in reality pro-racism are camouflaged by the stated reasons of obscenity, sex, or language."[23] Ellen Last made a similar observation about the textbook critics in Texas in 1978. Dorothy Thompson Weathersby made the same point concerning literature anthologies chosen for Tennessee in 1975. Carolyn Peterson noted: "There is no sure relationship between what is stated as objectionable and the real problem posed by a piece of literature. An NCTE representative at a censorship hearing in Anchorage, Alaska, was repeatedly told that it was the language in *Bless the Beasts and Children* that was objectionable, until the angry father broke down and admitted that he was afraid the book would turn his son against him since the book was against the killing of animals, the father's occupation."[24]

James Baxter wrote of a censorship campaign in the early 1960s, "The recent censorship campaign in Mississippi resulted in proposed legislation to reorganize the board and rating committees. The results definitely indicate that the motives were political rather than educational."[25] A more frequent hidden motive is racism. That a third or more of the thirty most frequently attacked books should deal with characters who are neither Anglo-Saxon nor white is strongly suggestive of racist motives. Not by a great deal does one-third of the more than 40,000 titles currently being published in the United States deal with so-called minority groups. In fact, there is probably no school library in the United States in which one-third of the books deal with minority people.

In a few cases objectors frankly state that they are opposed to books about Blacks or other minority people in the schools. As one teacher wrote about objections to *Black Like Me:* "In a rural community, people don't care to have their children read about Negroes."[26] A school board member in Loyal, Wisconsin, explaining why *Saturday Night Fever* was removed from the school library, said the book contained obscene language; furthermore, "the book describes life in a poor Italian section of New York and I don't think that it pertains to our style of life at all."[27] More often, however, it seems likely that the stated reason for objecting to accurate and realistic reports concerning the life of minority groups is bad language or obscenity, rather than the real reason, an objection to any material about Blacks or Indians, Italians or other groups.

Of the 11 books removed from the school library at Island

Trees, New York in February, 1976, seven dealt with Indians, Blacks, Puerto Ricans, and Jews. This removal was subject to an extended series of court battles resulting ultimately in a Supreme Court decision on June 25, 1982 that the students who protested the removal of the books had a right to a trial on the merits of their case.. No attention was paid to the distribution of subject matter in the books, either by the news reports or in the Supreme Court decision. It indicates something of the attitude of the Island Trees school board that it concentrated on books dealing in a realistic manner with the lives of Blacks, Indians, Puerto Ricans and Jews. The Island Trees school board charged the books with being "anti-American, anti-Christian, anti-Semitic, and just plain filthy."[28] The books so described were: *Down These Mean Streets, Best Short Stories of Negro Writers, Laughing Boy, Black Boy, A Hero Ain't Nothin' But a Sandwich, Soul on Ice, The Fixer, Slaughterhouse-Five, The Naked Ape, Go Ask Alice,* and *A Reader for Writers.*

A second set of hidden motives grows out of the belief that books should not be critical of this society. School books in particular should be optimistic, uplifting, supportive of traditional American values. That idea appears repeatedly in the Gablers' objections to the literary anthologies proposed for Texas in 1978. It also appears frequently in individual objections to various titles across the last three decades.

A typical illustration of a book being charged with obscenity, when the real reason for the charge seems likely to lie elsewhere, is the removal of *The Grapes of Wrath* from the Kanawha, Iowa, sophomore American literature class by order of the school board. The book was, however, allowed to remain in the school library. The action was taken as the result of a complaint by a parent who was a vice president of the local bank. The bank officer complained that the book was "profane, vulgar, and obscene."[29]

At approximately the same time the book was removed from use in the English class, the Committee on Peace and Justice of the Sioux City Diocese of the Roman Catholic church issued a report concerning land use in Iowa. The report stated that in the 14 northwestern counties of Iowa, 77 percent of the land was owned by absentee owners.[30] It may be coincidental that a banker should attack *The Grapes of Wrath* for being "profane, vulgar and obscene" and ignore the Jeffersonian agrarianism that runs through the book. Steinbeck's charge that capital is used to buy big tractors and drive farmers off the land may not have been apparent to the banker who complained about the book. But it is ironic that a novel with such a theme should be forbidden for study by high school students in a part of the country where the family farm is a dominant feature of life. It is an open question as to whether the book was censored because of a failure to understand it, or because it was understood too well.

It seems likely that an undercurrent of objection to books that point out the failures of this society to live up to its ideals is hidden by a charge that the books are obscene. Part of the problem lies in the failure to recognize satire. There is also a widespread belief that to discuss any subject or to use taboo language indicates approval of the subject or the language. Ellen Last has shown that any reference to a subject is regarded by the Gablers (and by a number of other critics) as approval of the ideas that are discussed. [31]

Thus such books as *The Magician*, which criticized several aspects of our society—the large, impersonal public high school, and lawyers, among other subjects—was attacked on obscenity grounds at Montello, Wisconsin. *Go Ask Alice* has been attacked all over the United States, though the parents of the girl whose life is portrayed in that book had the girl's autobiography published anonymously in the hope that it would deter other young Americans from the use of drugs. Almost every book written by or about minority members of this society is critical, either explicitly or implicitly, of the failure of this society. *Manchild in the Promised Land* suggests by its very title the gross contrast between reality and the utopian ideals that appear in many documents in our history, including such rituals as the pledge of allegiance with its statement calling for "liberty and justice for all" in this "one nation, under God." But this theme in *Manchild* is ignored by those critics of the book who call for its removal because of its alleged obscenity.

A classic case of ignoring the satiric content that is critical of this society, while charging a work of literature with obscenity occurred in Chelsea, Massachusetts in 1977. The book *Male and Female Under Eighteen*[32] contained a satiric poem which protests the reduction of women to sex objects by public, embarrassing comments. The poem was written by a fifteen-year-old high school student at Hunter High School in New York in 1973, Jody Caravaglia. The poem is as follows:

THE CITY TO A YOUNG GIRL

The city is
One million horny lip-smacking men
Screaming for my body.
The streets are long conveyor belts
Loaded with these suckling pigs.
All begging for
a lay
a little pussy
a bit of tit
a leg to rub against
a handful of ass
the connoisseurs of cunt
Every day, every night
Pressing in on me closer and closer.
I swat them off like flies
but they keep coming back
I'm a good piece of meat.

An offended father in Chelsea protested the inclusion of the book in the school library. A librarian, Sonja Coleman, defended the book, and it was ultimately restored to the library by a court decision. The poet, in the middle of the public controversy in Chelsea, wrote a telegram asserting that the book was not obscene, but rather: "The poem expresses feminine outrage against public lechery, an obscene, dehumanizing situation. It is anti-pornographic."[33] Some critics in Chelsea did recognize the thematic content of the poem, but insisted that the charges of the poem were not correct. A local newspaper publisher, Andrew Quigley, wrote in defense of the removal of the book from the school library: "A girl reading that without proper instruction could arrive at the opinion that every man walking down the street is considering her only as a sex object to be violated."[34] That is, of course, what the poem asserts. The main thrust of public objection to the poem in Chelsea, though, was to its alleged obscenity, and little attention was paid to the poem's protest against the situation of women in the United States.

In public controversies which emerge in places like Chelsea, defenders of challenged material are often asked to define obscenity. A possible answer is that obscenity is a legal term, and objectors to books or poems or plays should bring their charges in a legal arena. It is not the function of the school board or the library trustees to determine whether a work of literature is obscene. As implied in the introduction, I believe that the term "obscene" is fundamentally not definable. School boards should let the courts wrestle with this problem until further experience demonstrates the futility of basing legislation on so subjective a term.

Legal proscription of obscene literature is relatively new in the English speaking world, as Bryson and Detty have noted.[35] The first statutes against obscenity in the United States were passed in the 1840s and in England in the 1850s. In the ensuing decades the courts have found it very difficult to define obscenity; usually they have resorted to a circular kind of definition which begs the question. The obscene has been defined as the pornographic, the pornographic has been defined as lewd, the lewd has been defined as obscene. No referential definition has been established by the courts, in contrast to the crimes of murder, forgery, or arson. The 1973 Miller decision of the Supreme Court in effect gives up the effort to define obscenity and allows the jury in a given community to decide whether the indicated material is obscene. Obscenity continues to have no clear, statutory, referential definition, probably because the word refers essentially to a subjective reaction on the part of the reader or viewer.

The selection of a book, film, or periodical by a professional person—a teacher or librarian—for use in the schools is clear evidence that the material has been judged to be suitable for its intended use and is not therefore obscene. The burden of proof for a charge of obscenity should rest on the person who challenges the use of the material. A school board might properly assert that since obscenity is a legal concept, it will not entertain charges that school learning materials are obscene. The board should request that those charges be made in a court, not in an educational institution.

3/ Are censorship pressures increasing?

Much evidence suggests a steady increase in censorship pressures on the literary materials in the public schools since 1950. As Nelson and Roberts indicated in their report of school censorship, prior to 1963 the main targets of such groups as the DAR, the John Birch Society, the American Legion and, in the South, the White Citizens Council, were textbooks used in history or social studies classes. A few works of fiction were included in attacks by such groups but little concerted effort was made in the 1950s to remove the wide range of titles that became the object of attack in the 1960s and the 1970s, and which continue to generate attack. Nelson and Roberts listed several attacks on *The Catcher in the Rye* in 1960 but report very few attacks on works of fiction prior to 1960. Among those few works of literature were *Huckleberry Finn*, as noted, and *The Merchant of Venice*, removed from the public schools of Meriden, Connecticut in 1911, and in a few other places. [36]

The first effort to sample a cross-section of schools concerning censorship pressures occurred in Wisconsin in 1963. [37] This survey indicated that approximately 20 percent of the reporting schools had experienced censorship pressures. Beginning in 1966, a series of national surveys was carried out based on a sample of public high schools in the United States. [38] These surveys suggested an increasing degree of censorship pressure, as shown below.

FREQUENCY OF REPORT OF CHALLENGES TO SCHOOL LEARNING MATERIAL

	1966 Survey	1973 Survey	1977 Survey	1982 Survey
Books	20%	28%	30.0%	34%
Periodicals	na	na	8.5%	17%
Films	na	na	7.5%	8%

The basic question on these surveys was: "Has someone objected to a book or other learning material used in your school in the last year?" The word "censorship" did not appear in the questionnaires. The respondent was then asked who the objector was, what the objection was, and what the disposition of the case was. These are relatively objective questions. Their objectivity was designed to forestall the criticism that some teachers or librarians might be more sensitive to censorship than others, and therefore be more likely to report. It is conceivable that the increased number of reports may reflect, not increased censorship pressures, but increased sensitivity to the problem. However, since the questions are relatively objective, it seems likely that the resulting information is dependable.

Similar results have been obtained by other investigators, from other sources of information. L.B. Woods reported from information in the *Newsletter on Intellectual Freedom* that the number of items censored between 1966 and 1975 increased from 43 items in 1966 to 563 in 1975, or 13.1 times as many items in 1975 as in 1966.[39] The fullest account of legal cases dealing with school censorship problems was written by Joseph Bryson and Elizabeth Detty. They wrote in 1982: ". . . censorship is an ancient problem. However, public schools have been faced with more censorship problems and litigation in the past two decades than ever before in the history of the United States."[40] James Baxter wrote that organized criticism of textbook materials has become a rather frequent occurrence.[41] Judith Krug, of the Office for Intellectual Freedom of the American Library Association, has reported an increased number of requests for assistance in recent years.

In order to test the proposition that those teachers and librarians who were most sensitive to the issue answered the 1982 questionnaire, and less sensitive ones did not, a telephone survey was carried out to supplement the questionnaire survey. One hundred eighty-five school libraries were telephoned in May 1982. Forty schools could not be reached by telephone. Forty-one schools reported that the librarians had no telephone, or that there was no librarian, or, for miscellaneous reasons, that the librarian could not be reached. Fourteen librarians refused to be interviewed; one said it was against school policy; others would not explain. However, ninety librarians were interviewed by phone. Of those ninety, 25 percent reported challenges to school material. This is a smaller figure than the 34 percent who reported censorship pressure on the written questionnaire, but it is not greatly smaller; it confirms that there is substantial censorship pressure on the schools that, for a variety of reasons, did not answer the written questionnaire. It also made clear that some librarians answered the questionnaire for reasons other than the absence of censorship pressures. Since approximately the same population has been questioned in succeeding years with approximately the same set of questions, it seems probable that there is a reasonable degree of dependability in the report of increased censorship pressures on the literary material used in the public schools.

Carolyn Peterson, in her dissertation concerned with censorship in schools, used newspaper accounts, reports to the *Newsletter on Intellectual Freedom,* and other published reports, and concluded that the questionnaire method of gathering information had some advantages over relying on newspaper and journal accounts. She wrote: "The questionnaire as a research instrument may better expose the subtleties of self-censorship and selection based on student desires and abilities, than the newspaper/journal accounts which are more likely to emphasize the more flagrant and gross examples of censorship."[42]

An interesting evidence of concern by professional people is a great increase in articles in professional journals between 1950 and 1980. A count in five of the most frequently used periodical indexes on 75 topics that dealt with censorship under various rubrics yielded 871 articles written between 1940 and 1949. In the next decade 1,544 articles were published. In the following decade 2,787 articles were published. In the decade ending in 1980, 3,876 articles appeared on various aspects of censorship. It may be argued that this is not in itself evidence of increased censorship, but is only evidence of increased concern. However, when the data that have been accumulated by Krug, Woods, Baxter, Bryson and Detty, as well as the five surveys carried out by the present writer are considered, it seems evident that the increased concern by professional people reflects a real change in their working conditions—i.e., much more censorship pressure.

3 A SURVEY OF THE CENSORSHIP SITUATION: REGIONAL DIFFERENCES; RACE, CLASS, CULTURE; RESULTS

4/ Are there regional differences in the frequency of censorship?

An answer to this question must be tentative, but it does appear that the northeastern part of the United States has the highest incidence of censorship pressures on the schools. Note the table below.

FREQUENCY OF CHALLENGES TO ALL MEDIA BY REGIONS, 1982
Percent of Schools Reporting Challenges

Northeastern U.S.	56
Midwest	54
Plains	53.5
Mountain	53
Far West	54
Texas	52
The Old South	44

Several other sources of information, including earlier surveys by this writer, suggest a similar distribution of censorship pressures. L.B. Woods used a slightly different division of the United States than the one above, but reported the highest incidence of censorship in the New England states, followed by California and Hawaii, then the Pacific Northwest. The Middle

West, Plains and Mountain States were in a middle position; the Old South, together with Arizona and New Mexico, had the lowest incidence of reported censorship events.[1] This information contradicts the assumption many people make that censorship is most likely to occur in the southern states. Why the northeastern states report the highest frequency of censorship can only be conjectured. The most reasonable answer seems to be that schools in the northeastern part of the United States have the biggest and best libraries. The larger the library, the more frequently does someone find something to object to.

Many librarians believe that by careful selection, a euphemism for self-censorship, they can avoid outside censorship pressures; they argue therefore that the quality of the selection will determine the frequency of censorship, ignoring the impossibility of defining the term "the quality of the collection."

In order to test the proposition that the nature of the collection was related to the frequency of censorship, I listed 100 carefully selected titles on the 1977 and 1982 surveys, to sample the nature of the collections in school libraries. Librarians were asked to report how many of the titles were in the library. They were also asked to report the total number of volumes that circulated from the library.

The list of 100 titles included 50 that were known to have been challenged somewhere. The other 50 titles were an innocuous group, not known to have been challenged. The innocuous 50 were drawn from a list, prepared by Joyce Steward of the University of Wisconsin, of books that high school students reported they enjoyed reading. The list came from surveys of students in grades 7 to 12; the studies were carried out in 1972 and in 1977. I selected books most often mentioned by the students which were not the object of challenges. Presumably such books were likely to be in the school libraries, as indeed turned out to be the case. The 1977 list may be seen in *Dealing with Censorship* (p. 19). The 1982 list appears opposite. The lists include the percentage of responding libraries that contained each of the 100 books in their collection.

PERCENTAGE OF LIBRARIES HAVING EACH TITLE
(* indicates controversial title)

86	Across Five Aprils, I. Hunt
98	* Adventures of Huckleberry Finn, M. Twain
90	All Creatures Great and Small, J. Herriot
72	* Andersonville, M. Kantor
95	* Animal Farm, G. Orwell
73	Anna and the King of Siam, M. Landon
68	* Autobiography of Malcolm X, Malcolm X
82	* Bell for Adano, A.J. Hersey
97	* Bible
69	Big Sky, The, A.B. Guthrie Jr.
64	* Black Boy, R. Wright
84	* Black Like Me, J.H. Griffin
93	Born Free, J. Adamson
86	* Brave New World, A. Huxley
87	Bridge of San Luis Rey, T. Wilder
98	Call of the Wild, The, J. London
89	* Canterbury Tales, The, G. Chaucer
76	* Catcher in the Rye, The, J.D. Salinger
82	Christy, C. Marshall
93	Connecticut Yankee in King Arthur's Court, A, M. Twain
74	Cyrano De Bergerac, E. Rostand
97	David Copperfield, C. Dickens
92	Death Be Not Proud, J. Gunther
33	* Deliverance, J. Dickey
91	Don Quixote, M. Cervantes
26	* Down these Mean Streets, P. Thomas
74	Dropout, J. Eyerly
76	Eric, D. Lund
30	Escape from Freedom, E. Fromm
82	* Exodus, L. Uris
83	Fahrenheit 451, R. Bradbury
85	* Farewell to Arms, E. Hemingway
09	* Female Eunuch, The, G. Greer
51	* Fixer, The, Malamud
53	* Fountainhead, A. Rand
73	Giants in the Earth, O.E. Rolvaag
78	* Go Ask Alice, Anonymous
63	Go, Team, Go, J. Tunis
94	* Gone with the Wind, M. Mitchell
94	* Good Earth, The, P.S. Buck

86   * Grapes of Wrath, The, J. Steinbeck
48   Great Escape, The, P. Brickhill
62   Greek Way, The, E. Hamilton
75   * Hawaii, J. Michener
94   Hobbit, The, J.R. Tolkien
84   Hot Rod, H.G. Felsen
95   Iliad, The, Homer
92   Incredible Journey, The, S. Burnford
75   * Invisible Man, The, R. Ellison
97   Jane Eyre, C. Bronte
94   Johnny Tremain, E. Forbes
23   Joy in the Morning, E. Smith
86   Karen, M. Killilea
82   Lantern in Her Hand, A, B.S. Aldrich
57   * Learning Tree, The, G. Parks
63   Little Britches, R. Moody
56   Little House in the Big Woods, L. I. Wilder
89   * Lord of the Flies, W. Golding
89   Lord of the Rings, The, J.R. Tolkein
36   * Love and the Facts of Life, E.M. Duvall
67   * Love Story, E. Segal
60   Magnificent Obsession, L.C. Douglas
58   * Manchild in the Promised Land, C. Brown
44   * Mister Roberts, T. Heggen
83   Mrs. Mike, B.&N. Freedman
41   * Nigger, D. Gregory
90   * Nineteen Eighty-Four, G. Orwell
11   * O, Beulah Land, M.L. Settle
39   * Of Mice and Men, J. Steinbeck
96   * Old Man and the Sea, The, E. Hemingway
92   Old Yeller, F. Gipson
95   Oliver Twist, C. Dickens
68   * One Day in the Life of Ivan Denisovich, A. Solzhenitsyn
75   * On the Beach, N. Shute
67   * Other Side of the Mountain, The, E.G. Valens
90   * Outsiders, The, S.E. Hinton
79   * Ox-Bow Incident, W. Clark
95   Pearl, The, J. Steinbeck
94   Prince and the Pauper, The, M. Twain
74   Pygmalion, G.B. Shaw
78   Rascal, S. North
98   * Red Badge of Courage, The, S. Crane

94 * Scarlet Letter, The, N. Hawthorne
75 Scarlet Pimpernel, The, E. Orczy
87 * Separate Peace, A, J. Knowles
87 Seventeenth Summer, M. Daly
88 Shane, J. Schaefer
62 * Siddhartha, H. Hesse
55 * Slaughterhouse-Five, K. Vonnegut
66 * Stranger, The, A. Camus
25 * Studs Lonigan, J. Farrell
60 Swiftwater, P. Annixter
88 Swiss Family Robinson, The, J. Wyss
94 * To Kill a Mockingbird, H. Lee
78 To Sir with Love, E.R. Braithwaite
82 Travels with Charley, L. Steinbeck
79 Tuned Out, M. Wojciechowska
73 * The Ugly American, E. Burdick
75 * West Side Story, I. Shulman
96 Wuthering Heights, E. Bronte

The two lists of books permitted the establishment of a ratio of innocuous books to controversial books in the responding schools. Both in 1977 and in 1982 the ratio of controversial to non controversial books was approximately the same for librarians reporting censorship problems and for librarians reporting none.

RATIO OF CONTROVERSIAL TO NON-CONTROVERSIAL BOOKS

	1977	1982
Schools reporting censorship pressures	36/40	37/39
Schools not reporting censorship pressures	35/39	35/38

In each case, however, the schools reporting censorship pressures also reported more books than the schools reporting no censorship pressures, as noted below.

TOTAL NUMBER OF VOLUMES THAT CIRCULATED

	1977	1982
Schools reporting no censorship pressure	9,252	13,300
Schools reporting censorship pressure	10,812	14,230

In each case the data were analyzed to determine whether these figures were statistically significant. In 1977, the relationship was significant at the level of .035 on a T test; in 1982 the relationship was significant at the level of .011. It would seem, therefore, for the group of schools sampled in 1977 and 1982 that the size of the school library was more important than the (indefinable perhaps) quality of the books contained in the collection.

Since number of books is probably related to the size of the school, this relationship was also tested in 1982. The relationship between schools reporting censorship pressures and their size was examined with a Chi square test. Here the results were slightly less significant; the test yielded a relationship at the level of .058. Perhaps some smaller schools may have larger libraries than some larger schools. Apparently the size of the library is a more important characteristic of the kind of situation that produces censorship than the size of the school. There is a certain logic to this. Books seem to arouse controversy. The more books, the more likelihood of controversy. The best protection against censorship might therefore be to have no books.

If the hypothesis is correct that larger libraries are more likely to generate censorship than smaller libraries, one possible explanation emerges for the probability that censorship is more likely to occur in northern states than in southern. More money is spent on schools and libraries in the north than in the states of the Old South. Other explanations may also complement the belief that it is the library size that accounts for the greater frequency of censorship in the north than in the south. L.B. Woods suggested that "strong religious motives" in the south caused prior censorship to be exercised. He also pointed out that there are many rural schools in the south.[2] However, if the analysis above, based on the ratio of controversial books to non-controversial books, is correct, then the most important point may be the small size of rural libraries. Another explanation, which will be explored in more detail later, is that protest against book use is an essentially democratic activity, based on the belief that government should be by consent of the governed. Lower class citizens in the south, as W. J. Cash observed, are more likely to accept the authority of the state than are citizens in the north. A librarian, Mary Gail Wildman of Hattiesburg, Mississippi, is currently attempting to explore this question in a doctoral dissertation underway at the University of Mississippi. Her study may yield additional explanations.

5/ Do class, cultural and racial differences play a role in censorship situations?

While a final answer may not be available to this question, it seems likely that all of these factors are involved in censorship pressures on the schools.

Traditionally the American school system has been dominated by a white, middle class segment of the larger society. As demonstrated in the book *Elmtown's Youth*[3] the white middle class teaching staff has controlled the schools and has taken for granted a set of values that included the so-called standard or middle class dialect. A population more than half of which had non English-speaking background was expected to learn and use this dialect.

In the north, both in World War I and II, to know or to use German was regarded as unpatriotic. A law was passed in Nebraska forbidding the teaching of German. While that law was declared unconstitutional by the Supreme Court in the case of Meyer vs. Nebraska in 1923,[4] the spirit of the law pervaded the culture, as it still does with regard to bilingualism. In Texas for many years it was illegal to use Spanish in the public schools. Only recently has that situation changed. There are people still alive in Wisconsin who recall having paint thrown on their house in WW I, because people were believed to speak German in that house.

Class differences are not often discussed in American society, which claims equal status for all its citizens. Nevertheless, as Warner and others have pointed out, this is a strongly class-marked society.[5] The class divisions remain somewhat invisible; they are not often mentioned, but they are powerful. The janitor of the bank sees the president of the bank only at work. They live in different areas, attend different churches, dress differently, have different dialects, and their children attend different schools.

In a number of the public controversies over books, there has been a strong class element present. In Amherst, Wisconsin a group of local citizens objected to *Our Bodies, Ourselves* and certain other books on sex education. One of the charges was that the books taught masturbation. The rather conservative school board voted finally to keep the books, while adopting a provision that those parents who did not want their children to read those books could have that privilege.

The protest was led by a clergyman of a small fundamentalist local church. This church fulfills the description of the sect in the sociological terms that Ernst Troeltsch and others have used:

> . . . a sect is a schismatic group springing from and in opposition to an organized church and becoming independent of it. Finding its true authority in what it regards as a truer understanding of Scripture of primitive Christianity, it sustains a critical attitude toward the parent institution and indeed toward the patterns of contemporary culture in general, and seeks in its detachment a more positive realization of the Christian life. Developing sects find their fertile soil among the socially and economically insecure and tend to lose their sectarian features as the social and economic status of their membership improves.[6]

Several of the recent public controversies had as one of the proponents in the conflict a group that could well be characterized in Troeltsch's terms—in Kanawha County, West Virginia, in Tell City, Indiana and in Amherst, Wisconsin. An observer at Amherst suggested that in fact the real issue there was the conflict between insiders and outsiders. The school board at Amherst had previously refused permission for a local little theatre group to use the high school gymnasium for a drama presentation of *One Flew Over the Cuckoo's Nest*. Their commitment to First Amendment principles does not seem to be very strong. It is quite likely that they felt their authority as the in-group controlling the schools was threatened by the protests originating from members of a newly organized fundamentalist church. Two mainstream clergymen, one Catholic and one Lutheran, supported the questioned materials; they were regarded as members of the local in-group. The preacher of the complaining group was a local working man, who used what the schools regard as substandard language, and who identified himself as having only an eighth grade education.

It would seem quite reasonable to interpret the conflict at Amherst as essentially a class or cultural conflict over control of local institutions. That it concerned the right to read was probably incidental. A similar conclusion seems quite likely for the conflict at Kanawha County.

Class characteristics that have affected the school, in addition to the middle class dialect, include geographic distribution of housing by class and race patterns, class differences in typical vocations, in religion, and in moral values and standards.

The consolidation of school districts brought into a single school system students from widely varying economic and social backgrounds. The neighborhood school had for the most part a homogenous student population and parental constituency. The most obvious result of the great consolidation of school districts since 1950 has been the acres of school busses that may be seen somewhere in many school districts. About one-half of school children are now bussed for reasons that have nothing to do with race. About 2 percent are bussed for the purpose of integration. While bussing for purposes of integration has aroused much opposition, there has been relatively little criticism of bussing for reasons of presumed educational efficiency, not connected with integration. But this latter form of bussing laid the basis for community conflicts both within and without the school over the purposes of education and the materials to be used in the schools.

The Kanawha County conflict would in all probability not have occurred if the rural areas of the county had not been put in the same school district with the capital of West Virginia— Charleston. The conflict was certainly not anticipated by the legislature when it provided for the consolidation of the schools.

The conflict is largely between middle class parents and lower class parents, since, for the most part, the relatively small upper class in the United States does not send its children to the public schools.

The conflict at Wasco, California over the use of John Gardner's novel *Grendel* may well be an illustration of a conflict that was class based. The novel was used as part of a rather demanding small senior English class for largely college bound students. The school board represented a community increasingly dominated by working class citizens. Such a school board may object to materials used in college by students in a college bound class. Though the conflict may be seen by English teachers and librarians as a First Amendment issue, it should perhaps more accurately be described in terms of class conflict.

A variety of sources make clear that moral values are class related. Middle class moral standards differ significantly from the upper class on the one hand, and the lower class on the other, concerning drinking, violence, sex, the role of men and women, and the nature of the citizen's relationship to the government. However it is the set of differences between the middle class and the lower class that erupts in school controversies, especially concerning sex, since for the most part, the upper class is not interested in the public schools.

The Kinsey report showed that sex practices are class related. Thus lower class boys are reported to be less likely to masturbate and more likely to begin intercourse at an earlier age than middle class boys, for whom masturbation is more common. A number of other sex practices were shown by the Kinsey report to be class related, including fellatio and cunnilingus. The issue is further complicated by differences between the Catholic church, the mainstream Protestant churches and the more sect type churches over these issues. Masturbation is a sin in Catholic thought, but it is not regarded as a sin in mainstream Protestant thought. Since the sect type churches are largely drawn from lower class, or lower middle class, segments of the society, the lower class attitudes toward sex, as Kinsey has described them, become operative in conflicts over the use of sexually explicit materials in the schools.

Cal Thomas, in a recent book entitled *Book Burning*, (which describes none of the recent actual cases of book burning in the United States) quotes approvingly a letter to the editor of USA, which criticizes Blume's *Deenie* in the following words: "Masturbation was described in a how-to manner. Reference was made to petting, intercourse, and masturbation in a pornographic and titillating manner, encouraging children to experiment and assuring a good feeling when they do. . . ." The parent went on to say: "We complained. We said that we wanted *Deenie* and other books like it off the school shelves in the school libraries."[7]

The passage is notable for the intensity of feeling that it reveals. It is also typical of attacks on *Deenie* throughout the United States. The conflict between those who regard masturbation as a sin, and those who do not, presents great difficulties for school libraries, difficulties for which I see at the moment no real solution. As larger numbers of students move through the public schools and attain a high school education, some amelioration may occur. Also, if the centuries-old movement of the population from the lower class status to the middle class status continues, some additional amelioration of these conflicts may develop, but these are very long term considerations.

As Blacks came into the schools, and came in increasing numbers into middle class status, they began to object to materials they regarded as derogatory to Blacks. The substantial number of attacks on *The Adventures of Huckleberry Finn* have come to a significant degree from well-educated, middle class Black parents, who do not wish their children submitted to what they regard as insulting references to Blacks. A Black school official was responsible for the temporary removal of *The Adventures of Huckleberry Finn* from the Mark Twain Middle School, in Fairfax, Virginia. At the 1983 annual convention of NCTE an articulate and able Black woman parent, Margaret Allen of Pennsylvania State University, objected to *The Adventures of Huckleberry Finn* in the schools of State College, Pennsylvania, giving rise to an interesting study about the effect of that book on a student population. Middle class blacks also objected to *Daddy was a Number Runner* in Oakland, California, an objection that was supported by Ruth Love, the superintendent of schools in Oakland. The book was removed. Since white middle class parents can have books removed that they disapprove of, it is not surprising that Black middle class parents also bring pressures on the schools to remove books.

Those segments of the society that are fundamentally opposed to integration in the public schools and public institutions have mounted objections to such books as *The Learning Tree* that describe realistically the situation of Blacks or other minority members of the society. Ellen Last, L.B. Woods, and others believe that many objections to racist material are hidden under objections to language "—racially related attempts (at censorship) are subtly camouflaged by charges of bad language and/or obscenity."[8] Woods believed that *To Kill a Mockingbird* is "one of only a few titles censored strictly for racially inspired reasons".[9]

In short, racial conflicts have played a significant role and will probably continue to do so, in the controversies over learning materials in the schools. The Council on Interracial Books for Children presents a complicated form of the issue that race plays in books, as will be noted later.

6/ What are the results of the censorship pressures across the nation?

An examination of the available data suggests an ambiguous situation. On several of the four NCTE-WCTE surveys, a list of titles was included, with the request that the librarian report how many of those titles were in the school library. Note the chart on page 55. Only 21 percent of the 608 schools replying to the questionnaire in 1966 reported that they had *The Catcher in the Rye*.[10] By 1977, 76.5 percent of the schools reported having it,[11] and in 1982 the figure was similar, 76 percent. Published in 1951, *The Catcher in the Rye* did not make recommended lists for school titles until it was listed in the *Standard Catalogue for High School Librarians* in the 1963 Supplement. Its use in the schools preceded its inclusion in various recommended lists.

By 1969 *The Catcher in the Rye* had become the single most often attacked work of literature in the school libraries, as every student of this subject has indicated (Ahrens, Woods, Symula, Burress). It headed the list of frequently censored works of fiction until 1982, when it was supplanted in first place by *Go Ask Alice*, a tribute perhaps to increasing concern over the use of drugs by young people. No doubt also by 1982 some young people considered *The Catcher in the Rye* somewhat dated, with its heavy emphasis on the language usages of the 1940's.

Thus simultaneously, two things happened to *The Catcher in the Rye*; it became the most frequently censored book in school libraries, and it rapidly was ordered by a large proportion of school librarians.

Steinbeck's *The Grapes of Wrath* had a similar history in the public libraries, and to a lesser degree in the school libraries. In 1966, 54 percent of the schools on the survey reported having that book.[12] In 1982, 86 percent of the schools reported having *The Grapes of Wrath* in the school library. While no similar data currently exists concerning the books by Judy Blume, it is likely that her books reflect the same patterns as described above for *The Catcher in the Rye* and *The Grapes of Wrath*. Thus a history of censorship attempts is not necessarily a history of the general loss of the book from school classroom use, or from inclusion in the library.

Yet in many schools, on a rather unpredictable basis, students are denied the right to study or read some of the best books written in the twentieth century. Note the list below of the 48 most frequently challenged books in 1982. As a result of these challenges in 53.8 percent of the time, some form of censorship occurred in that the book was removed from classroom use, from the library, or from a list of recommended titles.

These denials represent a kind of bleeding of the lifeblood of the American school system. If education is a race between catastrophe and civilization, censorship of the materials listed below surely constitutes a serious handicap to the racers.

Not the least serious form of the handicap would be the substitution of bland, dull, irrelevant books for the living, quirky, passionate books that so often the censor attacks. One student reported checking out *Huckleberry Finn* and *Tom Sawyer* from the library. He started to read *Huckleberry Finn* while the librarian stamped his card. While he stood on the corner, waiting for the bus, he read. He read the book riding home on the bus, all through supper, and with a flashlight under the covers when his mother made him go to bed. Such experiences make lifetime readers. The books that the censors prefer—the McGuffey readers, or *Silas Marner*—are unlikely to generate that kind of commitment to reading.

One of the characteristics of the great literature that is so often attacked is a vigorous and definite point of view. The author's voice—his or her persona—gives a unique quality to the work. As Milton said, ". . . a good book is the precious life-

DISPOSITION OF CASES FOR THE 48 MOST
FREQUENTLY CHALLENGED BOOKS, 1982

Title	Request Denied	Some Form of Censorship	Pending
The Adventures of Huckleberry Finn	3	2	2
Anthology of New York Poets		2	
Are You in the House Alone?		3	
Ball Four Plus Ball Five	1	1	
Bellevue is a State of Mind	1	1	
Black Like Me	1	1	
Brave New World	2	1	
Catch Twenty-Two	2		
Catcher in the Rye	10	8	1
Chocolate War	2		
Daddy Was a Number Runner		2	
Electric Kool-Aid Acid Test		4	
The Exorcist	2	2	
Forever	5	8	
Go Ask Alice	18	16	
Grapes of Wrath	3	3	
Hard Feelings	2	1	
Headman	1	2	
A Hero Ain't Nothing But a Sandwich		7	
If Beale Street Could Talk		3	
I Hate To Talk About Your Mother	1	2	
I Know Why the Caged Bird Sings	1	1	
I, Pig	1	1	
It's OK If You Don't Love Me	1	5	
Johnny Got His Gun	2	1	
Killing Mr. Griffin	2		
The Learning Tree	2	3	
Lord of the Flies	1	2	
The Lottery		2	
Love Story		2	
Manchild in the Promised Land	1	2	
Mr. and Mrs. Bo Jo Jones	1	1	
My Darling, My Hamburger	4	1	
Native Son		2	
Nineteen Eighty-Four	1	1	
None of the Above	1	1	
All Books on the Occult	2	1	

Title	Request Denied	Some Form of Censorship	Pending
Of Mice and Men	3	6	
Our Bodies, Ourselves	8	8	
Run, Shelley, Run	2	1	
A Separate Peace		1	
Sex: Telling it Straight	1	1	
Slaughterhouse-Five	2	4	1
Summer of Forty-Two		2	
Then Again, Maybe I Won't	1	2	
To Kill a Mockingbird	2	1	
A Way of Love, A Way of Life	1	1	
Winning	1	2	
Totals	95	114	4
Percentage	44.5	53.8	1.7

blood of a master-spirit, embalmed and treasured up on purpose to a life beyond life." But the censorious attitude is one that either expects school books to have no point of view, or only the point of view of the censor. For a complex and diverse society such as the United States, with its origin in 50 or more ethnic groups, and with many religions, and with a variety of political positions, there might be safety in choosing a literature that is bland and uncommitted, but such a literature would be useless for preparing students for life in this country.

Another result of censorship pressure is the loss of some well-qualified teachers or librarians from the schools. Sonja Coleman, who defended the book which contained Jody Caravaglia's poem, was given tenure at Chelsea, Massachusetts, as a result of court action but resigned shortly afterwards. She was unemployed for a long time after leaving the Chelsea High School.[13] A young teacher in a Minneapolis suburb was harassed with many telephone calls, public attacks by a clergyman from the pulpit, and a school board reprimand, for using "A Coney Island of the mind #5." The poem was falsely charged with being unchristian. It had been previously taught for several years, and was suggested to the new teacher by the department chairperson. The new teacher left the profession after one year.[14]

Teachers have left or been fired for using books of the sort shown in the preceding table in several communities across the United States. In 1960 Mrs. Beatrice Levin resigned from teaching English at Tulsa, Oklahoma, because school administrators did not support her use of *Catcher in the Rye*.[15]

Another teacher was dismissed at Louisville, Kentucky, for using *Catcher* in 1960.[16] At Twin Lakes, Wisconsin, in 1962, six teachers were fired for objecting to the use of the McGuffey readers, as required by the school board.[17] In 1962 a high school teacher was fired at Wrenshall, Minnesota, for teaching *1984*. Court action restored his job.[18] In a few cases, legal action has protected the teacher, or recompensed the teacher for the lost job. In Clay County, Georgia, in 1971 an English teacher was fired for using an article from *Playboy* and for showing a surrealistic movie by Salvador Dali in the classroom. He was reinstated and paid $5,000 in damages after court action.[19]

A teacher was threatened with dismissal in 1969 at Ipswich, Massachusetts, for using an *Atlantic Monthly* article with a taboo word.[20] The teacher was protected by a First Circuit Appeals court decision. A first year English teacher, Marilyn Parducci, was dismissed for teaching *Welcome to the Monkey House* in Montgomery, Alabama in 1970. Court action restored her job.[21] John Fogarty was dismissed from an Idaho high school for using *One Flew Over the Cuckoo's Nest* in 1978.[22] Legal action resulted in some recompense to Fogarty. For the most part however, the teachers or librarians have left with little or no public recognition or recompense.

Nyla Ahrens' study of censorship showed that teachers experiencing censorship were better prepared, i.e., had more advanced degrees—masters, doctorate—than teachers who did not experience censorship. They had more recent training and were more likely to be liberal arts graduates, or university graduates, than graduates of teachers colleges. Thus it seems likely that teachers lost to the profession because of censorship controversies represent a loss of promising and well-educated persons. The effect of censorship controversies on those who remain in the profession is impossible to quantify. Nevertheless there is considerable evidence suggesting that some teachers retreat to a bland and noncontroversial stance in their classroom.

One librarian in returning the 1982 questionnaire unanswered, wrote: "Why would you expect librarians to answer such a controversial questionnaire when jobs are so scarce in times like these?" The fear represented by this answer is pervasive in the public schools, and understandable in the light of the experience of Sonja Coleman, John Fogarty and Marilyn Parducci. Yet significant numbers of librarians and teachers continue to order and use the materials their professional judgement calls for; otherwise all challenges would cease.

4 TWELVE REASONS FOR THE INCREASE IN CENSORSHIP*

TWELVE CHANGES IN AMERICAN SOCIETY and schools account for the growth of censorship pressures on literature texts in the public schools:

1/   Changes in the literature curriculum.
2/   The paperback revolution.
3/   The increasing numbers of students in school.
4/   The increased amount of education which students receive.
5/   The divisive nature of education.
6/   The success of the schools.
7/   The increase in reading by Americans.
8/   The increasing cost of education.
9/   The view of education as scapegoat.
10/   The role of education to reinforce democratic values.
11/   An increased willingness to protest government actions.
12/   Mistakes made by the schools.

1/ Changes in the Literature Curriculum

One reason why literature censorship increased after the 1950's was the effort of educators to fulfill the charge that appeared in an influential book published in 1935, by the National Council of

*This is an expanded version of an article which appeared as "Ten Reasons for the Recent Increase in School Censorship Pressures," in *Elementary School Guidance and Counseling*, vol. 17, no. 1 (October 1982), pp. 11–24.

Teachers of English, to make the literature curriculum reflect the emotional and intellectual range of students. Wilbur Hatfield, longtime executive secretary of NCTE, wrote this charge along with a number of objectives for the use of literature in the schools. He also suggested many titles that teachers could use to meet each objective.[1]

Hatfield suggested several hundred titles in all. In 1935 a teacher or school would have had a difficult time constructing a curriculum based on that selection of titles. A single, hard-bound anthology of selections determined by traditional publishers was the typical fare for secondary English literature classes in the 1930's. Moreover, it would have been almost impossible for a teacher to provide multiple copies of a story or poem for class use outside the anthology. The photocopying machine is a postwar phenomenon.

Dora Smith studied the curriculum in 1941 and reported that of 27 towns she visited:

> A few schools . . . provide a wealth of reading materials. Most of them, however . . . furnish a single literary compilation. . . . In general, the selections are traditional in content.[2]

Smith listed the titles most frequently supplied in quantities for reading in 18 representative high schools in New York State. Of the 31 titles on the list, 19 are British, 8 are American, 2 are Greek (*The Iliad* and *The Odyssey*), 1 is Norwegian (*Giants in the Earth*), and 1 is French (*Cyrano de Bergerac*). Smith concluded that the influence of the college entrance examinations determined to a very great degree the kind of books used to teach English literature through the early 1940s. She also pointed out that teachers gave little attention to "the reading abilities and interests of students in the lower half of an average group."[3]

Public school libraries were not well developed before 1950. Many smaller schools had no library at all, and even the larger schools had relatively few books. Those few were frequently arranged around the wall of a study hall. School librarians were largely an unknown part of school life. In view of the paucity of materials in the typical school library, a librarian would have had little to do.

Emerson's famous essay on the American scholar, which

called for an American literature, and by extension for the study of American literature by American students, had only slightly influenced the high school literature curriculum by 1940. In 1820, the famous British literary critic, Sidney Smith, wrote "Who reads an American book?" By 1940, a body of American literature had developed which was of worldwide importance. People all over the world read American books. U.S. Nobel prize winners, American books translated into many languages, a vigorous writing tradition and a substantial American publishing industry stimulated teachers to pay much more attention to American literature than they had in the past. Yet the American school curriculum in the 1930's was heavily influenced by British writers, an influence kept alive by the admissions tests for prestigious eastern colleges and universities.

Right wing critics have recently denigrated the schools by using the alleged decline of SAT scores based on averages; they have ignored the distribution of SAT scores by socioeconomic groups. Critics have kept alive the pressure to emphasize traditional British literary selections because the tests tended to emphasize British literature. Moreover the scholastic aptitude tests were heavily influenced by college entrance considerations and by the college English departments' emphasis on British literature. Thus they offered some support for attacks on the selection of contemporary American authors. These critics have their charges repeated in newspaper editorials and in speeches by politicians with little awareness of the larger issues described in this chapter.

In the curricular suggestions in his report of 1935, Hatfield attempted to bring things into a more appropriate balance. Hatfield's suggestions were not chauvinistic. He evidenced great concern to give students an awareness of other cultures and other literature. On his lists he included a number of British writers— Shakespeare, certainly, and several other British writers. But the proportion of American writers is far greater than the proportion suggested in Dora Smith's study cited above. Moreover, it is noteworthy that Hatfield's lists have a universal, international quality. He suggested titles from many cultures and many languages—Mukerji (*Gayneck*), tales from the Mahabharata and Ramayana, Cervantes, Sabatini, Stefansson, to mention the authors of only a very few of a wide and eclectic set of titles.

Moreover, he suggested titles which range across many interests and many levels of reading ability.

In the decades after 1940, the proportion of 14- to 19-year-olds who remained in school greatly increased. Students in the lower socioeconomic classes of American society contributed most of this increase. Hatfield was right in suggesting a variety of literary works to meet the diversity of interests and reading abilities that characterized the increasing proportion of young people who attended American high schools.

2/ The Paperback Revolution

The paperback revolution made it practical to implement the changes in curriculum that were suggested by Hatfield, Robert C. Pooley[4] and others and were advocated in the publications of the National Council of Teachers of English.

In the 1950's paperback books became available at 25 cents apiece, and a great many titles were published. Bantam Books estimated that 260 million copies were published in 1952.[5] Thus the schools could afford to buy several sets of various kinds of material. Between 1940 and 1960 book sales in the United States increased by 450 percent while the population of the country increased by only 37 percent.[6] Much of this increase in book sales was the result of the paperback revolution. English teachers began to use what the students actually wanted to read; they purchased such books as *Catcher in the Rye, A Coney Island of the Mind* and books about the occult along with hundreds of other contemporary titles. Classroom libraries of paperback books developed. The result was easy access to books that were believed by the teachers to be of interest to students. Robert Carlsen, in a series of articles and lectures based on his interviews with those persons he called "lifetime readers,"[7] emphasized the role that interest played in reading. People will read if they find material to read that interests them. So the question of student interest came to play a much more important role in book selection than had been previously the case.

Before the 1950's, the school libraries were believed to function chiefly to supplement the curriculum. There were encyclopedias, dictionaries, collections of Shakespeare's plays, reference works and some standard, largely British, novels or poets, though works by Hawthorne, Cooper and some other nineteenth century American writers occasionally found their way to the shelves of the school library. But with the changes in the literature curriculum advocated by Hatfield, Pooley, Carlsen, Dora Smith, Lou LaBrant and others,[8] schools began to recognize that an equally important function of the school library was to provide the same function that the public library does: To enable readers to find material they enjoy reading. Teachers and librarians developed the school libraries in the years following 1950 to fulfill this function of the library, as well as to complement the curriculum.

Many, including some librarians, still resist this notion. The recently adopted policy for selecting materials for the Racine, Wisconsin, public schools attempts to restrict the collection to material that supplements the curriculum. Other school libraries adopt the position that the only function of the library is to supply the best of books or to raise the reader's standards of taste. While this is a desirable goal, the road to that goal must include much material that may not be of the highest literary value. The somewhat elitist notion of the library's function suggested above ignores the evidence of Carlsen, and that of Fader described in *Hooked on Books*, of the power of reading interests to motivate people to read.[9]

The power of ephemeral books to motivate reading is described by the literary scholar Albert Guerard in his *Introduction to World Literature*. In that book he gives a theoretical explanation for the values of books of limited literary value. Carlsen, Fader, and Lou LaBrant demonstrated that many readers progress from books of lesser literary value to books of greater literary value if they are allowed to choose their own reading material from a wide range of possibilities. Thus libraries which refused to stock the Nancy Drew mysteries were acting in contradiction to the evidence of the process by which lifetime readers develop their skill. The evidence provided by such literary critics as Guerard and by such scholarly observers of the reading habits of young people as Carlsen and Fader suggest strong professional grounds for reviewing and acquiring popular books of ephemeral quality.

In general, the ideas of Hatfield, Pooley, Carlsen, Guerard, and Fader have won the day. Perhaps it could be said that the ideas of Ralph Waldo Emerson have won the day concerning literature selections for the high school. The libraries of the public schools are increasingly stocked with an eclectic set of books, across a wide range of reading interests, with a substantial, predominantly American set of authors and with a substantial representation of writers from the twentieth century.

That American schools should emphasize American writers seems self-evident, yet clearly some critics of the schools are still not ready to accept that proposition. Emily Dickinson had no trouble in deciding that the proper subject for American writers is the American landscape, as she wrote in her poem,

The Robin's my Criterion for Tune-
Because I grow-where Robins do-
But, were I Cuckoo born-
I'd swear by him-
The ode familiar-rules the Noon-
The Buttercup's, my Whim for Bloom-
Because, we're Orchard sprung-
But, were I Britain born,
I'd Daisies spurn-
None but the Nut-October fit-
Because, through dropping it,
The Seasons flit-I'm taught-
Without the Snow's Tableau
Winter, were lie-to me-
Because I see-New Englandly-
The Queen, discerns like me-
Provincially-

But many critics of the school system have found it hard to recognize that the proper subject for American students is primarily literature that deals with the American landscape and the American people. The paperback revolution made it possible to bring the contemporary writers of the United States into the schools and thereby to arouse the interest of the increasingly large number of students in the culture of this still new society—the

United States of America. More than half of these students, incidentally, were not originally from an English language background.

There is a certain irony in the fact that among the school critics have been several patriotic organizations—the Daughters of the American Revolution, the Sons of the American Revolution and various other groups. That they should resist developments in the school curriculum that emphasize American writers is a striking example of what might seem to be an irrational set of attitudes toward education. The forebears of these groups fought for the establishment of a new society, but their descendants do not wish the students in our schools to study the great literature that this new society has developed.

Of the several hundred titles listed in the appendix to this book which have become the object of attack in the public schools, most are by American writers and were written in the twentieth century. One would have thought that the DAR would encourage the use of American writers in the schools. However, as will be noted later, the DAR apparently takes offense at several of the values embodied in main stream American literature, such as the egalitarianism in Emily Dickinson's little poem:

> The Pedigree of Honey
> Does not concern the Bee-
> A Clover, any time, to him,
> Is Aristocracy-

From Emerson to Steinbeck, egalitarianism is a dominant strain in American literature. A group such as the DAR that as recently as the 1980's refused to allow a black woman to join its Washington, D.C. chapter may not be deeply committed to egalitarianism after all.

3/ The Increasing Numbers of Students in the Schools

We have been moderately successful in our effort made during the 20th century to offer opportunity for education to all young people. In 1900 a small proportion of young people attended school and did so for a relatively short school year. The average school year in 1900 was about 4½ months. Of 1000 fifth grade children in 1906 only 139 finished high school. Of 1000 fifth grade children in 1952, 604 finished high school. It was not until 1918 that all the states had passed compulsory attendance laws. Mississippi was the final state to pass such laws.[10] Today 90 percent of young people are in school, and they now attend for all the months between September and June. We have brought into the school Blacks, Native Americans, Hispanics, as well as various groups of handicapped children. Note the data below showing the steady increase in the proportion of students between the ages of 5 and 17 in school.[11]

	Enrolled	Attending
1870	55%	60%
1940	70%	70%
1970	90%	90%

Though we've succeeded in achieving educational opportunity for almost all young people, our failures get much attention. Dropout rates are still too high in some school districts. Some exceptional children receive only token education, but our failures should not obscure the substantial degree of success that we have achieved in pursuing the goal of educational opportunity for all.

It seems reasonable to believe that the events of Kanawha County, West Virginia, would not have occurred in earlier parts of this century when many rural children were unable to attend high school or had relatively few years of elementary school education. Before World War II, in Iowa for example, the lack of hard-surfaced roads made it difficult for rural high school students to get to school every day. In Wisconsin, even in the 1950's, rural schools gave children a "potato vacation" to help their parents with the harvest. Children in all the rural areas received similar vacations so they could help to do necessary work.

Two aspects of the growth in the student population have been important in censorship problems. The growth has come largely in the junior high and high school population. While censorship pressures have occurred in elementary schools, with for example a book that referred to the wedding of a black and a white rabbit, or with the Judy Blume books, most censorship problems occur in the junior high and senior high schools.

A second important aspect of the growth in school population is that it necessarily came from the lower socioeconomic sections of our society. Since these schools are primarily middle class institutions, the conflict in values between the differing social classes created the potential for serious conflicts over the purposes of education and the appropriate materials for use in the schools.

4/ The Increased Amount of Education Students Receive

With the increase in school population, a great many students now have more education than their parents. This is true not only in the first 12 years of education but also for college education. At the University of Wisconsin-Stevens Point, for example, approximately 80 percent of the students come from homes where their parents have little or no college background.[12] In fact, in Wisconsin more than one million adults did not have a high school diploma in 1980.[13] This situation, educating students whose parents have little education, results in complaints by those parents whose limited experience causes them to be surprised by the realities of education.

In a recent censorship controversy that I monitored in Amherst, one father, who was objecting to The Teenage Body Book, reported that his own education had ended at the eighth grade. Many of those advocating censorship have relatively little education and do not understand the concept of examining a book as a whole, or have little tolerance for opinions with which they disagree. The Gallup polls have regularly shown a consistent relationship between years of education and support for such civil liberties as freedom of the press, trial by jury, and separation of church and state.

As more young people move through the schools, the current censorship pressures may diminish.

5/ The Success of the Schools

It is also likely that the cause of attacks on schools is not because of their failures, but their success. When there is no hard news, newspaper editorials often lament the failure of the schools to teach students to read and write. The call for basic education rests on the assumption that schools are failing. I believe that this large generalization is of doubtful validity.

The National Assessment of Education does not support the proposition that the schools are failing. It is a truism of sociology that school test scores are related to socioeconomic status. The decline in SAT scores in all probability reflects the decreasing socioeconomic status of students rather than a real decline in basic skills.[14] In some high schools every graduating senior is asked to take the SAT test, whether the student took the college bound program or a vocational program. SAT reports of scores by states, data not often publicized, indicate that the states with the fewest students taking the test have the highest average scores. This supports the contention that the decline is illusory. In 1982 Egerton asserted:

> There has never been a time when a larger number or percentage of American young people completed the requirements of schooling, left with a greater and more diverse store of knowledge, and went on to advanced training in such a multitude of endeavors.[15]

That statement confirms my experience of 24 years at the University of Wisconsin-Stevens Point, where I have witnessed a steady increase in the ability of the average freshman to read and write.

6/ The Increase in Reading by Americans

A test of educational success that may be more valid than the SAT scores is the degree to which Americans read. There is considerable evidence that reading has steadily increased during the postwar decades. The previously cited study showed that while the population of the United States increased by 37 percent between 1940 and 1960, during that same period book sales increased by

445 percent, magazine sales by 110 percent, and newspaper sales by 45 percent.[16]

The 1978 Consumer Research Study on reading and book purchasing also shows an increase in reading by the population of this society.[17] A survey by Yankelovich, Skelly, and White in 1978 revealed the highest proportion yet recorded of positive replies to the question, Have you read a book in the last 6 months?[18] Between 1967 and 1984 the production of the U.S. book industry increased by 160 percent.[19]

One of the less publicized successes of the Great Society has been the effort to achieve access to a library for rural dwellers. Before 1965, a significant fraction of the population of the United States did not have legal access to a public library because the area where they lived did not tax the citizens to provide library service.[20] One Great Society piece of legislation, the Federal Library Services Act of 1956 which became in 1964 the Library Services and Construction Act, provided funds for the extension of library services to rural areas, which have taken advantage of this program to a substantial degree.

As an example, my community of Portage County, Wisconsin, had no rural library prior to 1965, when the City of Stevens Point began to provide library service to county people through buses and the periodic visits of a librarian to all parts of the county. For the fiscal year 1980–1981, 57 percent of the library use for the Stevens Point library was by rural people, and the county voted to take over financing and administering the library. In fact, by 1980, 99 percent of Wisconsin citizens were served by a public library, as is generally the case for the whole United States.[21]

Contrary to the usual assumption, the television age has not decreased people's interest in reading, nor has it decreased library use or book sales. In fact, as has been widely noted, the book industry has been a growth industry during the 1960's and 1970's. That would not have been possible if the schools had generally failed in establishing a population of persons who had mastered basic literacy. The schools have, in fact, produced a large population of people who can read and write and who do so in increasing numbers.

If schools had failed as abysmally as our critics suggest, we would not have the relatively high proportion of literate people who buy books, magazines, and newspapers and make increasing use of our libraries. It may well be that our success has evoked the vigorous criticism of recent years. If people were not reading books, why would anyone complain about books?

7/ The Divisive Nature of Education

That education is divisive is taught in classes in the philosophy of education, but often forgotten in actual practice. While teachers have an obligation to teach the values of the community, they also have an obligation to look searchingly at the community and its values. Much of what teachers teach in school stands in judgment of the community. Subjects of commercial value, such as vocational agriculture, are likely to be regarded with more tolerance than subjects with less obvious commercial value, such as English or history. Thus in classes in vocational agriculture, the instructor may point out the high rate of soil loss through local farming customs and may recommend terracing or no-till farming. Because of the commercial value of the class, such recommendations may create less conflict than judgments made in history or English classes about human losses in the community, along with recommendations for a more egalitarian society. Similarly, the reproductive cycle of the dairy cow may be taught in high school without complaint, but the reproductive cycle of human beings is taught in less than half of American school systems; and where it is taught, parents often complain.

The substantial literature of the Western world that criticizes racial prejudice, class prejudice, the glorification of war, and other tragic customs often produces complaint. Education is divisive. Those who profit from the status quo, who are frightened by change, or who cannot accept the function of education in accurately recording the past frequently attempt to reduce education to the indoctrination of students in the conventional beliefs of the local community.

8/ The Escalating Cost of Education

An eighth reason for the increasing frequency of attacks on the schools is the escalating cost of education. Inflation plays its role. Better educated teachers demand higher salaries, in contrast to the teachers in the rural schools before World War II who frequently had only a high school education or one or two years of education in a county normal school. In the 1950's and 1960's, most states began to require a four-year degree for entry into the teaching profession. Some school systems have begun to require a master's degree. These better-educated people demand, and merit, better pay. Most teachers however still make little money. In the late 1970's a right wing slogan was widely distributed across the country on bumper stickers and in other ways: "Is a teacher worth $34,000?" In fact in Wisconsin, which has moderately high salaries in comparison with other states, in 1978 high school teachers averaged slightly over $15,000 and elementary teachers averaged slightly under $15,000. These salaries were about equal to factory workers' salaries in those years.[22] Only a very few classroom teachers in the United States did in fact make $34,000 in 1978.

Cost for buildings and auxiliary services have certainly gone up, although contrary to the charges, most school buildings are not palaces. They are frequently built of cinder block, and are usually the most cheaply constructed public buildings in the community.

But whatever the cost of education, it is cheaper than the alternatives. For example, it cost about $26,800 a year to keep a person in the state penitentiaries of Wisconsin in 1983.[23] The cost is significantly higher in 1985. Yet because children do not vote and because we have an older, increasingly childless population, the schools are easy prey for politicians who want to cut taxes; to justify cutting educational budgets, they use the argument that the schools are failing.

9/ The View of Education as Scapegoat

A ninth basis for attacking the materials used in the schools is "scapegoating." Schools are blamed for all the ills of society. From the Gathings committee to the Gablers, a wide variety of voices have kept alive a chorus either blaming the schools, or the literature used in the schools, for all the ills of the contemporary world. Mel Gabler's charge that school textbooks are responsible for crime, violence, VD, and abortion is echoed again and again by school critics. A somewhat more moderate and perhaps more sophisticated form of the charges appeared in *Book Burning*.

Cal Thomas argues that the United States is suffering from a social, moral, and economic breakdown. To support this, he cites the high divorce rate, the one and one-half million abortions each year, a public school system which he asserts has a high degree of failure, and finally, "an epidemic of venereal disease." He concludes by saying that ". . . the root causes are . . . those who censor traditional values from textbooks, library shelves and bookstores."[24]

A similar charge was made by Carle (1978), who described the school as a hate factory. The essential message was vividly illustrated in chapter one with the nationally distributed cartoon entitled "Who is Destroying Your Children?" It shows small children going to school singing, "I love Mommy and Daddy, Jesus loves me, this I know, for the Bible tells me so." They are shown coming out of school saying, "I hate my . . . dumb parents. I'm pregnant, kick old people in the shins, down with America," and similar hateful sayings.

Few readers of this book would agree that schools are hate factories, but the assertion is widely made to explain all the ills of the day: drug addiction, abortion, alcoholism, teenage pregnancy, welfarism, and alleged declining rates of literacy. That the schools cause all of these problems is highly unlikely. It is more likely that changes in sexual behavior are caused by forces outside the schools. For example, the development of the automobile, which took courtship off front porches and out of the living room, played a more significant role in changing social customs than the books which young people read. The development of modern contraceptives and their easy availability changed sex customs. The commercialization of sex in advertising no doubt also played a role, when sexually provocative ads are used to sell cars, underwear, perfume, as well as trips to the sunny beaches of the Caribbean.

It should also be noted that puberty has developed at increasingly earlier ages in the United States. In 1900 the menarche occurred in American girls at age 14.3; in 1984 the average age was 12.9.[25] One interesting theory relates sexual maturity to better nutrition. When calories were withheld from some rats, they lived longer and their sexual maturity was significantly delayed. Could it be that if human beings cut their caloric intake in half, their life span might be greatly lengthened? Sexual maturity, however, might not then occur until age 30. Perhaps, therefore, we should suggest that instead of removing their children's books, parents instead cut their calories by half, or take away their driver's license!

However, as with other controversial subjects, the newspaper reports do not accurately reflect the complete situation with regard to teenage pregnancy. Since 1940, the number of babies born to unmarried teenagers has increased, tragically, but the number of teenage marriages has decreased, so that the total number of babies born to teenagers has declined.[26] Births per thousand women 15–19 years of age, married and unmarried in 1940 was 54.1; in 1976 it was 53.1.

In the past when teenagers married they dropped out of school; now the pregnant teenager, married or not, is likely to stay in school, thus tending to localize in the schools what is the result of social change outside the school. If schools prohibited attendance by pregnant teenagers, married or not, as they did in the past, there would be no imagery of pregnant teenagers associated with public schools. It is of course greatly disadvantageous for teenagers to become pregnant, but greatly to their advantage to remain in school, if for no other reason than the higher employability of high school graduates over eighth grade graduates. It is short-sighted of society to make the school a scapegoat because of its effort to assist these pregnant teenagers.

The scapegoating will no doubt continue, but if we make a better effort to stay in touch with our constituency, we can get a hearing for the view that we who work in the schools are not devils with horns and tails, but are ordinary human beings with children and grandchildren of our own, working for the best interests of the children and young people whom we teach.

10/ The Role of Education to Reinforce Democratic Values

A tenth reason for the pressures of the critics is the tendency of the schools to reinforce democratic values. We have not yet achieved a truly democratic republic; we are in process. This process has had a long history, both in the Old World and in the

New World. In the 17th century, voting was restricted to men of property. Shortly after the settlement in that colony, certain artisans were publicly lashed in Boston for politely petitioning the magistrates for the right to vote. The right to vote without a property requirement, not to pay taxes to the church, of women to vote, to strike, a free press—these and other rights have only slowly been achieved in the United States.

Much yet remains to be done to achieve a fully democratic republic. The school has been an effective agency in moving our society toward this goal. In accomplishing this, it took in immigrants from 50 or more language backgrounds, with differing colors and class status. The schools became both a means of personal advancement and a means of social progress. These efforts have been resisted across the centuries by those in our society who profit from the absence of a genuinely democratic society. Many still resist the further advances which we must make, if we are to fulfill the ideals of our founders.

By and large, the schools are effective at making clear our failures to live up to the great ideals embodied in our traditions and in such rituals as the pledge of allegiance to the flag, with its conclusion "one nation, under God, with liberty and justice for all."

The schools also equip large numbers of students with the skills necessary to work for a better society. We do teach people to read and write, with much more success than our critics give us credit for. If we did not, they would not be making such a hue and cry about the books we use. If the students could not read, who would care about the books available to them?

If our students were not learning to see through demagoguery, double talk, the faulty use of logic in the ad hominem argument, who would care about our teaching? We do have considerable success in teaching these essential skills for the citizens of our republic. Our critics want to stop us from teaching these skills.

11/ An Increased Willingness to Protest Government Actions

An eleventh reason for increasing pressure on the schools is the increasing tendency of Americans to protest actions of governmental agencies that they perceive as not working in their best interests. That was clearly the motive of most book protesters in Kanawha County. Saul Alinsky's Back of the Yards Movement in Chicago has had many a foster child in the last several decades; the Alinsky movement was a concerted effort to teach citizens how to organize to force governmental agencies to meet the desires and interests of the citizenry. [27]

We in the schools should not resist this movement. Instead we should carefully and thoughtfully respond to the critics. We should not forget that in the public schools we stand in the same relation to the citizens as other governmental agencies do. The taxpayers will have their way with the public schools in the long run. Let us work with the energies of the critics for the best possible results in our educational system.

12/ Mistakes Made by the Schools

I shall end this list of reasons for the increase in censorship with a reminder that schools have made more than a few mistakes and, like most other institutions in this society, have often been unwilling to admit these mistakes or to rectify them. With consolidation and growth of population, the schools have often become bureaucratic, hierarchical, and impersonal in dealing with people. Too often schools have dealt in a dehumanizing manner with parents as well as students.

It is not surprising that as a result many citizens have become angry. In almost every community, one can find aggrieved citizens who feel—frequently with some justice—that the schools have not listened to their complaint or have dealt with them summarily or unjustly. Recently in Wisconsin such an incident occurred with a farming couple who lived about a quarter of a mile from the main road down an isolated road lined with overarching evergreens. The school bus did not go down this road because the distance is slightly less to the main road than the required distance for bus pickup. This family had a second grade child, a little girl who was afraid to walk down the dark road in the early morning hours when the school bus came by. The parents asked for pickup at the house during the winter months when the child had to walk down that stretch of the road in the dark. The school board said no and understandably the family was angry.

Most of the readers of this book can think of a similar situation in which some good general principle influenced students and parents in an undesirable way. Like Procrustes, who constructed a bed in his tavern by the side of the road and then stretched the short ones to fit the bed and lopped the head or feet off those too long for the bed, we have constructed a system that sometimes makes the students fit the school rather than adapting the school to fit the students.

There have been several reports of persons who were motivated to form a group of censorious critics because they were rebuffed by a school administrator or teacher, sometimes with carelessness, sometimes with discourtesy. We have created some of our critics by our failures to recognize them as fellow human beings, by our failure to make clear what we have been doing, and by our failure to admit that we have, on occasion, made mistakes that we should rectify.

Undoubtedly, other reasons might be added to this list of factors that contributed to the growth of censorship pressure on the schools during the 1960's and 1970's, but these 12 reasons account to a considerable degree for the increase in censorship.

5 PUBLISHERS AS CENSORS

In March 1984, the parents of a ninth grade student in Roosevelt High School in Minneapolis learned that the version of *Romeo and Juliet* their son was using in school had been greatly expurgated. The play is contained in an anthology, *Arrangements in Literature* published by Scott, Foresman. Approximately 400 lines of the play were deleted and several words in the text were altered. The parents complained, correctly, that their son was being exposed to "secret censorship." This was an unusual complaint, since parents are generally more likely to call for censorship than to object to it.

That high school versions of Shakespeare are frequently expurgated has been a well kept secret to all but a few interested students of censorship on the American scene. As a teacher of Shakespeare in college classes, I have been aware for a number of years that the standard texts taught in college and university Shakespeare classes are not the same as the versions that appear in many high school anthologies. Unfortunately, what has been true of Shakespeare has also been true of Tennyson, Mark Twain, and many others. Though this discussion is primarily concerned with literature textbooks, what has been true of literature texts has, unfortunately, been true of science texts, especially concerning the issue of evolution.

There is nothing new in attacks either on Shakespeare or Mark Twain. It should be remembered that Shakespeare's plays had to be presented outside the City of London, since the Puritans who controlled the government of London made it illegal to present plays to the general public within the City. Therefore the Globe and other playhouses were built outside the City. In fact, the good Puritans who ran the city were so unhappy about the plays that the Lord Mayor of London wrote a letter to Queen Elizabeth urging her to outlaw the theater throughout England. The letter said of plays that:

> neither in politie nor in religion they are to be suffered in a Christian Commonwealth, specially beinge of that frame & matter as usually they are, conteining nothinge but prophane fables, lascivious matters, cozeninge devices, & scurrilus beehaviours, which are so set forth as that they move wholie to imitation & not to the avoydinge of those faults & vices which they represent.[1]

This letter was written in 1597 shortly after Shakespeare wrote *Romeo and Juliet*. Elizabeth loved the theater and paid no attention to the letter.

The complaints in the letter are in the language of the 16th century, but the substance of those complaints should seem familiar to anyone who has paid attention to the current wave of censorship activities. The terms, "prophane fables, lascivious matters, and scurrilus beehaviours" are older terms for the charges against literature that appear most frequently in any current study of censorship pressures—bad language, sexual references and immoral behavior.

The same impulse that characterized the Puritans in Shakespeare's London reappeared in England in the early part of the nineteenth century in the activities of Dr. Thomas Bowdler, as Noel Perrin reported in *Dr. Bowdler's Legacy*. Victorianism expressed itself in the work of Bowdler before Victoria came to the throne. The most famous of all expurgated books, *The Family Shakespeare*, edited by Bowdler, was published in Bath, England in 1807. Bowdler expurgated about 10 percent of what Shakespeare wrote. His sister, Harriet Bowdler, suggested that both moral and esthetic considerations should be taken into account in the publication of literature. She advocated omitting scenes that were "uninteresting or absurd." Bowdler himself reported that he cut out of Shakespeare "everything which may not with propriety be read aloud in a family." His cuts dealt largely with overtly sexual or religious allusions. Between 1807 and 1940, 100 or more texts appeared that bowdlerized Shakespeare. Such major publishers as the Oxford University Press, Cambridge University Press, and Ginn & Company published expurgated versions of Shakespeare; however, by 1940 most college texts were unexpurgated.

Perrin reported that hundreds of other titles have also been expurgated, including several versions of the Bible, *Gulliver's Travels*, and many collections of the standard English poets. In Milton's *Paradise Lost*, references to Satan's incest and Adam and Eve's nudity have been deleted. Noah Webster published a bowdlerized version of the Bible in 1833. His *Compendious Dictionary*, published in 1806, which relied heavily on Samuel Johnson's dictionary, omitted all the bawdy, 18th-century words that Johnson included.[2] These words did not come back into American dictionaries until after World War II. As has been noted earlier, the presence of those words caused the five most widely used dictionaries to be banned in Texas. James Squire reported that Merriam-Webster was asked to prepare a bowdlerized version of its dictionary for the Texas market but refused, a commendable illustration of principle that all publishers should follow.[3]

While publishers have long bowdlerized the works of standard writers, especially Shakespeare, and unfortunately, they continue to do so in publishing school anthologies, the expurgations, bowdlerizations, deletions, or emendations are generally unknown to the teachers or students who use the books. The publishers usually give no notice that the purchaser is not receiving the best text by current scholarly standards. In the Scott, Foresman text cited above, however, the teacher's guide does announce that the text of *Romeo and Juliet* has been cut by 404 lines. The students' text has no such notice, nor does it announce that some words are altered.

The broader definition used in this book asserts that any effort to prevent communication is censorship. This definition recognizes the power of publishers, the power of self-appointed pressure groups and the power of librarians, teachers and school administrators to prevent the fulfillment of the communication process, thus minimizing the ability of readers to decide for themselves the meaning or value of a given work. This broader definition recognizes the tendency of small groups to decide for the larger society what will be read or known.

In discussing the characteristics of censorship, several writers have pointed out that secrecy frequently accompanies censorship. That is certainly true of many standard high school anthologies. Secretly, the publishers prevent the full form of a play, novel, or poem, from reaching the teacher or student. As Dorothy Thompson Weathersby points out in her study of this subject, "It is very difficult for parents and educators to withstand silent censorship that they may not even realize exists."[4]

To publish a work and protest that it is a play by Shakespeare, or a novel by Mark Twain, while secretly changing the text of the work seems clearly nonprofessional, clearly in violation of the scholarly standards that obtain in colleges and universities and standards that ought to obtain in the publishing industry. Such an action seems quite appropriately described as censorship.

Two motives may be imagined for expurgating a text. One motive is the sincere, though mistaken belief that the text might corrupt the young, as the Lord Mayor of London wrote in 1597, and as the nationally known textbook critics, Mel and Norma Gabler continue to insist today.

The second motive for expurgating a text is commercial, the fear that the original text would prevent the sale of the book because of the activities of textbook critics such as the Gablers. Twenty states have various forms of statewide adoption of school texts. These states exercise great influence on the textbook choices of the other states. A text chosen in Texas will be very profitable to the publisher as Texas is such a large market where the 1983 textbook budget exceeded $60 million. Moreover, the cost of preparing a text is so great that publishers are unwilling to prepare one version of the text for Texas and another for the rest of the country.

Several other states which practice statewide textbook adoption, Tennessee and Mississippi for example, mirror the attitudes of the Gablers, thus increasing the influence in text selection of critics who have views that differ significantly from mainstream educators.

The censorious voices in Texas and Tennessee have had considerable effect, according to the two recent doctoral dissertations cited earlier; one by Dorothy Thompson Weathersby, (University of Tennessee, 1975) and the other by Ellen Last (University of Texas, 1984). That statewide adoption procedures are effective in shaping the literature available to high school students throughout the United States is shown by Last's observation that complaints in Texas have driven Shirley Jackson's "The Lottery" from all the major anthologies for the high schools. Weathersby pointed out that a version of *The Adventures of Huckleberry Finn* prepared for Tennessee omitted the passage in Chapter 18 in which in a daily ritual the Grangerford young men toasted their parents with a drink.[5] Perhaps deference to anti-alcohol feelings in Tennessee was responsible for that deletion; however, that text, with its deletion, is used nationally. The 1973 version is used in the high school in Stevens Point, Wisconsin, at this writing.

Weathersby reported ". . . publishers [are] reluctant to [discuss] this problem [and] did not answer [my questionnaire] or did not provide much information on what they did return."[6] In fact, the typical response of a major publisher to an inquiry concerning abridgment or censorship in anthologies is:

Dear Sir:

Thank you for your interest in our texts.

Sincerely yours,

In November 1982 when the National Council of Teachers of English held its annual convention in Washington, D.C., Steven Tchudi, then vice president of the Council, held a one-day workshop on the joint problems of teachers and publishers. A representative of the Association of American Publishers made a presentation to the assembled group; he used his forty-five minutes to make two points: one, that teachers should prepare better copy for submission of manuscripts, and two, that teachers should request fewer sample copies of texts for examination for classroom use. The issue of textbook censorship was not discussed by this AAP representative, nor would he answer any questions on that topic. This unresponsiveness of publishers to teachers, as noted by Weathersby, has been discovered by several other teachers facing censorship problems. The Montello, Wisconsin, case is a typical example. Neither Dell, publisher of *The Magician*, nor its parent company would offer any advice or assistance to the teacher using that book. As we have seen earlier the author of the book, Saul Stein, did advertise his willingness to provide a paperback copy of the book to any family in that school district in order to counteract a flyer that was distributed in the school district with excerpted out-of-context passages from the book. Letters of inquiry from the Minneapolis public schools also received generally unsatisfactory answers from a number of publishers, as will be noted later in this discussion.

Are the changes imposed by publishers important? Maureen F. Logan makes clear how the deletions in *Romeo and Juliet* distort the meaning of that play.[7] She compared the good Pelican text of *Romeo and Juliet* with two other versions, one published by Harcourt, Brace and World in 1963, and one by Harcourt Brace Jovanovich in 1980. The 1963 version was admittedly an abridged version with about 40 percent of the original 2994 lines (by Pelican line count); the 1980 version, in *Adventures in Reading*, Heritage Edition, printed 2676 lines. In this case, there was a notice that "This version omits trivial or ribald wordplay and especially difficult, static passages of poetry." The HBJ 1980 version in fact omitted about ten percent of the play. These omissions significantly distorted the play by making it more difficult to understand the characters of the Nurse and of Mercutio, Logan reports. Of the 318 omitted lines, 220 have sexual connotations. She is unable to explain why the other omitted lines were dropped; it would seem difficult to convince most Shakespeare scholars that those lines were "trivial" or "static." At least, HBJ announces it cut the play; most publishers of anthologies do not.

The Weathersby dissertation presents the fullest study currently available of censorship by publishers of high school literature textbooks. She examined 22 anthologies published by seven major publishing companies. She also made an effort to question publishers about their policies in editing high school anthologies. She did a massive amount of work comparing the original versions of the literary selections in the 22 anthologies with the textbook versions of those works.

Weathersby found that the publishers had silently omitted or altered many words or passages to which they presumably felt somebody might object. The expurgations she described parallel the objections commonly made to works used in the public schools today. The deletions removed material that dealt frankly or realistically with sex. Swearing or profanity was removed; material that dealt with minority groups was removed or rewritten, and any material that the editors apparently felt might be offensive to anybody was taken out. In addition, Weathersby found that the selection of authors emphasized white Anglo-Saxon males; only to a very limited degree were women or minority writers included. This is especially ironic since a number of the publishers have adopted guidelines for the elimination of racial and sexist language. For example, in 1970 Scott, Foresman began to use a pamphlet entitled *Guidelines for Improving the Image of Women in Text Books*. While these guidelines did not result in an immediate increase in the representation of women writers in the Scott, Foresman high school anthology of 1971, they may have ultimately influenced the selection of writers in later editions.

In examining the texts of Shakespeare, Weathersby found many examples of bowdlerizing. The only complete version of *Hamlet* that she found was in a Holt, Rinehart and Winston anthology.[8] A Scott, Foresman anthology omitted 119 lines from this play.[9] A passage often omitted from *Hamlet* is the play within a play in Act 3, Scene 2.

Hamlet.	Lady, shall I lie in your lap?
Ophelia.	No, my lord.
Hamlet.	I mean, my head upon your lap?
Ophelia.	Aye, my lord.
Hamlet.	Do you think I meant country matters?
Ophelia.	I think nothing, my lord.
Hamlet.	That's a fair thought to lie between maids' legs.
Ophelia.	What is, my lord?
Hamlet.	Nothing.
Ophelia.	You are merry, my lord.

These ten lines are frequently omitted from high school anthologies. Scott, Foresman omitted the passage cited above and in addition 109 other lines from its anthology *England in Literature*. Other passages omitted in the Scott, Foresman version of *Hamlet* are:

Player Queen:	A second time I kill my husband dead,
	When second husband kisses me in bed.
	(Act III, Scene 2, lines 194–195)

Hamlet: Nay, but to live
          in the rank sweat of an enseamed bed
          Stew'd in corruption, honeying and making love
          Over the nasty sty.
          (Act III, Scene 4, lines 92–95)

Weathersby also found many other examples of silent deletions: Eugene O'Neill's play *Beyond the Horizon*, a dramatic
version of *The Diary of Anne Frank*, *The Ox-Bow Incident* by
Walter Van Tilburg Clark, Bret Harte's *The Luck of Roaring
Camp*, Thomas Wolfe's essay "Circus and Dawn," and many
others. McGraw-Hill deleted the following sentence from the
dramatic version of Anne Frank's *Diary:* "No one's going to tell
us Dutchmen what to do with our own damn Jews." From the
Wolfe essay several paragraphs were omitted that present the
highly uncomplimentary picture of Blacks held by many persons
living in small towns in the South in the first half of this century.[10]

The editors of these anthologies displayed great concern
about language usage. Weathersby points out again and again
where "the language was cleaned up." Thus so-called swear
words—"My God," "Oh God," "For God's sake"—were frequently though inconsistently omitted or replaced with "By gum"
for "By God," "By heaven" for "By God," "Well" for "God," or
by many other euphemisms. Such words as "ass," "bastard," "son
of a bitch," and "nigger" clearly cause problems for the editors of
these various anthologies. A Singer anthology used the word
"slave" in place of "nigger" for a passage from *Huckleberry Finn.*
Scott, Foresman omitted the word "nigger" in rewriting the line
that appeared originally as Mark Twain wrote it:

" 'Betsy!' (this was a nigger woman), 'you' "

Scott, Foresman made it appear:

" 'Betsy, you fly around' "

McGraw Hill replaced the word "nigger" with the word "ser-
vant," or with the word "folks" or with the word "hand." Harcourt Brace Jovanovich chose to replace the word "negro" which
Mark Twain used in "The Private History of a Campaign that
Failed" with the word "slave."

Weathersby noted that an anthology by Ginn was the only

one that dealt openly with the word "nigger." It did this by including an essay from *American Literature* by Lionel Trilling on the novel *Huckleberry Finn*. Trilling explained why it was essential to use Mark Twain's own language and especially the word "nigger" in reprinting *Huckleberry Finn*.

> This is the only word for a Negro that a boy like Huck would know in his place and time—that is, an ignorant boy in the South before the Civil War. An American dictionary correctly describes it as "a vulgar and offensive term;" no decent person would think of using it, and all decent people feel that anyone who does use it thereby debases himself. It is right beyond question that the word should be driven out of the language, together with all the other words that have been used to express hostility and contempt for certain ethnic groups in our country, for the Irish, the Jews, the Italians, the Mexicans, and the Puerto Ricans, to mention only a few. But even if the vulgar contemptuous terms should be quite extirpated, the fact that they were once freely used ought not be suppressed. For it is a fact that forms part of our national history, and a national history is not made up of pleasant and creditable things only. And it is a part of the consciousness of themselves of each of the ethnic groups who have had to endure one or another degree of social disadvantage; it is something to be confronted and dealt with, not evaded or forgotten. [11]

One of the strangest sets of deletions that Weathersby reports concerns Tennyson's *Idylls of the King*. Scott, Foresman included the poem *Gareth and Lynette* in its tenth grade anthology. [12] However, Scott, Foresman presented only about 70 percent of the poem, omitting 419 lines and, incredibly, wrote new lines or joined two lines from different parts of the poem to bridge the cuts they made in the narrative. Weathersby reports at least seven alterations in the text of this poem, with no notice being given to the reader of these changes. At this writing, this text is still in use in at least one Wisconsin high school.

Weathersby points out that in the 22 anthologies she examined, the woman writer is relatively absent, though better represented than Blacks, Indians, or Jews. [13] Weathersby believed that there was a clear tendency in the texts to present women in the traditional roles of mother and wife. "They are generally shown as the passive members of the family who dispense love and understanding or who possess fear, innocence, and lack of intelligence." She believed that there was some effort by the Scott, Foresman editors to try to do more than the other publishers in "changing the role of women that literature textbooks have presented in the past."

One cannot avoid a degree of sympathy with the problem faced by editors who wish their texts to have the widest possible sale in a society where the Gablers expect texts to represent traditional nineteenth-century roles for men and women. Yet more than half of present women work outside the home, and a strong majority of the citizens favor freedom of choice with regard to abortion. According to the Weathersby analysis, the texts submitted for adoption in Tennessee generally present a nineteenth-century picture of women.

She said that "The twenty-two literature textbooks examined in this study contained little that parent, minority, religious, and patriotic groups can find objectionable."[14] In summarizing the general nature of the various expurgations and emendations that she found, Weathersby concluded: "This silent editing represents a serious threat to education because it does misrepresent the works and ideas that the publishers and educators select to be taught in the schools. The intellectual dishonesty that silent editing promotes is directly opposed to the ideals parents ask that the schools teach their children."[15]

Ellen Last's dissertation dealt with the pressure on the anthologies by critics from Texas, especially Mel and Norma Gabler. Last studied the ideas of those persons who criticized the high school literature anthologies that were considered for adoption in Texas in 1979. Seventeen critics filed 350 pages of criticism. The Gablers dominated the filings though one or two other persons also filed significant amounts of material. Other critics appeared before the Texas textbook committee to make oral complaints in addition to the written materials that were filed. Mrs. Mel Gabler and Mrs. Billy C. Hutcheson were responsible for nearly 70 percent of the oral arguments.

Ellen Last's dissertation is important because of the effect of Texas state adoptions on the rest of the United States. As she pointed out, "Because the state of Texas is the single largest market for secondary texts in the nation, and because its state adoption process has drawn a small but well organized group of inveterate protestors, the Texas textbook adoption process has begun to shape textbooks in use nationwide."

Publishers clearly strive to comply with the Texas critics but they then market texts prepared for Texas all over the United States. The success of the Texas critics was previously noted, illustrated by the disappearance of Shirley Jackson's short story, "The Lottery."

Ellen Last summarized the views of the Texas critics in the following fashion. "In summary, the textbook critics tend to view literature as a means of passing on a cultural tradition circumscribed by white, Protestant, nineteenth-century values." In applying this expectancy, the Gablers make clear their belief that "literature should be uplifting and optimistic, that it should express traditional views of the American family, the American economy, and the American social and political system. They insist that references to religious or ethical consideration should support a literalist, orthodox, Christian view."[16] Last points out that they fail to recognize satire, irony, or social protest as a significant part of the world of literature. For this and other reasons they object to much twentieth-century writing because they see in it only a rejection of traditional values of patriarchal white family life, capitalistic nationalism and fundamentalist, Protestant Christianity.

According to Last, their general statements about literature suggest that the Texas critics believe the following:

1/   The major objective in teaching literature is to convey the nation's traditional cultural heritage to its young people. An emphasis on contemporary literature subverts this goal.
2/   The American literary canon should consist of authors who were popular in their own times and who thus represent the thinking of Americans through the years. [For this reason, they object to Emily Dickinson].
3/   Editorial bias has created books in which the emphasis is on the wrong authors and the wrong ideas. This bias results in the inclusion of writers who are associated with Harvard University, with Unitarianism, and with left-wing, revolutionary, or humanistic groups or ideas. [Therefore, they object to Emerson, Thoreau, and Emily Dickinson].
4/   Values should not be examined in the classroom. Home-and-church taught values are threatened by the force of peer

pressure. These values include traditional views on self-re-liance, patriotism, authority, Christianity, the nuclear fami-ly, and on the superiority of white middle-class life and language as opposed to minority life and language. [There-fore they wish education to indoctrinate rather than prepare students to think for themselves.][17]

Some writers on the subject of the Gablers have com-mended the effort that they put into textbook analysis. Kenneth Taylor, for example, has said of the Gablers, "They do their homework thoroughly, know textbook content in impressive de-tail, and share their information with others. . . . Their review-ing processes might withstand public scrutiny better than those of many school systems."[18] Ellen Last's dissertation offers an oppor-tunity to test this proposition. Last analyzed the Texas critics' written presentations in an effort to understand the rhetorical characteristics of those presentations. She used four categories to analyze the various criticisms, based on the research concerning literary response by several scholars. The categories of literary response are:

1/ Personal statement
2/ Descriptive statement
3/ Interpretative statement
4/ Evaluative statement

In addition to the four categories listed above, she added two other categories: Category 5. Educational concerns; Category 6. Miscellaneous matters such as references to other authors. A rating system was used to classify written objections of the Texas critics under one or another of the categories listed above. She also made a computer search of the most frequently used words in the critical presentations.

With these methods of analysis, Last demonstrated rather conclusively that the Texas critics do not use professional or scholarly principles in literary evaluation. Her computer search, for instance, sought to find out the frequency with which 24 terms commonly used by literary critics appeared in this material. She found that only 9 appeared in the protests filed by the Texas objectors: poem, poet, style, play, character, theme, plot, satire, and language. Among words that do not appear are such terms as imagery, characterization, and irony. Thus, in place of the process of description and evaluation that characterizes scholarly or literary discussions, the Gablers "frequently use short emotional rejections of the literary selections."

> Foolishness, Ridiculous. This is ridiculous, nonsense and a waste of time. These stories do not reconcile with the definition of "literature." Gutter level ideas. No literary value.[19]

A list of the writers objected to by the Texas critics include Thoreau, Emerson, Hawthorne, Melville, Poe, Cather, Crane, Dickinson, Twain, Wharton, Steinbeck, Lewis, Hemingway, Anderson, Sandburg, Frost, Pound, Amy Lowell, Robert Lowell, Tennessee Williams, William Carlos Williams, Baldwin, Hughes, and Millay. Note that of these writers, 18 are 20th-century writers; the others are generally from New England and the North. The seven nineteenth-century writers reflect the opposition of the Texas critics to what they perceive to be a Harvard and Unitarian bias in the literary selections presented in Texas in 1978.

It is interesting to compare the findings of Weathersby on the content of the anthologies used in Tennessee with the protests of the Texas critics, as described by Last. The parallelism is quite noteworthy. Weathersby found that the editors tended to remove or rewrite objectionable word choices or language, such as "Oh God, By God, bastard, nigger." As Last pointed out: criticism of improper language—whether vulgar, profane or nonstandard—recurs as an important feature in the Texas critics' evaluation of literature. "They frequently attack words that they perceive to be profanity, such as the phrase, 'Good Lord,' as well as vulgar or grammatically incorrect expressions."

Weathersby found that the publishers of the 22 anthologies she examined tended to remove all material that criticized the racism of this society. The Texas critics also strongly objected to material that in their reverse psychology was considered discriminatory, because it criticized the white race for its treatment of Blacks.

The Weathersby study found relatively few selections from

women writers, thus supporting the stereotype of the patriarchal society.

That the Tennessee texts parallel Texas ideas with regard to racial and ethnic differences is not surprising. Last's belief was that some objections to language and dialect usages in the materials submitted for adoption in Texas concealed race prejudice. She asserted that . . . "the expressed concern for language may mask other unstated feelings . . . the protestors frequently attack works containing dialect forms, especially those by black writers." In commenting on a poem entitled "Minority Poem," in which the poet addresses her "little brotha," one critic ostensibly based her attack on the assumption that the poet was unable to spell the word correctly. It seems likely that this is a hidden form of racism. [20]

Weathersby pointed out that in 22 anthologies there were only four selections that dealt with the Jewish experience, that no modern Native American writers are represented, and that the only presentation of Native Americans reflects the nineteenth century views of Cooper and Parkman. In the Scott, Foresman text *Man In Literature* dealing with a story about a Malay, a significant omission is a paragraph which includes the statement that "people are alike on the inside no matter what color they are outside."

Weathersby also noted that a Singer text omitted several lines from Carson McCullers' play *Member of the Wedding*, lines that showed the "more sensitive issues from a black's point of view." She found only 4 stories in the 22 anthologies that show the workings of race prejudice and commented that "At a time when racial harmony is nonexistent in many American high schools, this lack of material . . . is more than oversight; it is dangerous."[21] It is, however, harmonious with the expectancies of the Texas critics.

Weathersby found no references that dealt with drugs, and references to drinking alcohol were nonexistent in the texts chosen for inclusion or were deleted, as in the previously cited case of *Huckleberry Finn*. Very little material descriptive of the variety of American views about religion was presented. Franklin's doubt about religion in his *Autobiography* is omitted from the school texts. Thus nothing offensive to the Texas prescription of material that supports fundamentalist, Protestant, Christian ideas is found. In fact, Weathersby asserts, "Very little material that might be construed as critical of American values can be found"[22] in these anthologies. These books therefore fit the Texas prescription that makes English classes "a refuge from reality, not a place to explore reality," to use the accurate observation of Last. Furthermore, because of their attitude toward literature, the Texas critics are unable to distinguish between a realistic presentation of some aspect of life, and advocacy of whatever is being presented. In Last's view of the Texas critics, "Attacks on the content of stories and poems imply a belief that content equals advocacy."[23]

There is considerable evidence of the continuing national relevance of these studies completed in 1975 in Tennessee and in 1978 in Texas. Anthologies tend to stay in use for a number of years because of their high cost. The Stevens Point, Wisconsin Area High School, a well-managed school with some two thousand students, currently uses a 1973 edition of the Harcourt Brace Jovanovich *Adventures in American Literature*. In fact, in the Stevens Point high school, literary anthologies published in 1958 are still available for use. Inquiries at several other Central Wisconsin high schools yielded similar reports. The 1973 HBJ anthology is a traditional survey of American literature with approximately 70 authors. The selections begin with William Bradford and end with such writers as John Updike and James Baldwin. This 1973 anthology contains 57 male writers, 9 women writers and 3 black writers—the same disproportionate selection of men and women writers that Weathersby found in the text adopted for use in Tennessee. As Weathersby noted, minority writers are only slightly represented. There are no Native American writers and no writers that reflect Jewish experience.

Meanwhile, at least some expurgation of materials is evident. Benjamin Franklin's autobiography is frequently represented in high school anthologies with a passage in which Franklin describes his attempt to acquire 13 virtues. He made a chart and attempted week by week to improve his ability to live up to the various virtues he set for himself. In the original text Franklin specified after each virtue what its application meant. Thus Virtue #11, Tranquility, he described as: "Be not disturbed at trifles, or at accidents common or available." Virtue #12 is Chas-

ANALYSIS OF CONTRIBUTORS TO THREE HBJ ANTHOLOGIES

	Men	Women	Blacks	Jews	Native Americans	Hispanics	Asian Americans
1973	57	9	3	0	0	0	0
1980	81	17	14	0	2	4	0
1985	85	24	14	1	2	5	0

THE UNITED STATES IN LITERATURE (SCOTT, FORESMAN)

	Men	Women	Blacks	Jews	Native Americans	Hispanics	Asian Americans
1979	77	47	18	2	10	13	2

tity. In the original text Franklin described that virtue in the following language. "Rarely use venery but for health or offspring, never to dullness, weakness, or the injury of your own or another's peace or reputation." This passage is omitted from the 1973, from the 1980, and from the 1985 editions of the Harcourt Brace Jovanovich anthology, *Adventures in American Literature*.

An even older English textbook is still in use in another central Wisconsin high school. *Advanced Composition: A Book of Models for Writing*, published by Harcourt Brace and World in 1961, contains Faulkner's short story "Barn Burning." As written by Faulkner, this story of a Southern sharecropper and his son used the word "nigger" several times. As published by Harcourt Brace and World, the word was dropped or became "Negro," an obvious anachronism when spoken by Abner Snopes, an uneducated sharecropper. In addition, the editors chose to emend a phrase describing two of Snopes' daughters: ". . . the sisters sitting with spread heavy thighs in two chairs over the cold hearth. . . ." The words "spread heavy thighs" were omitted by the editors. In context the three words are hardly noticeable; taken out of context they seem much more suggestive. No notice is given to the reader of these deletions.

Faulkner was still alive in 1961; it would be interesting to know if he approved these changes. In 1945 he was asked for permission to include "Two Soldiers" in a high school anthology, to be bowdlerized in four places, deleting "hell" and "nigger." He wrote a letter seeming to agree but required that the editor put an asterisk and an explanatory footnote at each deletion. He wrote, "This may be good for the children. . . . It will be teaching them at an early and tender age to be ever on guard to protect and shield their elders and teachers from certain of the simple facts of life."[24] However, Houghton Mifflin did include the words but footnoted them to explain that Faulkner had refused permission to delete the words, but he would not use those words "except in the mouths of the kind of people in his story."[25]

Another egregious and ironic example of censorship by a publisher is the report by Ray Bradbury that a version of his work *Fahrenheit 451*, which is an attack on censorship, was bowdlerized for a high school edition without his knowledge. An example was the deletion of a reference to abortion in Montag's speech on page 91 of the 1972 Ballantine edition of the novel. No notice is given to the reader of the deletion. Bradbury wrote in a later Ballantine edition, which is not bowdlerized, (1979) that "some cubbyhole editors . . . fearful of contaminating the young, had, bit by bit, censored some 75 separate sections from the novel. Students, reading the novel, which after all deals with censorship and book burnings in the future, write to tell me of this exquisite irony." Fahrenheit 451 is the temperature at which book paper burns. Bradbury also wrote that there are many ways to burn books. He suggested that almost every point of view is represented by people who believe they have "the right, the duty to douse the kerosene, light the fuse." As Bradbury correctly notes, the ultimate result, if each minority takes out of books what it objects to, will be empty books, "the minds shut and the libraries closed forever."

> Fire-Captain Beatty, in my novel *Fahrenheit 451*, described how the books were burned first by minorities, each ripping a page or a paragraph from this book, then that, until the day came when the books were empty and the minds shut and the libraries closed forever.[26]

So Faulkner may not have known that the 1961 anthology bowdlerized "Barn Burning." But clearly a new task for teachers is to make sure they are using books or short stories as the authors actually wrote them; the alternative as Bradbury wrote, with some hyperbole, is a set of stories that are "slenderized, starved, blue penciled, leached and bled white, resembling every other story."[27]

I have had several reports of teachers who were embarrassed to discover by reading aloud to a class that the school text was abridged without notice. The discovery came because a bright student had an unabridged copy of the book obtained from the library or brought from home. Those who abridge books give insufficient credit to the intelligence of American high school students.

There is some evidence, however, of changes in editorial practices since 1975. It would appear from the selection of authors in the three Harcourt, Brace Jovanovich American literature texts described above, as well as in other anthologies, that there is a movement toward a broader representation of American writers.

Some of the editorial changes in the various texts are hard to understand. For example, Mark Twain used the word "negro" in lower case when he published a humorous sketch of his brief Civil War experience entitled "The Campaign that Failed," in *The Century Magazine*, December, 1885. But when Harcourt Brace Jovanovich reprinted the sketch in *Adventures in American Literature* (1973) the word "slave" is substituted. No notice or explanation is given to the reader for the substitution. It is odd that a simple explanation relying on the truth does not seem satisfactory to the publishers. If education has any chief governing principle it ought to be truthfulness. Truth is a hard word, and no doubt must often be prefaced with the word "probable." But if anyone questions a word in a text, the answer ought to be "This, in truth, is what Mark Twain wrote."

Another difficult question is why this selection is included in a work that only devotes twenty pages to the writing of Mark Twain. This limited selection is a sharp illustration of Weathersby's point that the anthologies tend to misrepresent the literature they include. No one reading these twenty pages would have the faintest idea of Mark Twain as a vigorous satirist of this society, a severe critic of slavery, and a severe critic of superstition in religion as illustrated by the misuse of the Bible in the episode in *Huckleberry Finn* in which a Bible is opened and placed upside down on the chest of a dying man.

These few pages give no impression of the Mark Twain who wrote "The War Prayer," *The Mysterious Stranger, Pudd'nhead Wilson*; nor does the student have any impression of the lyrical power of the symbolism of the river in *Huckleberry Finn*. One speculates that the selection "The Campaign" was included because of a strictly commercial motive. Not having been printed in Mark Twain's collected works, it may have been out of copyright so could be printed with no cost to the publisher.

That the reports of Weathersby and Last are still relevant in 1985 is made clear by the recent experience in Minneapolis. When Margaret Reed, English Language Arts Director for the Minneapolis public schools, wrote to various publishers inquiring about abridged or bowdlerized versions of Shakespeare, she received answers from several publishers defending their abridged versions. Several publishers offered an argument that relied on sophistry, or deception. These publishers pointed out that it is difficult to know exactly what actually was the original text as written by Shakespeare. This is certainly true but is quite irrelevant to the concern expressed by the parent in Minneapolis or by teachers generally. The problem of establishing the best possible text is quite irrelevant to the various omissions in *Romeo and Juliet* or in other plays as they are typically published in high school anthologies.

There is no question that Shakespeare wrote the porter scene in *Macbeth*, or that he wrote the scene in *Hamlet* (Act III, Scene 2) in which Hamlet asks Ophelia if he may lie in her lap, or that he wrote Act 3, Scene 3, in *Julius Caesar*, in which the poet Cinna is torn to death by a mob.

There is no doubt that Shakespeare wrote various lines in *Romeo and Juliet* in which Mercutio and the nurse reveal the animality of their character with sensual references to sexuality, in marked contrast to the characters of Romeo and Juliet, whose attitude toward love and sex is shown to be clearly human and religious. To remove the passages referred to above would do significant damage to the full intent of the plays in which they occur and would prevent a full experience of the realities of a Shakespeare play.

It is quite deceptive to assert that because of some degree of scholarly uncertainty about what Shakespeare wrote, it is permissible to omit such lines as mentioned above. The real reason for the omission is fear of such critics as the Gablers or their followers in the various states and fear of resulting loss of sales.

One publisher's representative, after using the argument that
there are some ambiguities in the texts, wrote

> As you note some of our cuts have to do with passages of a
> specifically sexual nature. Since sex is felt by many to be a private
> matter, since viewpoints about sex vary widely, and since [our
> text] is intended to be used nationwide in the ninth grade, the
> authors [Shakespeare?] and editors deleted some references to the
> sexual act itself and to various parts of the human anatomy. Our
> deletions in [our text] do not mean that students are deprived of
> reading, listening to or seeing the whole work; many classes sup-
> plement their study by seeing the film or attending a live perfor-
> mance.

The argument that the school may censor a work because it may
be found elsewhere has been specifically rejected by various
courts when advocates of school censorship offered it. "Since this
is a pluralistic society," the editor continued, "we try to consider
the sensitivities of many kinds of students when preparing our
texts, not only in sexual matters, but in matters relating to race
and religion as well."

   This argument asserts that it is permissible or necessary in a
pluralistic society to reduce the content of the text to the lowest
possible level of controversiality, again an argument that various
courts have rejected as a basis for the selection of school materials. Furthermore, the argument that in a pluralistic society, the
various deletions are required exactly reverses the proper conclusion. In a pluralistic society the maximum opportunity for difference of opinion should be provided. To bowdlerize or expur-
gate a text denies that maximum opportunity.

   That the bowdlerization of Shakespeare still continues is
illustrated by the omission of the following lines from the play
Macbeth, as it is printed in many recent anthologies.

Macduff.   What three things does drink especially provoke?
Porter.   Marry, sir, nose-pointing, sleep and urine. Lechery, sir,
           it provokes and unprovokes. It provoked the desire, but it
           takes away the performance. Therefore much drink may
           be said to be an equivocator with lechery. It makes him
           and it mars him, it sets him on and it takes him off, it

persuades him and disheartens him, makes him stand to
and not stand to; in conclusion, equivocates him in a
sleep and giving him the lie, leaves him.

Macduff.   I believe drink gave thee the lie last night.

Porter.   That it did, sir, i' the very throat on me. But I requitted
him for his lie, and I think being too strong for him,
though he took up my legs sometime, yet I made a shift
to cast him.

Macduff.   Is thy master stirring?

Shakespeare did write this passage, and if the play is going to be
taught it ought to be taught as Shakespeare wrote it. If high
school students are incapable of dealing with the complete *Macbeth*, then perhaps the play ought not be taught at all. In addition to the McDougal, Littell anthologies, others that silently
abridge the porter scene are: *England in Literature*, 7th Edition, Scott, Foresman, 1985; *British and Western Literature*,
McGraw-Hill, 1979; *Adventures in English Literature*, Harcourt Brace Jovanovich, 1985; and *English Literature*, Ginn,
1984.

An unsigned communication from the publisher,
McDougal, Littell, reports the omission of this passage because:
"The language has vulgar sexual offenses that create problems
in the classroom." In addition, the publisher asserted that
"These abridgments occur in every textbook because they have
been requested by teachers and heads of English departments."
In fact this, and the other abridgments described above do *not*
occur in college textbooks, nor do they occur in the single volume paperback issues of the various plays. Many teachers report
that these paperback copies of individual plays are increasingly
used in place of the anthologies and cause no trouble.

It is apparent that the bowdlerization of Shakespeare still
continues. Clearly the findings of Weathersby and Last describe
the contemporary world of textbook publishing.

Two books have pointed out the tendency of publishers to
censor the materials they include in literature anthologies. James
J. Lynch and Bertrand Evans published *A Study of High School
English Textbooks* in 1963. They were aware that significant
deletions and emendations occurred in the substantial number of
literature textbooks which they examined. In polite fashion they

suggested that "short stories should be published in their full text" and that "Shakespeare's texts should be treated with utmost respect." They also recommended that "a noticeable advance would result from the editor's resolutions *never* to abridge, simplify, adapt, or alter a poem."[28] Relatively little attention was paid to the Lynch and Evans report, perhaps in part because their study was sponsored by the Council for Basic Education. This organization is regarded by some teachers as having views that are not appropriate to the comprehensive high schools that characterize the United States. Furthermore, Lynch and Evans, as well as the Council for Basic Education, have nothing like the political power exercised by the Gablers who stand at the choke point in education as described above. Ginn and Company did publish a high school anthology in the 1960's based on the recommendations of Lynch and Evans. Unfortunately, it had a relatively small sale and was discontinued.[29]

Another study of textbooks appeared in the book *The Censors and the Schools* by Jack Nelson and Gene Roberts, Jr. also in 1963. Nelson and Roberts tended to emphasize social studies and history texts rather than the high school literature anthologies, but they make fully clear the degree to which publishers respond with timidity to critics. They illustrated this with a report that a Macmillan civics text got into final proof with a picture of an integrated playground; a salesman spotted it and screamed. Macmillan, with a gesture of rebuke to the editor responsible, remade the book with a different picture, thus avoiding any protest from those who opposed integration in the schools.[30] Nelson and Roberts' report of the policies followed by the publishers demonstrates the accuracy of the Weathersby study.

If parents do not want their children to read a Shakespeare play as it was written by Shakespeare, they should have the opportunity to request an alternate assignment for their children. If some parents do not want their children to become acquainted with Shakespeare, that is their right. But neither they, nor a publisher, nor the public schools should impose on *all* the students or teachers the limitations that some parents may prefer. It is clearly not the proper function of publishers to act as a bowdlerizing agent for puritanical parents. To deny to all students in American high schools the opportunity to know Shakespeare plays as they actually are, according to the best scholarship, is to play the role of the censor. In a democratic society neither the publishers nor the public schools should censor the works of Shakespeare, Tennyson, Mark Twain or any other writer. Censorship in our society is profoundly unpatriotic. Publishers and public schools that have the benefits of this democratic republic have every obligation to live up to its ideals.

Though Weathersby and Last use the term censorship for the various activities they describe in their studies, from a different perspective it might seem that either cultural lag or cultural conflict is at work.

Seen in terms of cultural lag, the textbook conflict could be related to the great changes that occurred in American literature after 1900. In that year, Theodore Dreiser's *Sister Carrie* was published, but not distributed, because the wife of the publisher saw the book after it was printed and regarded it as quite immoral. However, another publisher did print and distribute the book, thus beginning a struggle for the acceptance of a much more realistic literature.

William Dean Howells, approaching the end of a long career, cast a vote for the genteel tradition in a famous article for *Harpers Bazaar*, in 1902, "What Should Girls Read?" arguing that nothing should be published that was unfit for the eyes of a teen-aged girl, a view that is still extant in some quarters.

As late as 1930 Dreiser's *An American Tragedy* was held to be "lewd and obscene" in a court in Massachusetts, and a book seller was convicted for selling the book. In the 1940s Lillian Smith's *Strange Fruit* was censored in Massachusetts; about the same time, Edmund Wilson's *Memoirs of Hecate County* was banned in New York.

However, by 1933 James Joyce's *Ulysses* was freed from censorship by Judge Learned Hand, and in the early 1960s the three most egregious cases of questionable books were found not to be obscene in various federal courts: *Lady Chatterley's Lover*, *The Tropic of Cancer*, and *Fanny Hill or Memoirs of a Woman of Pleasure*. The inclusion of the last work is particularly interesting, since it was one that Anthony Comstock bragged of banning in his long career devoted to protecting the citizens of this country from reading so-called immoral books. But on March 21, 1966 the Supreme Court held the book not to be obscene. These three books established parameters of freedom for authors, publishers, and booksellers with almost no limitations. Charles Rembar, who defended *Fanny Hill* before the Supreme Court, said after these decisions that no book purchased by a library would hereafter be deemed obscene by the courts, perhaps an overly optimistic belief.[31]

But this freedom did not extend to the public schools. Prior to World War II little of contemporary American literature was available in the schools of the United States, as Dora Smith demonstrated. As she noted, of the 31 most frequently ordered titles of class sets for 18 representative New York state high schools, only eight were written by authors from the United States. Those authors were Edith Wharton, Carl Sandburg, Nathaniel Hawthorne, Eugene O'Neill, Edna Ferber, Booth Tarkington (*The Turmoil*), Paul De Kruif (*The Microbe Hunters*), and Owen Wister (*The Virginian*). So much for introducing students to the writings of Dreiser, Dos Passos, Steinbeck, Sinclair Lewis, Fitzgerald, Thomas Wolfe, Ellen Glasgow, and Elizabeth Maddox Roberts. It would be quite unrealistic to expect representatives of the Harlem Renaissance to have been in the list, or for Faulkner to have been represented. As Dora Smith said in summarizing her study, "The teaching of high school literature was very traditional, greatly influenced by the college entrance exams." "Traditional" also meant greatly influenced by British writers.[32]

Following World War II, with the rise of the paperback and the entrance of a new generation of teachers, many of whom had studied American literature in college, twentieth century literature began to come into the classroom. The use of that literature has occasioned many complaints. Respondents to the Ahrens study of 1965 listed 52 titles as the objects of attempted censorship. The authors were predominantly twentieth-century American; they included Pearl Buck, Walter Van Tilburg Clark, Dos Passos, Howard Fast, William Faulkner, Alfred Guthrie, Ernest Hemingway, Harper Lee, Arthur Miller, Lillian Smith, Herman Wouk, and John Steinbeck. Clearly, the literature of the twentieth century had come into the classroom and clearly many people disapproved of that fact. The Gablers, and other Texas critics, still disapprove of the use of twentieth century writers. Note again the twentieth century writers objected to in the 1978 hearings in Texas: Edith Wharton, John Steinbeck,

Sinclair Lewis, Ernest Hemingway, Carl Sandburg, Robert Frost, Ezra Pound, Amy Lowell, Robert Lowell, Tennessee Williams, William Carlos Williams, James Baldwin, Langston Hughes, and Edna St. Vincent Millay.

These writers were in all probability slightly or never taught in American high schools before 1950. The slowness with which the critics accept the writers of the twentieth century could accurately be described as cultural lag. While it is unrealistic to expect the schools to lead the way in cultural change, should they never reflect changes in literary modes, as the Gablers expect them never to do?

In a recent article in the *Washington Post*, Nicholas Lemann has argued that the "American South is dead." If that were so, then it is likely that the Gablers would not have the power to influence textbooks, which in fact they do. In 1940 Wilbur Cash wrote a minor American classic, entitled *The Mind of the South*. In that work he traced chronologically the development of several major features of Southern culture. Among the characteristics he reported were the following:

a) a vigorous class structure, with lower classes as docile followers of the leadings of the ruling class, even against the best interests of the lower class. Cash refers to "the masses whose historical role it was merely to follow where they were led;"

b) an intense individualism which in the 20th century saw any collective effort at problem solving as Marxist; any effort to improve the status of blacks raised "the bogy of the Red Revolution;"

c) a distrust of authority beyond the barest minimum, and a tendency toward vigilantism;

d) the rise of evangelical Protestantism with significant influence by the fundamentalist clergymen;

e) women's role restricted largely to the home; women regarded as the protectors of moral and cultural values;

f) any criticism of the established social institutions regarded as disloyalty;

g) considerable effort to keep blacks in their places, in spite of pressures for social change;

h) violence as a continuing part of Southern culture; vio-

lence as socially acceptable in all its forms. Lynching,
Cash believed, occurred because the ruling class either
"consented quietly or more often, definitely approved."[33] Other evidences of the Southern attitude
toward violence were the emphasis on capital punishment, military schools, the high degree of interest or
social approval of military careers, and the high rate of
homicide in Southern states as compared to the other
states. In 1935, according to the FBI, the eleven former
states of the Confederacy had a murder rate of 21.9 per
100,000 in all towns ranging from 10,000 to over
250,000. In New England the murder rate was 1.3 per
100,000. In the north central states the rate was 4.5 per
100,000.[34]

i)   opposition to science and the new learning, especially
     by the evangelical preachers: "From the pulpit the word
     went forth that infidelity and a new paganism masking
     under the name of Science was sweeping the world."[35]

Cash summarizes his report of the mind of the South by
saying that "The very commonest white indeed, saw [the new
learning] as a menace to his interests, or at least to his ego, once it
had been called to his attention by his masters. . . . Perhaps he
also resented the new learning and the new freedom of ideas [in
the twentieth century] as tending to widen the gulf between himself and those who went in for them."[36] Cash observed that this
attitude motivated a "patriotic will to hold rigidly to ancient
patterns."[37]

Other students of American culture showed the results of
the Southern tendency to view modern science with suspicion
and distrust. Two scientists from Wesleyan University, Robert H.
Knapp and Hubert B. Goodrich, studied the education of American scientists and attempted to discover the educational origin of
those persons who received a Ph.D. in science between 1880 and
1950. They reported in *Origins of American Scientists*[38] that
overwhelmingly these scientists came from the church-related
liberal arts colleges of the North. The proportion that came from
the eleven states of the Confederacy was minuscule. The fundamentalist objection to science clearly has had a powerful effect on
education in the South. According to a recent report by Wayne

Moyer, former executive secretary of the American Association of Teachers of Biology, fundamentalist attitudes toward science still powerfully influence textbook content and teaching in the high schools of the South and of the nation.[39] It is clear that the Southern, fundamentalist attitudes toward science still have power, and have greatly influenced science teaching throughout the nation through the Texas adoption procedures.

In noticing the sense in which the Texas critics represent a lingering nineteenth century Southern culture, in conflict with Northern, more rational, pragmatic attitudes, the resistance to objective science teaching should be taken into account.

Last has emphasized the objections of one of the Texas critics, Mrs. Billy C. Hutcheson, to the New England writers who played so important a role in American literature and education. Mrs. Hutcheson wrote several pages of objections to what she termed a group of "objectionable writers connected in some fashion with Harvard University. Those who had not attended still had pieces [of literature] presented that followed the same pattern of distastefulness." She referred to the influence of William Ellery Channing and of Transcendentalist thought on later writers. It is certainly correct that the Transcendentalist school greatly influenced the American writers. Emerson's influence, not only on literature, but on education, would be hard to exaggerate. Mrs. Hutcheson is quite correct in seeing reflections of Transcendentalist thought in twentieth century literature. Last comments of the Hutcheson references to a "Harvard connection . . . [that] they include so many underlying assumptions that they move beyond the level of objections to individual authors to a generalized level of complaint against an entire world view. . . ."

Mrs. Hutcheson's objections are the most fully explicit illustration of the cultural conflict between a Northern rationalist, democratic, pragmatic culture and a Southern traditional, class-bound, anti-scientific culture. Fundamentally the Texas critics, with some degree of cooperation from the publishers, wish to use censorship to prevent the spread of the Northern-based culture they find so objectionable.

In summary, it seems clear that high school texts continue to be bowdlerized. This is most vigorously true for Shakespeare's plays, but to a considerable degree other bodies of literature, both

English and American, have been silently edited to prevent criticism. However, in spite of the Texas critics, changes have occurred in American literature texts and seem likely to continue. Some change has already begun in Texas; if the public continues to object, as did two parents in Minneapolis, perhaps we may finally have accurate, representative texts in our high schools.

6 CENSORSHIP BY THE LEFT

THE TERMS LEFT AND RIGHT are rather unsatisfactory, but they do indicate roughly an orientation that is useful for discussing social problems. Two groups that may be considered on the left are militant liberals and militant feminists. Some members of each of these groups are willing to use censorship in support of their causes.

One organization actively concerned to eliminate racism and sexism in children's literature is the Council on Interracial Books for Children (CIBC). This organization publishes a bulletin which evaluates children's literature. The *Bulletin* regularly denies that the organization advocates censorship. In defense of that view Howard Meyer insists that only governmental officers can censor and therefore CIBC or other private citizens cannot be said to engage in censorship activities.[1] The Council asserts that its chief goal is consciousness raising to eliminate racism and sexism in children's literature.

The goal is certainly a worthy one; racism is such a destructive characteristic of this society that one can only applaud efforts to eliminate it. However a careful examination of 16 volumes of the CIBC *Bulletin* raises troublesome issues—so troublesome in fact that it becomes difficult to escape the conclusion that the verb *eliminate* creates a presumption that leads to censoriousness and ultimately to censorship. However, it should be noted that consciousness-raising to eliminate racism and sexism has in practice led to several groups seeking to have public school teachers and public librarians act as their surrogates and remove the material to which the various groups object. Public school teachers and public librarians are government officers; their actions, if

116

they complied with the requests of the objectors, would certainly seem to fit the definition of censorship stated by Howard Meyer.

It is noteworthy that Dr. Robert B. Moore, educational director of CIBC, as reported in the CIBC *Bulletin*,[2] proposed at a conference in 1977, that under Title IX, federal regulations be established to insure that all new textbooks and supplementary materials purchased by public elementary and secondary school systems be free of sex bias. That seems quite clearly to fit Howard Meyer's definition of censorship as "interference by government agencies." It would be interesting to know whether, given the attitudes of the Reagan administration toward education, CIBC still wishes the federal government to regulate the purchase of books for secondary and elementary schools. Former Secretary of Education Terrell Bell suggested that all that is needed in the elementary schools is the Bible and the McGuffey readers.

It should also be remembered that a characteristic of censorship is its tendency to judge a publication by a single episode, use of language or another single aspect of the work, instead of considering a publication "as a whole" before judgements can be made about it, as literary critics have insisted almost universally, and as the Supreme court said in 1973. A judgement about a work based solely on whether it contains racist or sexist language or episodes does seem to fit the pattern that censors have frequently used.

The essentially negative method of approach suggested by the CIBC asserted goal with its key verb—eliminate—suggests a dangerous philosophy for the public schools and libraries. The dangers of such a negative approach are illustrated in a story by Hawthorne entitled "The Birthmark." This is the story of a scientist who marries a beautiful woman, named Georgia. Unfortunately Georgia is marred by a birthmark on her cheek. Her husband determines to use his scientific skill to remove the birthmark; he has some slight degree of success with a potion he gives her. A stronger potion is more effective and a still stronger one is very effective. It removes the birthmark, but it also removes her. She dies as a result of his efforts.

This is a real danger in the essentially negative approach to literature followed by CIBC. There is some evidence that in fact the ultimate values of literature may get lost in the negative approach represented by the publications of the Council. The Council does some important positive things which seem very worthwhile, such as assisting in the publication of works by un- published minority group writers, but the great emphasis on fault-finding or severe criticism of children's literature has its dangers. One danger is the failure to remember that the real reason for the existence of literature is to give pleasure. An in- teresting letter to the *Bulletin* of the CIBC, after complimenting the magazine as a helpful consciousness-raiser, then makes the poignant comment: "Where's the joy? Your editors seem to have a great reverence for kids, but do you really like children's books? . . . occasional reviews by children's literature specialists who are true 'bookfreaks' and not politically motivated would add new dimension to your publication."[3] The editors are to be com- plimented for publishing this dissent, but after reading almost all issues of the *Bulletin*, I have seen no evidence that the suggestion was adopted.

That the ultimate purpose of literature may be lost in the critical approach of CIBC is also suggested by a statement that Dr. Moore of the Council made in connection with fairy tales in an article entitled "From Rags to Witches." In this article, he wrote, "Concerned parents and educators should work to liberate homes and schools from such potentially destructive materials as fairy tales [*Cinderalla, Red Riding Hood, Rumpelstiltskin, The Ugly Duckling, Hansel and Gretel,* and others are mentioned by Dr. Moore] and to provide children with more progressive and equal- ly enjoyable tales." He said further that "fairy tales like much of western world literature contain many values and assumptions which reinforce unhealthy and destructive images for the read- er."[4] Passages such as this convey the impression that the *Bul- letin* is indeed biased against literature.

The verb "liberate" in the passage cited above should be noted. "Liberate" is a euphemism that appears elsewhere in the *Bulletin* for "to get rid of." In Vol. 6, no. 1 and 2, (1975) p. 6, appears the headline, "Liberate Your Libraries." Under this headline are listed four books about Latin America which are given unfavorable reviews. Eight other books are given favorable reviews. It would be difficult to avoid the conclusion that the *Bulletin* wishes librarians either not to purchase the unfavorable titles or to get rid of them. Incidentally, one of the four titles given an unfavorable review is Oscar Lewis, *"La Vida": A Puerto Rican Family in the Culture of Poverty—San Juan and New York.*

Other writers that advocate consciousness-raising like CIBC, are willing frankly to advocate censorship. An example is found in, *How Communities and American Indian Parents Can Identify and Remove Culturally Biased Books From Schools,* written by Rebecca Robbins, and distributed by ERIC (Educational Resources Information Center) in 1979. Robbins suggests: "In order *to remove* textbooks from use in the classroom the problem of biased material must first be identified." A set of criteria for identifying biased material is then included. Elsewhere in the document is the sentence: "Support for the *removal* of objectionable material may be obtained from"—followed by a list of agencies. (Italics mine)

That much American literature is biased against the American Indian is unquestionably true, including work by such writers as Longfellow, Cooper, Elizabeth Maddox Roberts, Hemingway, and a host of others. Is there no alternative to decent treatment for Indians, except by removing most of the books from our libraries?

Milton in the *Areopagitica* pointed out that to remove all "scandalous" books already printed would "require the time of not a few overseers." To remove objectionable material from libraries would in fact be an impossible task. It is impossible not only because of the time required, but also, as Milton pointed out, removing so-called bad books would also get rid of the best books for good and evil are inextricably mingled in all human affairs and human books. "Suppose," said Milton, "we could expel sin by this means [censorship]; look how much we thus expel of sin, so much we expel of virtue; for the matter of them both is the same; remove that, and ye remove them both alike." Milton was right; to get rid of all books in American literature biased against the Indian would be to get rid of most American literature.

Editors of CIBC publications are aware, I think, of the deep commitment to what may be termed unsatisfactorily a liberal position against censorship. Thus CIBC publications appear to avoid the term in contrast to the Robbins publication cited above, while at the same time suggesting as strongly as possible that in fact various books be eliminated, or not purchased. An example of this strategy, one that suggests censorship but does not state the word, is found in an editorial in *The Bulletin.*

> It seems to us that there has been a abdication of responsibility for protecting children from the pernicious effects of such racist and otherwise anti-human books. Unsafe cars are recalled by the manufacturer. Dangerous drugs are taken off the market by the FDA. Children's clothing that contains hazardous chemicals is also removed. But who in the publishing world assumes responsibility for the damaging effects of children's books once they are published?
>
> What can be done about such books? The most effective course, we believe, is to promote consciousness-raising activities for the children's book-buying public—librarians, teachers, parents—and alert them to the nature of racist materials so they will no longer purchase or disseminate such materials. Just as important is the need to provide children with the skills and insights needed to detect racist and other anti-human content so that they will develop into adults capable of dealing effectively with these societal ills. We also urge racism awareness programs for writers, editors and publishers, so that new books for children will promote values that are consciously anti-racist and pro-human.
>
> But for books *already* published, isn't it time that publishers accept their responsibility for "recalling" or otherwise dealing with books that they themselves acknowledge to be inaccurate and/or racist? Does social responsibility end once a book leaves the printing press? Is the profit motive inviolate and never to be challenged? And for all of us—librarians, parents, teachers, editors—as we increase our awareness, are we to be bound by our past insensitivity?
>
> As Michael Dorris has said in another context in this *Bulletin*, there may be no simple or easy solution, but the problem does need to be addressed. We don't suggest that we have the answers, but we do presume to pose substantive questions. We ask for input from our readers on these crucial issues.[5]

The passage seems to be a clear call for publishers, librarians, and teachers to get rid of "racist" and "sexist" books. The word censorship is not used, but the idea is very clearly stated.

That some people are acting on such a call is shown by a

variety of evidence. An example is the previously noted episode at the Mark Twain Intermediate School in Fairfax, Virginia where *The Adventures of Huckleberry Finn* was ordered removed from the library by the principal. The deputy school superintendent ordered the book returned to the library, but provided that it could not be made required reading. The charges made against the book were that the book is racist, that it implies that Blacks cannot be trusted and are not human and that anybody who teaches the book is racist.

Huckleberry Finn has also been challenged at Houston, Texas; Davenport, Iowa; Philadelphia, Pennsylvania; State College, Pennsylvania and in a number of other places, as telephone calls to the national office of the National Council of Teachers of English show—calls from teachers or librarians who want assistance in defending the book *Huckleberry Finn*. It was challenged at New Trier High School in Winnetka, Illinois, and was placed on an optional reading list, thus preventing teachers from assigning that book as part of a course in American literature.

Dr. Robert Moore argued that this action was not censorship in a discussion of censorship and guidelines at the National Council of Teachers of English convention at Cincinnati in 1980. Moore asserted that "black parents and black students, indeed all parents and all students have every right to protest a state agency requiring students to read a book that contains racist and derogatory depictions of third world people." Dr. Moore paid no attention in his discussion to the fact that putting the title on an optional reading list prevented it from being taught as a class assignment. To prevent a book from being taught as a class assignment because of the allegation that the book—*The Adventures of Huckleberry Finn* in this case—is racist is surely an act of censorship. It is not at all unusual to assign books that contain ideas which may be offensive or inaccurate. Such books may be taught for a variety of reasons, perhaps to recognize the offensive idea, or perhaps because the book contains compensating virtues of high value. It may also be the case that the book does not contain the alleged offensive ideas in the minds of many readers.

It is sad to hear educated whites speak of this novel as derogatory to Blacks. As a student of American literature, I cannot think of any book better designed to acquaint students with the process by which white Americans slowly became aware of the monstrous cruelty of slavery than *Huckleberry Finn*. Mark Twain as critic of our society made the superstitions and tyrannies that still govern too many Americans quite clear, in detailed and realistic fashion. The continuing relevance of the book is illustrated by the episode in which Huck's father announces he will never vote again, because he has just learned of an educated Black who is a college professor and who can actually vote in Ohio. The effort in the Congress in 1984–1985 to extend the Civil Rights Voting Act shows how relevant *Huckleberry Finn* continues to be. Many citizens still do not want blacks to vote, though they may not say so publicly.

In practice any student who objected on grounds of conscience should not be required to read *Huckleberry Finn* or any other book, but any Black student who omitted reading *Huckleberry Finn* would be prevented from access to an insight into the white culture that would be seriously limiting to the fullest education. And if complaints from parents prevent teachers from assigning this book to other people's children, the term censorship clearly applies. Parents should be able to control only their own children's reading.

There is considerable evidence that a number of books are challenged and sometimes removed from the schools and libraries because they are charged with being racist or sexist. For example in Howard County, Maryland, *Kookanoo and the Kangaroo*, a book describing the life of an aboriginal boy in Australia, was removed from all elementary school libraries because it was charged that "it would be hard for primary youngsters to make a distinction between aborigines in Australia and Black children in the United States." Moreover the book included the word "piccaninny" which, a complainant said, would result in "lessening of racial esteem for the black child."[6] Members of the National Organization for Women (NOW) in Montgomery County, Maryland protested the use of *Back to School with Betsy* because it contained racial slurs. Among other books objected to was *Male and Female Under 18*, the book which was the occasion of the Chelsea, Massachusetts case decided by Judge Joseph Tauro in the United States District Court for Massachusetts. In another episode members of NOW in Montgomery County, Maryland objected to *The Dog Next Door and Other Stories*, a second grade reader which was allegedly riddled with sexism. As a result, the school board of Montgomery County voted not to purchase more copies of the book and not to have existing copies rebound.[7] The Multi-Cultural Non-Sexist Advisory Committee of Cedar Rapids, Iowa recommended permanent removal of more than one hundred books from the Kenwood Elementary School Library of Cedar Rapids. The books were deemed "discriminatory, racist, sexist, or biased against handicapped people." They were not however removed.

In 1976 the Commissioner of Education for the state of Texas removed five dictionaries from the list approved for state adoption, because of objections to the books. Two groups filed bills of particulars against these dictionaries. One was the National Organization for Women, which implied the books were sexist—that is, demeaning to women. They objected in particular to the definitions of several words, including 1) woman, definition number five, because it implied weakness or passivity. They also objected to 2) womanish, 3) machismo, 4) macho; NOW also complained because chairperson was not listed. A further objection was that fewer women than men worked on the dictionaries, and the women were concentrated in lower positions. The various groups were successful in having the five dictionaries removed from the recommended list for the state of Texas.[8]

The removal of sexist or racist books has been noted by representatives of the Moral Majority, who accuse teachers and librarians of being hypocrites in acting as censors themselves but in preventing the censorship of obscene or pornographic material that is offensive to the position held by the Moral Majority. Michael Farris, President of the Moral Majority for the state of Washington, said in a speech at a conference of The American Library Association in the summer of 1981 at San Francisco, that when he did some searching to find *Little Black Sambo* or *Nicodemus and Sally*, he could not find them in the public library.

> They were thrown away, they were buried because they were considered racist. . . . Librarians, I would submit, have censored *Little Black Sambo* and *Nicodemus and Sally*, but they would call it censorship if I suggested (that a sex education book called) *Growing Up Feeling Good* should be removed from the open shelves of the Spokane Public Library.

But what is the great constitutional distinction between book burning and book burying? Book burying was the practice in Richland, Washington recently to bury thousands of dollars worth of textbooks which were banned because the books were deemed by women's liberation forces to be sexist. Intellectual hypocrisy is a better description of the move to remove *Little Black Sambo* and promote *Growing Up Feeling Good* in the name of Freedom.

In a TV debate on Station KOMO in Seattle, Farris implied that he would not object to teachers and librarians removing racist or sexist books if they would support the efforts of the Moral Majority to remove sexually offensive materials. I do not myself think teachers and librarians should enter into such a collusive arrangement to violate the spirit at least, if not the letter, of the First Amendment.

There is the further danger of establishing a precedent that may well be used against those who wish to stock libraries with books more fully representative of the lives of contemporary women and of contemporary members of various ethnic groups. For every book that is challenged by the left because it is racist or sexist, it is likely there are fifty or a hundred books that are challenged by the right because they are allegedly pornographic, or obscene, or depict sex too frankly, such as *Show Me*, or *Our Bodies, Ourselves* or because, in fact, they depict too vigorously the harsh and unfair treatment that minority group people are subjected to in this country, such as *The Learning Tree*.

Of the twenty most frequently attacked books in high schools between 1965 and 1977 none were attacked because they were racist or sexist. However one-third were attacked because they depicted minority group people in ways that constituted a vigorous protest against racism. Those books are *To Kill A Mockingbird, Black Like Me, Hawaii, Manchild in the Promised Land, One Flew Over the Cuckoo's Nest, Diary of a Young Girl,* and *The Ugly American.*

If English teachers and librarians want support for keeping books like these in the library, they will have to convince the general public that they deal in a consistent way with book ordering and book use. In short, they cannot practice censorship themselves.

The First Amendment was adopted as a set of ground rules for people who in the past had disagreed violently about matters of morality. Quakers were hanged in Boston by Congregationalists, Baptists were whipped and jailed in Virginia by Episcopalians, and newspaper editors were tried for sedition for criticizing the government. The First Amendment is a form of conflict management. It provides means by which those of us who disagree with each other are allowed to do so. Since persons in the front lines of equalitarianism are probably in a minority it is in their best interest to protect the First Amendment for reasons of prudence or practicality.

There is also a moral argument for First Amendment practices of permitting apparently mistaken or wrong or offensive materials to be published and distributed. That argument was well stated by Immanuel Kant who said that one of the moral principles that should govern our conduct is to act so that the maxim by which we act we could will to be a universal maxim for all other persons similarly situated. If I wish freedom to read and write as I think best, I must support that freedom for all others, even those with whom I disagree.

One of the reasons listed for eliminating racism and sexism from children's literature is the belief that "Research shows the children's attitudes and achievements are affected by race and sex bias in books, and that non-biased books can make a difference."9 An article entitled "How Books Influence Children: What the Research Shows" by Patricia B. Campbell and Jeana Wirtenberg argues that children's literature does indeed affect the attitude and behavior of children. Campbell and Wirtenberg list twenty-three references. Richard Beach offers a considerably fuller discussion of the effect of reading on the reader in an article entitled "Issues of Censorship and Research on Effects of and Response to Reading." Beach based his article on an examination of 113 references including some of the same references used by Campbell and Wirtenberg.

Beach observes that:

> the research findings do not provide definitive answers as to the need for censorship. Nor do the researchers pretend that they can empirically define what constitutes desirable or undesirable reading; those decisions are made by the advocates or critics of cen-

sorship based on their own beliefs and values. Even if empirical evidence were conclusive that reading has no undesirable effects on readers, such a finding would not lessen demands for censorship . . . as long as people strongly believe in certain values and the need to defend those values, censorship will exist.[10]

Beach makes several relevant observations: 1/ He suggests that the older assumption that there is a single correct meaning residing in the work itself is probably not accurate and that a more accurate assumption may be that the meaning of a work evolves from the interplay of reader and work. Thus a work may mean different things to different readers. 2/ The assumption that because a critic responds to a particular work in a particular manner, others who read that work will respond in the same manner seems doubtful. The research on reading indicates that a) readers respond in a highly individualized manner to works; b) the same reader responds differently to different works; and c) differences in readers' responses are due to differences in readers' personality, sex, literary training, age, reading ability, cognitive development, and other characteristics. 3/ His third observation is that it is widely held that reading changes people. Beach reports that the research on the effects of reading is somewhat inconclusive; the trend indicates that reading does not have much long term effect on readers' attitudes or behavior. This suggests that readers' attitudes or behavior are symptomatic of stable aspects of personality which are influenced more by parents, peers, schooling, and cultural socialization than by reading.

In discussing the research on this subject, Beach makes two important generalizations: 1/ An overriding problem is that most studies examine change in attitude or values over a short time period. This runs counter to much social science research indicating that people's values or attitudes change only gradually over a long term. Because readers therefore impose a stable set of values on their reading, they respond positively to aspects of reading that reinforce their values and suppress aspects that threaten their values. 2/ Research which shows that reading produces significant change has relatively unsophisticated design, and is susceptible to the influence of researcher expectation. He ascribes these defects to such references mentioned by Wirtenberg as H. Tauran's doctoral dissertation on the subject, "The

Influence of Reading on the Attitudes of Third Graders Toward Eskimos," and F.L. Fisher's doctoral dissertation on "The Influence of Reading and Discussion on the Attitudes of Fifth Graders toward American Indians."

The most extreme form of expressions of racism raises difficult questions—scatological ethnic jokes, for example, which are fairly prevalent in folklore. There must be considerable leeway for disagreement about the presence or absence of racism in a given work. One reason for not drawing rigid lines is that reasonable people may disagree about presence of racism or its effect on the reader, even when, as various articles in the CIBC *Bulletin* allege, some may think it to be clearly present as in the *Merchant of Venice, Huckleberry Finn, Mary Poppins, Sounder,* or *The Cay.*

An issue of the *Bulletin* of CIBC was devoted to an analysis of children's books on Asian-American themes.[11] Sixty-six such books were published between 1945 and 1975. Eleven Asian-Americans reviewed these books; seven Asian-American authors wrote eleven of the sixty-six books. The reviewers established criteria that were a fairly detailed description of racism and sexism. By these criteria the critics found almost all of the books unsatisfactory except books written by Lawrence Yep and Taro Yashima. "The major conclusion was that, with one, or perhaps two exceptions, the sixty-six books are racist, sexist, and elitist. . . ."[12]

Presumably of these sixty-six books only one or two might be purchased by librarians. Racism and sexism with regard to Asian-Americans would be eliminated from the libraries but so would sixty-three books about or by Asian-Americans.

Two of the books by Asian-Americans were based on the author's experiences in the American concentration camps of World War II. These books are severely criticized by the reviewers who allege that the authors have been brainwashed into accepting the camp experience, and they do not, therefore, make sufficiently clear, by the reviewer's criteria, what an outrageous part of American history the camp experience was. Quite coincidentally, I have known two Japanese-Americans who were in the concentration camps. Both seemed to have the same attitude toward their experience that the reviewers disapprove of in the two books mentioned in the CIBC *Bulletin*.

Should young people and our society generally be denied the opportunity to learn of the reaction that seems to have been held by at least some Japanese-Americans about their experience in the concentration camps? Who is to decide that? The proponents of the CIBC point of view? Or a large cross section of teachers, librarians, and other persons? An interesting illustration of the difficulty of determining whether a given book is racist or not lies in the candid admission of an unidentified writer who described the criteria by which the critics reviewed the sixty-six books. "The fine line between stereotyping and authenticity is often hard to see. In most cases the former draws upon the latter as a base, exploiting and vulgarizing it, and frequently a stereotype escapes notice altogether because it is so subtle." The implication is quite clear here and elsewhere that only those whose consciousness has been sufficiently raised can detect the racism. If you do not detect the racism, you have not been sufficiently sensitized.

One aspect of consciousness-raising to eliminate racism or sexism has developed from the ideas of Edward Sapir and B.L. Whorf. Whorf argued that the structure of language controls members of the culture who use that language. Whorf's ideas provide the theoretical basis for abandoning such words as chairman, policeman, fireman, and other similar words.[13] The belief in this theory has led to the development of guidelines used by various publishers and publishing organizations. An example is *The Handbook of Nonsexist Writing for Writers, Editors and Speakers* by Casey Miller and Kate Swift.[14]

The ideas expressed in books of this kind have led to several incidents of censorship. In 1977, the NCTE accepted for publication a collection of papers presented at a conference in stylistics. NCTE staff persons preparing the papers for publication asked the author of one paper, a distinguished professor at the University of Illinois—Chicago Circle, to change two words—"policeman" and "chairman" to "police officer" and "chair." The author refused, and the paper was not published, thus denying to all English teachers the contributions to knowledge made by this researcher, because he used two presumably offensive words. After tumultuous debate, in two annual sessions of the NCTE, its guidelines were amended to prevent such actions in the future by prefacing NCTE publications with a statement that authors were responsible for their own language.

The linquist Joshua Whatmough has argued in his book, *Language: A Modern Synthesis*, that the theories of Sapir and Whorf are wrong, that language use follows reality—it does not control reality. Whorf tried to relate what he believed to be absolute categories with regard to tense and other grammatical features of English to what he regarded as the absolutist characteristics of the American culture concerning moral values—right versus wrong. Whorf contrasted the American culture with the Navaho culture in which Whorf saw grammatical structures that are relative and a culture that Whorf perceived to be relativistic. In short, Whorf believed that the English language had absolute categories, and caused or contributed to an American culture with absolute categories—right versus wrong. Whorf also believed that Navaho had relativistic language categories, and caused or contributed to a Navaho culture that was relativistic in nature. The linguist Whatmough disagreed with Whorf. Whatmough pointed out that relativity theory did in fact develop in an Indo-European language with its supposed absolute grammatical structures rather than in Navaho with its supposed relativistic structures. Whatmough says: "The theory that linguistic behavior controls non-linguistic behavior in all its details is erected on an unfounded assumption . . . and when appeal is made to language of totally different cultures and structures, namely North American Indian, the supposed 'message' is so distorted by transmission as to be useless for the argument. . . ."[15]

Several efforts have been made to test the Whorfian thesis empirically. These efforts attempt to break out of the circularity in the argument for linguistic relativity as illustrated by the following quotation from Bourne, Ekstrand, and Dominowski, "The language determined the outlook which determined verbal behavior, thus the circularity of evidence."[16]

An example of empirical testing concerns the differing ways that various languages code the color spectrum. In English "green" and "blue" refer to light wavelengths of about $520\mu m$ and $470\mu m$, respectively. In Japanese the word "ao" refers to both wavelengths. Proponents of censoring sexist language often refer to the 40 or more words that Eskimos have for various kinds of snow. In order to test empirically the effect of these linguistic differences on perception and cognition, speakers of English and speakers of Zuni were asked to discriminate between various colors. Other comparisons have been made between speakers of

Wolof and speakers of French in terms both of color discrimination and shape discrimination. The experiments did not show that language controlled the ability to discriminate between colors and shapes.

There is a substantial literature on experiments of the sort described above as is noted in the linguistic section of the bibliography appended below. Insup Taylor summarized the literature in the following words: "The current consensus among psychologists . . . regarding the principle of linguistic relativity is that . . . language reflects rather than determines cognition."[17] Taylor also points out that Roger Brown's comparison of Japanese data with American data showed that "both languages share the same basic semantic dimensions [which is] a major disconfirmation of Whorf's linguistic relativity."[18]

The belief that by changing language it is possible to change reality is strongly embedded in our culture. However, the change in language from "graveyard" to "cemetery" to "memorial park" did not soften the losses from death. It seems likely that the fireman who insisted on nursing her baby at the fire station in Iowa City, Iowa, and who won the right to do so by a lawsuit, did more to change the relationship between words and reality than an effort to replace the word "fireman" with the word "firefighter." It is likely that the efforts of Patricia Merdan, a student from the University of Wisconsin–Stevens Point, who went to Oklahoma as a missionary for the Equal Rights Amendment may have more effect on the status of women than the concern that liberals have expressed over a set of black marks on white paper or a set of symbolic sounds. Language follows reality. To change language, it is necessary to change the reality that the language refers to. Censorious persons should study the distinction that linguists make between sign and symbol. Signs, like the red rash that is symptomatic of measles, are inseparable from reality. Language is symbolic, and is therefore quite distinct from or separable from reality. Much censorship confuses sign and symbol.

Because they confuse sign and symbol, many censors believe in magic. They are like the little boy in *Ali Baba and The Forty Thieves* who said the magic word and opened a door to great treasure. Words are symbols; not signs. Signs are direct evidence of reality. Deer tracks show the presence of deer; a red rash shows the presence of measles. Tracks and red rash are not symbolic (though of course the words that refer to them are). Censors believe, however, that to use objectionable words will somehow bring about the presence of that to which they object. So the censor objects to words that refer to whatever aspect of reality he or she dislikes, whether that be to the status of women—or to references to sex.

Censorship should occur only when there is a clear, definite, and immediate relationship between the allegedly harmful language and the asserted social harm. It cannot be said that the 21 books dealing with psycholinguistics in the appended bibliography offer the clear and definite evidence of the harmful effect of language structures or vocabulary necessary to justify censorship of either racist or sexist terms.

Alternatives to censorship of racist or sexist terms

One of the characteristics of the censor who acts on moral grounds is the belief that something effective has been accomplished by the act of censorship. In fact, in most cases only symbolic representations have been removed. The moral evil remains. The act of censorship is a red herring that prevents attention to the moral evils reflected symbolically in the novel, play or film.

As an instructor of classes in non-violence at the University of Wisconsin-Stevens Point, I use a variety of materials describing the ideas of the great proponents of non-violent action against the various evils of this world. I include such Old Testament books as Micah, Isaiah, Jeremiah, such other writers as Tolstoy, or Thoreau and such practitioners of non-violent action as Gandhi, Martin Luther King, and Saul Alinsky. None of these proponents of non-violent protest advocate censorship as an effective means of overcoming evil. One of the powerful statements against censorship may be found in Jeremiah 36. In this passage Jeremiah's criticisms of the evils of his day are being read to the king, who cuts them off the scroll and burns them in a brazier; "yet they were not afraid," reports the text, implying they should have been afraid.

Gene Sharp in his three volume work, *The Dynamics of Non-Violent Action*, describes in Volume II 198 different methods of non-violent action that have been used historically. None of these include either censorship or changes in language use, such as abandoning the word "colored" for "Negro" or "Black." While Gandhi did use the term "children of God"—or "Harijan" for the untouchables of India there is no report that he advocated or practiced the censorship of the word "untouchable." Instead he devoted his life to working for and with the untouchables in direct social action to improve their lot.

It is highly likely that the willingness of northern liberals to say "Black" rather than "Negro" had an infinitesimal effect on the status of Blacks as compared to the direct non-violent, brave action of Rosa Parks, or Martin Luther King, or of the young Blacks who sat at restaurant counters in Greensboro, North Carolina in 1961, or the bravery of Violet Liuzzo who was killed when she took the family car to help provide food for King and his marchers from Selma to Montgomery, Alabama. Schwerner, Cheney, Goodman—who died at Philadelphia, Mississippi in 1964 in helping Blacks to vote—made an immeasurable effort to atone for white mistreatment of Blacks. They did not call for linguistic changes.

When scholars and scientists approach social pathologies in an effort to understand their causes, they do not list books or reading as a causative factor, as for example in the Glueck study of delinquent boys or in the many studies of race prejudice or anti-Semitism by Gordon Allport, or such members of the Frankfort school as T.W. Adorno, Max Horkheimer, and Bruno Bettelheim. The studies by the Frankfort school found that instead of reading as a cause of anti-Semitism authoritarian family life was an important factor. Other scholars have found economic conflict as a cause of race prejudice.[19]

The evil of race prejudice, anti-Semitism, or of a subordinate status for women, will not be overcome by changing the structure of the language or by eliminating actual or presumed racist books.

A positive philosophy for book selection and use is illustrated by the media standards of the Wisconsin Department of Public Instruction: ". . . All students shall be provided access to a current, balanced collection of books, basic reference materials, texts, periodicals, and audiovisual materials which depict in an accurate and unbiased way the cultural diversity and pluralistic nature of American Society. . . ."

There is no call here to rid the libraries of offensive books. There is a call to present material on a wide range of positions on all the controversial subjects that divide our society. That means including books that present women in a traditional role as well as including Ms. Magazine. It means including Soul on Ice, or The Learning Tree, as well as traditional works such as Huckleberry Finn, The Deerslayer, Elizabeth Maddox Roberts' The Great Meadow, and other similar novels that deal with the American Indian.

An illustration of how the positive principle stated might affect the selection of material occurred in a 1977 meeting of the Board of Directors of the National Council of Teachers of English. At this meeting the Council's Commission on Minority Group Literature offered a resolution calling for the schools to enhance their curricular offerings and learning resource materials with additional offerings that accurately represented the life of minority group people in this society. There was at the end of the report a sentence calling for screening the libraries to remove objectionable material. After considerable debate, there was almost unanimous approval, including the approval of most members of the Commission on Minority Group Literature, that the final sentence be modified, and that the resolution be a positive call for action but that there be no call to rid the libraries of sexist or racist materials. As modified, the positive call for action was adopted almost unanimously.

Both the National Council of Teachers of English and such state affiliates as the Wisconsin Council of Teachers of English have taken positive action to improve teaching with regard to ethnic differences and the role of women. In the early 1960's among the several dozen candidates for a position at Stevens Point was one candidate who offered competence in knowledge of Black literature. We were fortunate to hire Abraham Chapman, who initiated courses in Black literature at Stevens Point, whose bibliography of Black literature was published by the Wisconsin Council of Teachers of English, and whose book Black Voices grew out of his courses at Stevens Point. Courses in the literature about and by Native Americans were also initiated in the early 1960's at Stevens Point; bibliographies were published by the Wisconsin Council of Teachers of English and are still available for the elementary schools and for the secondary schools. The National Council of Teachers of English has pub-

lished similar bibliographies in full length form for Black literature, and for literature by and about Native Americans. These
actions are positive, and involve no suggestion that excellence in
education rests on attacking or removing books presently in print,
or presently in libraries.

Equalitarians of all political positions should agree on
positive actions both in book selection and in use, in accord with
the philosophy stated above, and thus form common ground
against the critics of the right, who are currently making vigorous
efforts to roll back our country from the limited degree of desegregation and democratization attained in recent years.

7 SECULAR HUMANISM

IN THE 1970s complaints about books began to be orchestrated
by the charge that they taught "secular humanism." With this
charge, school critics went beyond their challenges to single
books on the charge of obscenity, to a generalized attack on the
core curriculum of the public schools.

The charge of secular humanism had its earliest popular
exposition in pamphlets by Onalee McGraw, *Secular Humanism
and the Schools: The Issue Whose Time Has Come* (1976), as well
as in such books by Tim LaHaye as *The Battle for the Mind*
(1980).

The term "secular humanism" has been given many meanings by critics of the schools. A frequently stated definition is that
it refers to ideas or activities in the schools that are "anti God,
anti-Christian, and anti-patriotic." This phrase suggests the critics intend a religious dimension to the charge—i.e., atheism—
and a political dimension—i.e., a lack of patriotism, as the critics define patriotism.

What does the word "secular" mean?

The term "secular" is of Latin origin, referring originally to "a
generation" or "an age." In Christian Latin it came to refer to the
world. It might therefore be used to refer to secular clergy, who
lived in the world, as opposed to cloistered clergy who lived in a
convent or monastery. According to the *Oxford English Dictionary*, however, a more general meaning of the word secular is,
"belonging to the world and its affairs, as distinguished from the
church and religion, civil, lay, temporal. Chiefly used as a nega-

135

tive term, with the meaning non-ecclesiastical, non-religious, or
non-sacred."

In these three specific senses, the American public school
system is secular. It is in the world, it is not ecclesiastical, it is not
religious, and not sacred. The reasons for these qualities are well
known. They lie in the First Amendment to the Constitution
with its separation of church and state.

The writers of the constitution lived less than 200 years
from the time of Archbishop Laud who in the 1620s and 1630s
had the ears of religious dissenters in England cut off. Closer in
time were the activities of Congregationalists who hanged
Quakers in Boston in the 1650s. Still closer to the experience of
the writers of the constitution were the activities of the defenders
of the Episcopalian church in Virginia who whipped Baptists for
their religious activities in the years immediately before the writing of the Constitution. It is not accidental that the First Amendment included protection of freedom of speech and freedom from
state control of institutions of religion in the same article.

Milton's great defense of freedom of thought and freedom
from censorship in the *Areopagitica* was part of his religious
beliefs. Milton was a Puritan of the Puritans. An essential feature
of his thought was an absolute individualism, an individualism
which insisted that each person must be in control of his own life
and that salvation is an individual matter. This individualism has
as one of its important sources in Protestant thought, Luther's
tract *On The Liberty of the Christian Man.* Individualism appeared in a variety of ways in Puritan thought in New England.
The first important American book to be published, the *Bay
Psalm Book* explained in the preface that the Bible should be
translated into every language so that each person could read and
decide for himself what it meant: "now no protestant doubteth
but that all the books of the Scripture should by God's ordinancy
be extant in the mother tongue of each nation, that they may be
understood of all."

Roger Williams, the first American Baptist, argued in his
book, *The Bloody Tenent of Persecution* that church and state
should be separate, that the civil powers should have no control
over the church. Williams used a famous metaphor, comparing
life to travel on a ship, in which religion is represented by the
mariners who navigate the ship across the ocean. If a head of

state, a prince were aboard the ship, should he have the right to give orders concerning the navigation of the ship? No, said Williams, since he has none of the arts of navigation. Only those who are skilled in managing the ship should control it. This "similitude" as Williams called it, suggests that it is not the duty of the civil magistrate to see that the church does its duty; it is not the duty of the magistrate "to establish the true religion, or to suppress and punish the false" or "to correct, punish, and reform [religion] by the civil sword."

The founding fathers, consistent with Williams' views, wished to prevent the powers of the state from enforcing doctrinal religious ideas or practices on the citizenry.

For these reasons, the founding fathers laid the basis for a relationship between church and state that is not hostile but rather is neutral to dogmatic, doctrinal or denominational or institutional aspects of religion.

This long heritage started with Luther, and the notion that religious unity is necessary for national unity, as illustrated by the proverb—cuius regio eius religio—which is to say, the religion of the ruler should be the religion of the state. In the newly-established states of the new world the process of separating church from state was slow. In the 1840s Thoreau had to "sign off" to be free from paying church taxes in Massachusetts. In the 1890s the Wisconsin Supreme Court interpreted the Wisconsin Constitution to prohibit prayer and Bible reading in the public schools as part of a religious exercise, a decision quite acceptable to a state with significant membership in Catholic, Lutheran and other churches. In fact, each group welcomed the decision, since they were at odds over both the particular translation of the Bible to be used, and the specific language of the prayers to be offered. Other states, such as Illinois and Pennsylvania, continued religious exercises directed by those state officials who operate the public schools—the teachers and administrators.

The relatively low crime rate, relatively honest and efficient government, and generally high level of public morality in Wisconsin during the last ninety years suggests that no public harm has come from prohibiting devotional religious services in Wisconsin schools. On the other hand, devotional religious services in the Illinois public schools through much of the twentieth century apparently failed to prevent Al Capone and the rise of organized crime in Chicago, nor did those exercises prevent a proverbially graft ridden government in the city of Chicago.

Several states continued prayer and Bible reading, until the Abington Township v. Schempp Supreme Court decision of 1963 brought all the states into conformity with Wisconsin in prohibiting such devotional exercises in the public schools. Although school critics often falsely charge that the Supreme Court has censored the Bible, such court decisions do not prohibit the use of the Bible as literature, nor do they prohibit the study of religion in history or social studies classes. In fact, the various surveys that I conducted show that almost every school library reported having the Bible in its collection, which is quite consistent with the 1963 Court decision: "In addition it might well be said that one's education is not complete without a study of comparative religion or the history of religion and its relationship to the advancement of civilization. It certainly may be said that the Bible is worthy of study for its literary and historic qualities. Nothing we have said here indicates that such study of the Bible or of religion, when presented objectively as part of a secular program of education, may not be effected consistently. . . ."[1]

American public schools are indeed secular institutions, as the Court decision cited above implies. The schools are in the world, they are not operated by or in churches or convents, they are non-ecclesiastical, non-denominational, non-sectarian. In these limited or restricted senses of the word, they are not religious, in contrast to the parochial schools operated by the Catholic church, the Lutheran church, and various other denominations. But though the public schools are non-religious in these limited senses, they are clearly *not* hostile to religion, as the Court decision makes clear. They are not hostile to religion in the broader sense of the word either. Religion is an activity in the lives of individuals, and of society, by means of which human beings find meaning in life and relate themselves to the transcendental aspects of the universe.

The public schools are not hostile to organized church groups with whom many informal interactions take place. The public schools are not guilty of hostility toward traditional Christianity, nor have they adopted secular humanism as an alternate faith which they are attempting to impose on society. Neither the public schools nor the great majority of public school teachers are hostile to religion or to theistic attitudes toward reality, as most people know who have any working acquaintance with the schools or school teachers, or who have any acquaintance with contemporary mainstream church life.

What does "Humanism" mean?

The term "humanism" may be defined in many ways. The *Encyclopedia of Philosophy* lists six definitions, one of which may be illustrated by the Humanist Manifesto so often cited by critics of the schools. This definition of humanism may be labeled as secular in the sense that it is completely non-theistic. A second definition, which is also non-theistic, refers to communism. A third non-theistic definition refers to existentialism, illustrated by the ideas of Sartre and his followers. A fourth definition is that of pragmatism, in the sense of the Greek philosopher Protagoras, who made man the measure of all things. A fifth definition refers to personalism, which "affirms man's capacity to contemplate the eternal truths, or in general, to enter a relationship with transcendent reality."[2]

However, it is the sixth definition of humanism that is relevant to the public schools. This describes a historic movement originating in the Renaissance in the second half of the 14th century, which had its theological basis in the ideas of St. Thomas Aquinas, with his demonstration that reason is compatible with grace. As H.C. Gardiner puts it in *New Catholic Encyclopedia*, "St. Thomas Aquinas laid the basis for Christian humanism with his teaching that philosophy is distinct from theology and that human reason has its own value and consistency apart from grace and must build the understructure for the life of grace."[3]

Humanism in the Renaissance was a movement based on the efforts of a group of priests to develop a system of education for the new world of the Renaissance. The term humanism in this sense came from the word "humanitas," which meant the education of man and referred to what the Greeks called "paideia," the education favored by those who considered the liberal arts to be . . . the disciplines proper to man which differentiate him from the animals."[4] This educational system emphasized human freedom, though a freedom within a cosmic order which man has to accept. This philosophy of education did not have an anti-religious or anti-Christian character. Indeed humanism revitalized the traditional questions concerning religion by its emphasis on man's capacities. These religious discussions had tolerance of other points of view as one of their goals. "For the humanists . . . the attitude of tolerance derived from their conviction of the fundamental unity of all the religious beliefs of mankind. . . ."[5] It may be that one of the reasons for the antipathy of the school critics to modern education is this heritage of tolerance for differing points of view that to some degree is implicit in education.

Though the Renaissance humanists were less interested in science than in literature, in language, and in religion, they developed attitudes toward the natural world and toward the use of reason that contributed to the development of science. The humanistic philosophy of education included science; typical college organizations today include the sciences in liberal arts colleges, as an ongoing expression of the humanistic philosophy of education.

Many writers on the subject of humanism as a philosophy of education emphasize the degree to which it is concerned with literature and the storage of information. The early humanists laid the basis for the great libraries of the Western world, such as the Vatican library. We owe the skill of librarianship to those humanists. They developed librarianship—the indexing or cataloging of books without which our libraries would be virtually unusable, because of the mass of material they contain. The humanist Erasmus devoted much time to indexing books. The index to a book or to a library is an almost indispensable instrument and the development of indexing made libraries the great intellectual tools that they are.

The collection of manuscripts gave rise to the question of selection versus censorship. A priest, Johannes Pfefferkorn (1469–1524), argued that Jewish documents should be destroyed because they were a threat to Christian thought. However, another priest, Johann Reuchlin (1455–1522), argued that to understand the Old Testament it was necessary to collect and study Hebrew manuscripts, not destroy them. Reuchlin published the first Hebrew grammar for Christians in 1506, typical of the humanist concern for literacy—and literacy in several languages. Reuchlin's views generally were followed, as a fortunate precedent for libraries and librarianship.

Another significant element in the humanistic philosophy of education was its concern for historiography. As Nicola Abbagnano pointed out, "The discovery of documentary falsifications and false attributions, the need to discover texts and revive them in authentic form by studying and collating codices, and the attempt to understand the personalities of the literary men and the philosophers of the past in their own worlds are all the indications of humanism's fundamental concern for historicity."[6] In this respect, the fundamental compatibility of Christianity with humanism is well illustrated in the Christian belief that God acts in history, that Jesus was a historic figure, and that the accumulation of accurate historic information contributes to the growth of understanding and faith. History by its very nature requires the exercise of reason.

Humanism as a philosophy of education played a significant role in developing the vernacular languages. As those languages developed in Europe, writers and teachers made use of Latin terms, modes of thought, and literary types derived from their study of the classics. Thus the "inkhorn terms" of Shakespeare gave his writing some of its distinctive quality and added many Latinate words to the English language

Rather paradoxically the humanistic impulse to revive the learning of the past resulted in the movement to use the vernacular languages for the education of human beings in the present. Thus the movement in American colleges in the nineteenth century by the progressivists who wished to emphasize the English language and the study of science is one of the many evidences of the continuing influence of humanism on education. The distinguished Roman Catholic scholar, Father Walter J. Ong, suggests that the "humanities" have rather slowly become a significant element in all levels of education. That the humanistic impulse still continues is suggested by Father Ong's statement that "In the extent, depth, and maturity of academic literary and cultural studies, humanism, for all its weaknesses, is in a far stronger condition today than ever, most notably in the U.S."[7]

The belief that the word "humanism" automatically and

exclusively refers only to atheism is not supported by the scholarly discussions of this subject. Even the quite conservative *Encyclopedia of the Lutheran Church* refers to the "center of all true humanism, Christ Jesus. . . ."[8]

Humanism influenced northern Europe through the work of Erasmus, religious reformers Philipp Melanchthon and Ulrich Zwingli, as well as through the work of Martin Luther. Erasmus' influence has been given more attention than is the case for these other Protestant reformers. Examples of humanistic attitudes may be found in Luther's tract "On the Liberty of Christian Men." A specific example of a humanistic attitude may be found in Luther's 8th sermon, preached at Wittenberg in 1522. In that sermon Luther discussed images in the light of the commandment found in Exodus 20:4 which prohibits making images in a far more sweeping form than is usually recognized.

> You shall not make yourself a graven image, or any likeness of anything that is in heaven above, or that is in the earth beneath, or that is in the water under the earth;

In his sermon Luther demonstrated an attitude toward images parallel to the ideas expressed by Milton in the *Areopagitica*. Luther argued that images should not be destroyed, an important issue because Protestants were in fact destroying images in Catholic churches at the time. Images should not be worshipped but they need not be destroyed. "If no service is done to God by erecting them they would have fallen all of themselves." Even such objectionable images as serpents should not be destroyed. Luther pointed out that while Paul preached in Athens against idols he overthrew none by force. Luther also said that the apostle Luke writing about images in the book of Acts "wanted to show that outward things could do no harm to faith if only the heart does not cleave to them." Books contain images; the imagery in books is constructed of words. To many people the imagery in books is as objectionable as the images of idols that the early Christians met in Greece and other Mediterranean cities. But Milton argues, just as did Luther, that it is the attitude of the reader that is all important. Images, whether constructed of stone or of words, can only affect viewers to the degree that they choose to acquiesce in the influence of the image on their lives.

Both Melanchthon and Zwingli were religious scholars who had the same interest in the classics as did the Italian scholars. Zwingli, a Swiss Protestant reformer, studied Greek and Hebrew and emphasized the importance of recovering the ancient classic documents. He was greatly concerned with civil rights and the democratization of society. Through Zwingli humanistic influences came into the Reformed churches and complemented the influence of humanism at Oxford and Cambridge. Zwingli's influence played a significant role in the development of congregationalism in the new world.

Humanism as a philosophy of education began to affect the English-speaking world as early as 1437, when an Italian schoolmaster Frulovisi came to England. He brought with him an interest in the new learning of the Renaissance. By the year 1500 a number of humanists were active in England or English universities, especially at Oxford. They included such eminent worthies as William Grocyn, a theologian and preacher. His student, Thomas Linacre, was particularly interested in medicine and largely founded what is now the Royal College of Physicians in London in 1518. Other important Oxford humanists were John Colet and William Lily. All of these men were clergymen, deeply interested in linguistic scholarship and in education. Colet became the Dean (principal clergyman) of St. Paul's in London, where he founded St. Paul's school. William Lily was its first headmaster and later John Milton was a student there.

Histories of English literature describe the work of these Oxford humanists in greater detail than is appropriate here. One such text describes them in the following language: "They were all saintly souls, living abstemious lives, possessing an incredible ardor for learning and extraordinary powers of administration."[9] That the humanistic education John Milton received at St. Paul's school predisposed him toward atheism is amply contradicted by *Paradise Lost*. This, the greatest religious poem in English, is a poem that for many generations of readers presented a more vivid picture of our first parents than did the book of Genesis itself.

The humanistic philosophy of education that dominated the great English universities was brought to the New World by clergymen who referred to it in their sermons and relied upon it in establishing the first American university, Harvard. There is a direct line of succession between these great English universities whose graduates founded Harvard and most modern colleges. Most academicians can trace their education to a teacher who was a graduate of Harvard, or who was taught by a graduate of Harvard. A similar line of succession may be shown in the Lutheran colleges for academics who are culturally descended from Luther and the Lutheran theologian and humanist Philipp Melanchthon.

Samuel Eliot Morison in two books on the history of Harvard College has shown the influence of humanistic education on the curriculum of that school. As Perry Miller wrote, "Thanks to the labors of Professor Morison we may now rest assured that the Puritans of New England were the descendants of Erasmus [a Catholic priest] and Colet [an Episcopalian clergyman]."[10]

Miller demonstrated the influence of Renaissance humanism on the Puritans in several ways. He wrote:

> That a Puritan writer could be devoted to classical literature is demonstrated most conspicuously by John Milton. The miraculous fusion of Puritanism and Hellenism which he achieved is unique only in his grandeur of expression; the same combination of religious dogma with the classics, of Protestant theology and ancient morality was the aim of the curriculum at Harvard College, and it was sustained, though on a rudimentary or pedestrian level, in the sermons of Yankee parsons throughout the seventeenth century.
>
> The humanist learning had already become a regular part of the studies in the English universities when the men who were to be ministers and magistrates in New England matriculated there.[11]

One example is the Puritan clergyman Increase Mather, who preached a sermon in 1677 in which he asserted that the Massachusetts legislature must take care of the public schools and of Harvard College, "that so there might be able instruments raised up for the propagating of Truth in succeeding Generations. And some have well & truly observed, that the Interest of Religion and good Literature, hath risen and fallen together."[12]

Another example of humanism in Puritan writing is John Wise's *Vindication of the Government of New-England Churches* (1717).[13] This is a defense of a democratic government for churches and by extension a defence of democracy in general. In the course of his argument, Wise asserted that every human being contained within himself "right reason" received from God as an "emanation of His Wisdom: (Proverbs 20:27. The spirit of man is the candle of the Lord, searching out the inward parts of the belly.)" Wise used several other Biblical quotations to support his argument that all human beings contain within themselves a dependable rational function: "And the light was the light of men, which lighteth every man which cometh into the world."[14] (John 1:9) He argued further:

> That which is to be drawn from man's reason, flowing from the true current of that faculty—when unperverted—may be said to be the law of nature: on which account, the Holy Scriptures declare it written on men's hearts. . . . (Rom. 2. 14) "These having not a law, are a law to themselves." So that the meaning is: when we acknowledge the law of nature to be the dictate of right reason, we must mean that the understanding of man is endowed with such a power as to be able, from the contemplation of human condition, to discover a necessity of living agreeably with this law. . . .[15]

Wise was a typical humanist in his willingness to quote classic authors to support his view that human beings contained a principle of rationality within themselves: "Therefore," says Plutarch, "to follow God and obey reason is the same thing."[16]

A second relevant point that Wise made was his insistence on the equality of all human beings. Not being stupid, he didn't argue that all human beings were of equal height, weight, color, or intelligence. He did argue that "all men are born free" and made equal by nature:

> Thus every man must be acknowledged equal to every man since all subjection and all command are equally banished on both sides; and considering all men thus at liberty, every man has a prerogative to judge for himself, viz. what shall be most for his behoof, happiness and well-being. . . . it follows as a command of the law of nature that every man esteem and treat another as one who is naturally his equal, or who is a man as well as he. There be many popular or plausible reasons that greatly illustrate this equality: viz. that we all derive our being from one stock, the same common father of [the] human race. . . .
> And also, that our bodies are composed of matter, frail,

brittle, and liable to be destroyed by (a) thousand accidents. We all owe our existence to the same method of propagation. The noblest mortal, in his entrance onto the stage of life, is not distinguished by any pomp or of passage from the lowest of mankind; and our life hastens to the same general mark: death observes no ceremony, but knocks as loud at the barriers of the Court as at the door of the cottage. . . . For that it is a command of nature's law that no man . . . shall arrogate to himself a larger share than his fellows, but shall admit others to equal privileges with himself.[17]

Onalee McGraw quotes the attorney William B. Bell concerning the Supreme Court's constitutional definition of religion: "for the court theistic belief is but one sort of religion: nontheistic belief may equally qualify as 'religion. . . .'"[18] To apply this definition of religion to the public schools puts them in a quandary. If the schools teach specific theistic dogmas they violate the First Amendment. If they do not teach specific theistic dogmas the right wing critics accuse them of teaching secular humanism and thus violating the First Amendment. This is highly illogical. To refrain from saying "I believe in God" at the beginning of each school day does not support the conclusion that the teacher who thus refrains is an atheist. There is a distinct tendency in the right wing fundamentalists toward a faith in verbalism. They wish to reduce religion to verbal formulas. In this respect, they ignore the principle enunciated by Jesus in Matthew 23:25: "Woe to you, scribes and Pharisees: hypocrites, for you cleanse the outside of the cup and of the plate, but inside they are full of extortion and rapacity." The principle this passage suggests is that it is the reality of righteousness that matters, not the outer appearance.

The school critics have a long list of subjects or methods which they regard as evidence that the schools are in fact teaching the belief of secular humanism. The list is lengthy and varies from one critic to another. A list published by the *Eagle Forum* is reproduced on pages 148–149.

That the list inhibits the teaching of literature is illustrated by attacks on the play *Romeo and Juliet*, which concludes with two young people committing suicide. Suicide is, tragically, a relatively common cause of death among young people today. There were five suicides in the 1984–85 school year at a moderately sized central Wisconsin high school. It is, however, extremely unlikely that Shakespeare's play, *Romeo and Juliet*, or class discussions of suicide are responsible for the current wave of suicides among teenagers. In this matter, as in a number of other subjects previously discussed—VD, teenage pregnancy, drug addiction—the schools are made the scapegoat for social problems largely beyond their control.

The effort to proscribe the use of autobiographies, diaries and journals will surely come to be thought of as one of the strangest fears of the radical right wing. Orwell's *1984* begins with Winston Smith starting to write a journal—an activity strictly forbidden in the world of Big Brother. The reasons are clear. Journal writing is an important method by which the writer develops a sense of self-awareness, a sense of inner integrity. The Western world from the time of the prophet Isaiah has regarded the development of the inner self as of the highest importance. For that reason the schools have regularly used great diaries and journals from the past and have encouraged students to write their own journals. The *Confessions* of Augustine is found in many high school libraries, especially in those libraries that have the Great Books collection. Many other diaries are studied in literature classes. Franklin's *Autobiography*, John Woolman's *Journal*, the *Diary* of Anne Frank and Lincoln Steffen's reminiscences are only a few of the many literary works in the category of the personal journal. The usefulness of journal or diary writing is well established by experience in the schools. Yet the school critics would, if they could, prevent the use of this valuable and traditional method of instruction.

Another of the characteristics of secular humanism, according to the critics, is a belief in, or the teaching of, evolution, yet many members of the Christian churches see no conflict between evolution and their own faith. The Gablers report, however, that "evolution is the cornerstone of humanistic education."[19] The Gablers and other school critics rest their case on the fact that the Humanist Manifesto of the American Humanist Association (AHA) also supports a belief in evolution. This argument, as with several other subjects, exhibits the logical fallacy of the undistributed middle, or more simply guilt by association. The Humanist Manifesto has attracted little attention, except among the school critics, who believe that the 3000 members of AHA

The following letter is reprinted from *The Phyllis Schlafly Report*, January 1985.

TO: School Board President

Dear _____

    I am the parent of _____who attends _____ School. Under U.S. legislation and court decisions, parents have the primary responsibility for their children's education, and pupils have certain rights which the schools may not deny. Parents have the right to assure that their children's beliefs and moral values are not undermined by the schools. Pupils have the right to have and to hold their values, and moral standards without direct or indirect manipulation by the schools through curricula, textbooks, audio-visual materials, or supplementary assignments.
    Accordingly, I hereby request that my child be involved in NO school activities or materials listed below unless I have first reviewed all the relevant materials and have given my written consent for their use:
    Psychological and psychiatric treatment that is designed to affect behavioral, emotional, or attitudinal characteristics of an individual or group;
    Values clarification, use of moral dilemmas, discussion of religious or moral standards, role-playing or open-ended discussions of situations involving moral issues, and survival games including life/death decision exercises;
    Death education, including abortion, euthanasia, suicide, use of violence, and discussions of death and dying;
    Curricula pertaining to alcohol and drugs;
    Instruction in nuclear war, nuclear policy, and nuclear classroom games;
    Anti-nationalistic, one-world government or globalism curricula;
    Discussion and testing on interpersonal relationships; discussions of attitudes toward parents and parenting;
    Education in human sexuality, including premarital sex, extra-marital sex, contraception, abortion, homosexuality, group sex and marriages, prostitution, incest, masturbation, bestiality, divorce, population control, and roles of males and females; sex behavior and attitudes of student and family;
    Pornography and any materials containing profanity and/or sexual explicitness;
    Guided fantasy techniques, hypnotic techniques; imagery and suggestology;
    Organic evolution, including the idea that man has developed from previous or lower types of living things;
    Discussions of witchcraft and the occult, the supernatural, and Eastern mysticism;
    Political affiliations and beliefs of student and family; personal religious beliefs and practices;

Mental and psychological problems and self-incriminating behavior potentially embarrassing to the student or family;

Critical appraisals of other individuals with whom the child has family relationships;

Legally recognized privileged and analogous relationships, such as those of lawyers, physicians, and ministers;

Income, including the student's role in family activities and finances;

Nonacademic personality tests; questionnaires on personal and family life and attitudes;

Autobiography assignments; log books, diaries, and personal journals;

Contrived incidents for self-revelation; sensitivity training, group encounter sessions, talk-ins, magic circle techniques, self-evaluation and auto-criticism; strategies designed for self-disclosure (e.g., zig-zag);

Sociograms; sociodrama; psychodrama; blindfold walks; isolation techniques.

The purpose of this letter is to preserve my child's rights under the Protection of Pupil Rights Amendment (the Hatch Amendment) to the General Education Provisions Act, and under its regulations as published in the *Federal Register* of Sept. 6, 1984, which became effective Nov. 12, 1984. These regulations provide a procedure for filing complaints first at the local level, and then with the U.S. Department of Education. If a voluntary remedy fails, federal funds can be withdrawn from those in violation of the law. I respectfully ask you to send me a substantive response to this letter attaching a copy of your policy statement on procedures for parental permission on requirements, to notify all my child's teachers, and to keep a copy of this letter in my child's permanent file. Thank you for your cooperation.

Sincerely,

Copy to School Principal

Written by the Maryland Coalition of Concerned Parents on Privacy Rights on Public Schools and distributed by Phyllis Schlafly and Eagle Forum.

represent and speak for the several hundred thousand school teachers in the United States, teachers who may be Catholic, Lutheran, Presbyterian, Methodist, Baptist, Jewish or even Buddhist.

Though the Schlafly report does not list bussing or school desegregation as evidence of secular humanism, the drive toward equalitarianism in the public schools is regarded by the school critics as evidence of secular humanism. As noted previously, a substantial proportion of the books most frequently objected to deal with minority group people. One of these books, *The Learning Tree* by Gordon Parks, has been explicitly charged with teaching secular humanism by parents in the Mead school district, a district near Spokane, Washington. In addition to teaching secular humanism, the book was said to insult Christianity and to contain pornography. The charge was filed in a district court in Washington.

In fact, the book is a slightly fictionalized account of the author's life as he grew up in southeastern Kansas. As a native of southern Kansas who grew up at approximately the same time, I can bear witness to the essential truthfulness of the book's account of black life in those years.

The Moral Majority of Washington state paid legal fees and provided a lawyer for the lawsuit (Grove vs. Mead). Michael Farris, reported to be executive director of Moral Majority for the state of Washington, was the attorney.[20]

The complaining student was assigned the book in her public high school sophomore literature class. The student read part of the book and found it offensive to her Christian faith. She was assigned another book and given permission to leave the classroom during discussion of *The Learning Tree*. The student's mother brought suit, contending that use of the book violated the religion clause of the First Amendment. She contended that the book inhibited her religion and promoted the religion of secular humanism.

The district court rejected the charge that the book promoted secular humanism. The court also held that since the student was given an alternate assignment and allowed to leave the room while *The Learning Tree* was being discussed, the student's constitutional rights were not violated.

School critics argue that since the Abington v. Schempp case held that students could be embarrassed by leaving the room for religious services, they should not be compelled to leave the room to avoid a discussion of a book of which they disapprove. But there are ample traditional reasons for dividing classes when academic reasons make that appropriate. The two situations seem quite different. The ninth U.S. circuit court of appeals upheld the district court decision. Judge Eugene Wright wrote in a 3–0 decision: "The state interest in providing well-rounded public education would be critically impeded by accommodation of Mrs. Carolyn Grove's wishes." The appeals court found that using the book did not violate the Groves' religious rights because the girl was assigned an alternate book as soon as she and her mother objected and was given permission to avoid class discussions.

In a concurring opinion Judge William Canby wrote that school officials' selection and retention of the book did not signal government endorsement of what some may perceive as anti-Christian elements in the book. "Inclusion of *The Learning Tree* as representative of a particular literary genre neither inhibits nor instills, but simply informs and educates students on a particular social outlook forged in the crucible of black rural life," Judge Canby wrote. "To include the work no more communicates governmental endorsement of the author's or characters' religious views than to assign *Paradise Lost*, *Pilgrim's Progress* or *The Divine Comedy* conveys endorsement or approval of Milton's, Bunyan's or Dante's Christianity."[21]

The strongest argument of the school critics for the charge that the schools teach secular humanism is the charge that the American Humanist Association and the Humanist Manifesto assert a number of the same beliefs that appear in the public schools. This is the logical fallacy of the undistributed middle. Some teachers agree with members of the AHA concerning evolution, equalitarianism, and moral relativity. That some teachers agree with some humanists at certain points is not evidence that those teachers of the public school system are to be identified with the AHA or its non-theistic beliefs.

A widely circulated definition of humanism appears in a brochure entitled "Is Humanism Molesting Your Child?" This brochure was published by the Pro-Family Forum of Fort Worth Texas. No author is listed. It is distributed also by the Gablers as an insert in their *Handbook No. 1, Humanism.*

The brochure lists the ten following basic beliefs of humanism:

1/   Denies the deity of God, the inspiration of the Bible, and the divinity of Jesus Christ.
2/   Denies the existence of the soul, life after death, salvation and heaven, damnation and hell.
3/   Denies the biblical account of creation.
4/   Believes that there are no absolutes, no right no wrong— that moral values are self-determined and situational. Do your own thing, "as long as it does not harm anyone else."
5/   Believes in removal of distinctive roles of male and female.
6/   Believes in sexual freedom between consenting individuals, regardless of age, including premarital sex, homosexuality, lesbianism, and incest.
7/   Believes in the right to abortion, euthanasia (mercy killing), and suicide.
8/   Believes in equal distribution of America's wealth to reduce poverty and bring about equality.
9/   Believes in control of the environment, control of energy and its limitation.
10/   Believes in removal of American patriotism and the free enterprise system, disarmament, and the creation of a one-world socialistic government.

Articles 1–3

The first three articles in this alleged catechism deal with subjects that are constitutionally forbidden in the public schools as matters of dogma. Those articles could be discussed in a description of Christianity in classes in history, social studies, or comparative religion. The absence of attention to these articles does not, however, tell us anything about the beliefs of school teachers or of the purposes of American public schools. Article number three, the denial of the biblical account of creation, is typical of the entire approach. For one thing, it deals with the Bible in a simplistic and uninformed fashion. There are many accounts of creation in the Bible including references in the following places: Genesis 1, 2:1–3; Genesis 2:4–25; Genesis 5; Psalms 104; Proverbs 8; John 1.

These references may be interpreted in a variety of ways. It is typical of the charge of secular humanism that a disagreement with the interpretation of the critics is labeled secular humanism, i.e., atheism. Substantial numbers of practicing Christians find no difficulty in accepting whatever interpretation of evolution seems most persuasive to them. Some school critics, however, deny the right of Christians to decide this matter for themselves by alleging that to believe in any form of evolution is automatically un-Christian.

Article 4—Moral Relativity

Article four asserts that secular humanism is based on moral relativity or situation ethics and that the schools by using such books as *Values Clarification* indoctrinate students into moral relativity. Onalee McGraw also discusses this charge at some length.

The prevailing climate of opinion in the United States concerning ethics does substantially accept moral relativity. School critics regularly advance the Ten Commandments as the ideal of an absolute ethical standard, yet Catholics find no difficulty in reconciling the commandment against making a graven image and installing crucifixes with an image of Christ in their churches. Large numbers of Americans find no conflict between the sixth commandment, "Thou shalt not kill," and the imposition of capital punishment by many states. Texas, the Gablers' home state, has executed several people in recent years. A number of people are currently awaiting execution in Texas and several other states. Nor do many Americans see a conflict between the sixth commandment and killing in time of war. Many Americans believe that it was morally correct to drop the atom bomb on the Japanese cities, in spite of the sixth commandment. The New Testament prohibits divorce, and in the words of Jesus says that whoever marries a divorced woman commits adultery. (Matthew 5:32) However, large numbers of Americans, many of whom are church members, and in every state in the union, accept divorce as a normal part of twentieth-century life.

These accommodations with the absolute principles laid down in the Bible can fairly be described as growing out of an atmosphere of moral relativity. Put another way, many Americans believe that changing situations require changes in moral principles in dealing with crime by capital punishment or international conflicts by war or family conflicts by divorce. It is not surprising that the climate of opinion in the public schools reflects generally an ethical standard of moral relativity. It is however false to assert that those who practice moral relativity are thereby secular humanists, i.e., atheists.

In discussing moral relativity the Pro-Family brochure lists seven stages from *Values Clarification*. These seven stages amount essentially to the processes by which an individual learns to choose and act freely and regularly on the values found of greatest importance. These stages of moral development represent the systematization of a tradition that might be illustrated by the writings and actions of many of the western world's most admired figures including Jesus Christ.

Other examples that might be cited are Socrates, Augustine, Luther, Milton, Franklin, and Ralph Waldo Emerson. Franklin's autobiography with its description of his systematic effort to attain virtue illustrates the point well. Emerson's essay "Self Reliance" is another example. The term "self reliance" well describes the essential thrust of *Values Clarification*.

Onalee McGraw's description of secular humanism contains a similar analysis. McGraw cites Lawrence Kohlberg's six stages of moral development as an alleged illustration of secular humanism. Kohlberg's analysis describes a process beginning with the self-centered ego gratification of the small child and continuing through the pressures toward conformity with the peers of the adolescent and, unfortunately, of many adults. The final stage of moral maturity that Kohlberg describes results in obedience to the inner voice of conscience.

Kohlberg's final stage of moral maturity seems remarkably consistent with the "new covenant" announced by Jeremiah in Chapter 31:31–34. In a powerfully concrete passage Jeremiah said:

Behold the days are coming, says the Lord, when I will make a new covenant with the house of Israel and the house of Judah, not like the covenant which I made with their fathers when I took them by the hand to bring them out of the land of Egypt, my covenant which they broke, though I was their husband, says the Lord. But this is the covenant which I will make with the house of Israel after those days, says the Lord: I will put my law within them, and I will write it upon their hearts; and I will be their God, and they shall be my people. And no longer shall each man teach his neighbor and each his brother, saying, "Know the Lord," for they shall know me, from the least of them to the greatest, says the Lord; for I will forgive their iniquity, and I will remember their sin no more.

The charge of moral relativity distorts the realities of our society and the relationship of moral education in the public schools to the main stream ethical traditions that our society has derived from its Biblical sources. Henry Steele Commager has pointed out that the contemporary world may no longer accept the complex Puritan theology; nevertheless the power of Puritanism remains today. Commager wrote:

> Two centuries of reaction could not dissolve the Puritan inheritance of respect for the individual and for the dignity of man, of recognition of the ultimate authority of reason, of allegiance to principles rather than to persons, to the doctrine of government by compact and by consent, and to spiritual and moral democracy. These things, along with Puritanism's deepseated moral purpose, its ceaseless search for salvation, its passion for righteousness and for justice, and its subordination of material to spiritual ends, entered into the current of secular thought and retained their vitality long after the theological and metaphysical arguments which sustained them had been forgotten.[22]

Article 5—The Roles of Male and Female

Article five asserts that secular humanists believe in the removal of the distinctive roles of male and female. It is patently obvious that this charge has nothing to do with the presence or absence of theistic or non-theistic systems of belief. What it reflects is the nineteenth century Southern belief that the place of women is in the home, a belief remarkably violated by Phyllis Schlafly, Onalee McGraw, Norma Gabler and several other leaders of the school critics. The dissertations by Dorothy Thompson Weathersby and Ellen Last amply demonstrate this point. If the school critics spoke German, they would probably describe the duty of women in terms of "kinder, kirche, and kuchen."

However, from the *Wall Street Journal* to most small town newspapers, there is evidence on every hand that the hundred-year-old effort of American women to move into the mainstream of American society has had substantial success. The school critics would reverse, if they could, the processes that started at Seneca Falls, New York in 1849 when a famous meeting was held to publicize the effort of American women to achieve equal rights with men. It is an index of the distance that women have come that they debated in 1849 whether to ask for the right to vote. It took 70 years to achieve that right; the school critics would no doubt take it away if they could.

That the belief in equal rights for women is an evidence of secular humanism, i.e. atheism, is contradicted by the membership of most churches on Sunday morning. Those Protestant churches, including the Episcopalian church, that have ordained women to the clergy give the lie to the charge that equal rights for women is a sign of atheism. Westminster Cathedral in London recently appointed the first woman verger in the history of that institution; the United Methodist Church in the United States recently appointed the first woman bishop in the history of Christendom. Neither the Anglicans nor the Methodists can seriously be charged with atheism as a result of these appointments.

The belief that the most distinctive human traits are non-sex-related is a theme in Western world literature from Plato's *Symposium* through the androgynous characters of Shakespeare to much twentieth-century writing. The term androgyny refers to the belief that the most admirable human qualities are neither male nor female, but exist in varying combinations in either sex. Shakespeare's frequent use of disguises illustrates androgyny in, for example, the play *As You Like It,* in which a woman disguises herself as a man and then pretends to be a woman. If all the 20th century books that reflect the aspirations and abilities of women for full equality with men were removed from school and public libraries, these libraries would be decimated indeed. The 800 titles in the appendix of this book suggest, however, that if the Gablers, Schlaflys, the Moral Majority, Pro-Family Forum people and other school critics get their way, that will indeed be the ultimate result of this battle of the books.

Article 6—Attitudes Toward Sex

Article six is a mixture of charges, some of which represent realities for which there is substantial public support and others of which have no public support at all. The Pro-Family charge that secular humanists believe in the right of incest can only come from people who have no conscience. No evidence at all exists that the American Humanist Association or any school teacher anywhere in the United States has advocated either incest as a right or the right of adults to have sex with children, which is meant by the phrase "regardless of age." These charges are contemptible and should earn public disgust for the people who make them.

Article six also asserts that secular humanists believe in sexual freedom for "homosexuality, lesbianism." As a generalization concerning the public schools, this has little substance; a few teachers across the United States have asserted their right outside the classroom to make their sexual identity public and to work for equal rights for homosexuals. No persuasive evidence is presented by the Gablers that there is any general movement in the public schools advocating either homosexuality or lesbianism. In fact, most school children in the public schools still have little or no sex education, even of the most innocuous kind.

The main thrust of Article six is an objection to the belief that there should be sexual freedom between consenting adults, and as noted above the phrases are added in a mean-spirited fashion "regardless of age" and "incest." Ignoring these two phrases, many people will agree with the action of the Wisconsin state legislature in establishing as a statutory principle in Wisconsin the rights of consenting adults freely to engage in sexual behavior. There may be here, as elsewhere in the battle of the books, regional differences at work. If so, given the tendency of the schools to reflect the climate of opinion in whatever community they exist, it is highly doubtful that school teachers or the curriculum do advocate sexual freedom for consenting adults in these states that have not, as did the Wisconsin legislature, established as a statutory principle sexual freedom for consenting adults.

Article 7—Abortion, Euthanasia, Suicide

Article seven, which asserts that secular humanists believe in the right to abortion, euthanasia and suicide may or may not be true of members of the American Humanist Association. As a generalization about the public schools it is groundless; as is usually the case, no documentation exists to support this charge. While it is true that some materials used in the schools describe suicide, for example *Romeo and Juliet*, it is difficult to take seriously any critic of the American schools who fails to recognize that *Romeo and Juliet* is a tragedy, or who fails to recognize that the play is a lament for the death of two attractive young people whose parents and society failed them in their time of need. Yet in several places in the United States *Romeo and Juliet* is currently under attack because it describes teenage suicide.

It is possible to construe the book *Go Ask Alice*, which is currently the most frequently attacked book in the schools, as concluding with a suicide. It can hardly be said that the book presents any inducements to the reader for engaging in the life of drug addiction which ended in the central character's death. In fact, the parents of the girl involved are reported to have had the book published, anonymously, in the hope that it would deter other young people from drugs and the death to which the drugs led.

The terrible tragedy of teenage suicide, which has reached almost epidemic proportions, is not the fault of the public schools. For this tragic reality the schools are being made the scapegoat.

Gablers' *Handbook No. I, Humanism* contains no evidence of any significant movement in the public schools in support of euthanasia. So far as I am aware, the advocacy of euthanasia rarely or never appears in the 800 books which have been the object of attack across the last three decades. Probably the charge appears, as do other charges in these 10 articles, as a reflection of the prejudices of the school critics, with little or no regard either to the realities of school life or to the realities of the material used in the schools.

The charge that secular humanists believe in the right of abortion may or may not be true of the members of the American Humanist Association. Whatever may be the case for the AHA, public advocacy of the right of abortion must be nearly nonexistent among public school teachers. Some sex education materials describe abortion. Contrary to the views of the critics, description of a reality is not advocacy.

The Supreme Court has said that the right to an abortion is constitutionally protected within certain limits. Gallup polls reveal that a substantial majority of the public believe this decision to be correct. Undoubtedly some unknown proportion of school teachers agree with the general public concerning abortion. That many teachers may agree that abortion is an individual right does not mean that those teachers use time in classes in English, mathematics, economics, history, social studies or physical education to advocate the right to an abortion. If teachers have in fact abused their position and misused class time in English or mathematics to advocate abortion rights, they should be, and in all probability would be, reprimanded. I know, however, of no such cases and doubt if any significant number exist.

Thus with Article seven the Pro-Family Forum brochure has put together a miscellaneous set of charges, two of which have no grounds—suicide and euthanasia—and a third which represents a distortion of existing realities.

Article 8—Equalitarianism

Article eight charges secular humanists and school teachers with advocating an equal distribution of American wealth to relieve poverty and bring about equality. As with other articles, the fear and guilt feelings of the right wing extremists are made evident by this charge. They project upon the public schools what they think ought to be done or what they fear might be done.

It is certainly true that there is a strong impulse toward equalitarianism in the American public school system. The ultimate source of this value, as of the other basic values in our public school system, is our Judeo-Christian tradition. The prophet Amos criticized the world of his day for forgetting the "covenant of brotherhood." The book of Ruth shows that foreign women (Ruth) or foreigners generally are equal in virtue to

Hebrew people. Many passages in the New Testament insist on the oneness of the humankind, the equal value of all human beings as children of God. One of the many evidences of the Biblical influence on our literature is the recurrent theme of human equality. It is present in the medieval morality play *Everyman*, as well as in the prayer by the great priest and poet John Donne who wrote these famous lines in his well-loved meditation XVII:

> No man is an island entire of itself; every man is a piece of the continent, a part of the main. If a clod be washed away by the sea, Europe is the less, as well as if a promontory were, as well as if a manor of thy friend's or of thine own were. Any man's death diminishes me, because I am involved in mankind, and therefore never send to know for whom the bell tolls; it tolls for thee.

Equalitarianism is implicit in Milton's *Paradise Lost* just as Puritan preachers such as John Wise took equalitarianism as their theme for sermons. Dozens of twentieth century American novels, plays and poems assert implicitly or explicitly the equality of humankind. To eliminate materials containing the notion of equality from school libraries would leave many shelves bare. That equalitarianism, defined as a belief in the equal worth of all human beings, is strongly present in public school learning materials, is certainly true. Only critics who are profoundly ignorant of our Judeo-Christian tradition and of the dependence of our literature on the Bible would condemn the schools for the equalitarianism that runs through them.

Even the Supreme Court decision of the 1890's which declared segregation legal used the phrase "separate but equal," thus at least giving lip service to equalitarianism. The 1954 Supreme Court decision which prohibited segregation did so on the grounds that "separate but equal" did not result in equal education for all. An impulse toward equalitarianism was strongly present in the 1954 decision.

The increasing effort to admit handicapped students, to provide bilingual education for non-English speakers, to provide food programs in the public schools, all grow out of the widely held desire to give equal opportunity to all children and young people. None of these programs lead to advocating equal distribution of wealth. No documents are provided by the school critics showing that the extensive literature of education contains such an advocacy, nor is there any evidence of any number of school teachers using their classrooms specifically to urge the equal distribution of wealth.

The phrase in Article eight "to reduce poverty" does not distinguish between theists and non-theists. The recent pastoral letter of the Roman Catholic bishops which asserts that the measure of success of an economic program is the degree to which it ends poverty hardly justifies asserting that those bishops are atheists. A concern with the poor has characterized Christianity since Jesus delivered his first sermon. We are told in Luke 4:18 that Jesus began his first sermon with the following words:

> The Spirit of the Lord is upon me, because he hath anointed me to preach the gospel to the poor; he hath sent me to heal the brokenhearted, to preach deliverance to the captives, and recovering of sight to the blind, to set at liberty them that are bruised. . . .

Mary's Magnificat expresses similar views:

> And Mary said, "My soul magnifies the Lord, and my spirit rejoices in God my Savior, for he has regarded the low estate of his handmaiden. For behold, henceforth all generations will call me blessed; for he who is mighty has done great things for me, and holy is his name. And his mercy is on those who fear him from generation to generation. He has shown strength with his arm, he has scattered the proud in the imagination of their hearts, he has put down the mighty from their thrones, and exalted those of low degree; he has filled the hungry with good things, and the rich he has sent empty away.

That the Christian forms of humanism strongly present in the public schools should express themselves with a special concern for poor children is natural. Many a teacher has surreptitiously provided books, lunch money, clothing and other kinds of support for poverty-stricken students. This generalization has its many exceptions, no doubt, but it is certainly true that both individually and institutionally efforts have been made to ameliorate proverty in society and especially the effects of poverty on school children.

Article 9—Control of the Environment

The ninth item that supposedly characterizes humanism, i.e. atheism, is its asserted belief in control of the environment. This is an extraordinarily curious charge since a well-remembered passage in the book of Genesis reports that God commanded mankind "to have dominion over the fish of the sea, and over the cattle, and over all the earth, and over every creeping thing that creeps on the earth." Chapter 2, verse 15 of Genesis reports that God "took the man and put him in the Garden of Eden to till it and keep it." These passages from Genesis make clear that it was God's will from the time of his creation that mankind should control the environment.

It seems likely that Article nine is a badly phrased objection to the twentieth-century impulse to conserve the environment. It is also likely that Article nine reflects the desire of right wing extremists to exploit the environment rather than to conserve it. Thus those segments of our society that oppose control of strip mining, that oppose action to prevent acid rain, that oppose action to clean up polluted air, that oppose protecting wilderness areas use this article to attack the schools. This article is another reflection of the tendency of school critics to define secular humanism in ways that express whatever prejudices the school critics may feel.

The impulse to protect the environment has its sources in the most venerable parts of Judeo-Christian history. The Psalms are full of references to man's duty to act as trustee and steward of the natural world. "The earth is the Lord's and the fulness thereof" (Psalm 24:1). Man cannot rule the earth; it belongs to God; man is to till—i.e., cultivate, preserve the earth. English literature, dependent as it is so powerfully on the Bible, is full of references to the fact that man, because of his short life, cannot own the earth but must hold it in trust for ensuing generations.

It is not surprising that a theme which runs through our literature from the Bible through Shakespeare to Faulkner, should be reflected in the activities of the public schools. Many schools in a variety of ways try to help children learn to love nature (difficult as that must be in inner city schools) and to protect the environment. That tradition is very old in American public schools.

In the 1930's I took vocational agriculture in a Kansas high school. The teacher, a church-going Republican, emphasized vigorously the importance of conserving the environment, especially the soil. The teacher had no trouble in relating the importance of soil conservation to the Old Testament notion that we are trustees and stewards of the land, not absolute owners, and therefore we have the duty to conserve the soil and to hand it on to the next generation preserved and not despoiled.

National Arbor Day, school forests, the community planting of particular trees or of flowering shrubs (redbuds in a small Kansas town, for example) are activities frequently carried out through the public schools. These and similar activities illustrate the ongoing impulse in many schools to teach respect for the natural world, to teach students to be sensitive to the need to protect and conserve the environment, "to till and keep the earth," as the Bible puts it.

This charge, that belief in controlling the environment is a sign of secular humanism betrays ignorance of the Bible and is an obvious effort to protect the interests of those right wing extremists who wish to exploit the environment in a fashion utterly without conscience.

Article 10—Secular Humanists Are Unpatriotic

Article ten asserts that humanists and the schools believe in removal of American patriotism and the free enterprise system among other charges. Much of this article is simply false, unsupported by any documented evidence and relying on the propaganda device of the big lie. The high proportion of American school teachers who have been veterans of one or another of the twentieth century wars has certainly proved their patriotism by their service. There must be very few students in the public schools who have not had several veterans for teachers. A substantial fraction of the great wave of veterans who descended on the colleges after WWII became school teachers. While that group of persons is now approaching retirement they constituted a significant fraction of the teaching staff across the last three decades. That they have been tricked into, or consented to, the removal of patriotism from the public schools is inconceivable. The charge that schools are attempting to remove patriotism is an outrageous falsehood.

The charge that humanists and the schools believe in the removal of the free enterprise system may or may not be true for some members of the three thousand people who belong to the American Humanist Association. It is certainly not true for the American public schools. This charge must be dealt with along with the implication that secular humanists and the public schools support socialism. Socialism may well be discussed in history or social studies classes but the school critics provide no evidence of a general tendency towards advocacy of socialism in such classes. The school critics, the Gablers in particular, are unable to distinguish between reporting and advocacy, as Last's dissertation abundantly documents. To advocate support for any political position—democratic, republican, socialist—would certainly be a violation of professional standards and in most cases, would result in a reprimand to the teacher.

In any case, socialism is not very popular in this society, as the election returns demonstrate regularly. Only those right wing extremists who believe that the post office, the public roads, the public schools or hot lunch programs are forms of socialism would charge the public schools with advocating socialism.

The charge of advocating a one-world government needs careful attention. The Old Testament calls for a one-world government in several places including Isaiah 2:1–5 and Micah 4:1–4:

> It shall come to pass in the latter days that the mountain of the house of the Lord shall be established as the highest of the mountains, and shall be raised up above the hills; and peoples shall flow to it, and many nations shall come and say: "Come, let us go up to the mountain of the Lord, to the house of the God of Jacob; that he may teach us his ways and we may walk in his paths." For out of Zion shall go forth the law, and the word of the Lord from Jerusalem. He shall judge between many peoples, and shall decide for strong nations afar off; and they shall beat their swords into plowshares, and their spears into pruning hooks; nation shall not lift up sword against nation, neither shall they learn war any more; but they shall sit every man under his vine and under his fig tree, and none shall make them afraid; for the mouth of the Lord of hosts has spoken.

The most dramatic evidence that we live in one world is the picture of planet earth taken from the moon. All science rests on the assumption that the entire universe is governed by the same laws. The most distant source of light is divisible into the same parts of the spectrum as the light on earth that comes from our sun. Not surprisingly, the public schools reflect in many ways the impulse toward unity, toward wholeness, that is suggested both by our religious heritage and by the principles of science. The literature that is taught frequently implies the attractiveness of those forces in the universe that unify life and the humankind. Note the familiar poem by Tennyson:

Flower in the Crannied Wall

Flower in the crannied wall,
I pluck you out of the crannies,
I hold you here, root and all, in my hand,
Little flower—but if I could understand
What you are, root and all, and all in all,
I should know what God and man is.

Another frequently taught poem is Vachel Lindsay's "Abraham Lincoln Walks at Midnight"—one of the many illustrations of the tendency of literature in English to embody the oneness of humankind. Lindsay's poem uses vigorous imagery to describe Abraham Lincoln as a symbol of the unity of the United States. Lindsay suggests that the spirit of Lincoln continues to motivate human beings to work for a world of peace, a world in which nationalistic enmities have come to an end.

Abraham Lincoln Walks at Midnight
In Springfield, Illinois

A bronzed, land man! His suit of ancient black,
A famous high top-hat and plain worn shawl
Make him the quaint great figure that men love,
The prairie-lawyer, master of us all.

. . . .

His head is bowed. He thinks of men and kings.
Yea, when the sick world cries, how can he sleep?

Too many peasants fight, they know not why,
Too many homesteads in black terror weep.

The sins of all the war-lords burn his heart.
He sees the dreadnaughts scouring every main.
He carries on his shawl-wrapped shoulders now
The bitterness, the folly and the pain.

He cannot rest until a spirit-dawn
Shall come;—the shining hope of Europe free:
A league of sober folk, the Workers' Earth,
Bringing long peace to Cornland, Alp and Sea.

It breaks his heart that kings must murder still,
That all his hours of travail here for men
Seem yet in vain. And who will bring white peace
That he may sleep upon his hill again?

Many activities go on in the public schools that grow out of the impulse to recognize the oneness of the world in which we live. There are exchanges of students, the study of foreign languages, and various celebrations of the effort to establish a peaceful world order. The League of Nations, the United Nations, as well as various other international organizations have long received sympathetic response in the public schools. Few teachers who cooperate in these activities believe that they are unpatriotic in doing so. Since membership in the United Nations is part of the national policy of the United States, appropriate school activities growing out of U.N. membership can hardly be called unpatriotic.

To put the matter as clearly as possible, the Gablers, the McGraws, the Pro-Family Forum, and their various offshoots are attacking the central core of education in the United States. They are opposed to ideas that started with Aquinas, that reason is compatible with a theistic position, indeed that God gave reason to man, that reason expresses itself in the study of science, of history, of religion, of foreign languages and of literature. The humanistic tradition lives vigorously today in the literary heritage of the English speaking world, as well as in the ongoing efforts of each new generation of writers. From Milton to Faulkner or Ferlinghetti, humanistic ideas of equality, tolerance, the worth of every individual person, a sense of wonder at the natural world, the impulse to understand ourselves and the cosmic order in which we live, together with humility at the limitations of our understanding—these elements of the humanistic tradition reoccur in our literature generation after generation.

Just as Milton and several generations of Puritan preachers found no conflict between this humanistic set of impulses and their religious faith, so have several generations of teachers in the public schools believed that in teaching the humanities with its emphasis on tolerance, its recognition of diversity, its assertion of the equal worth of all human beings, they were in accord with the basic principles of whatever faith they professed.

The critics are right that humanism is present in the American educational system, but they are wrong in their assertion that the educational philosophy of humanism is atheistic. As demonstrated above, the origins of humanistic education lie in Christian thought and may correctly be described as a philosophy of education that is essentially compatible with theism.

8 CONCLUSION

THIS BOOK must be regarded as an interim report, since it is likely that the issues considered here are not going to be resolved in the near future. As the preceding discussion has suggested, the critics of the schools are well organized, have substantial funds, and are very persistent; in all probability, these issues will continue to concern this society for a long time.

Establishing Rapport with the Community

In dealing with those issues several principles seem useful. While resort to the law has been carried out by both the school critics and the defenders of the public schools, it seems likely that the issues will ultimately be resolved in the court of public opinion. As Mr. O'Dooley said, the Supreme Court follows the election returns. The public schools have only slowly adopted strategies and tactics designed to win support from the broad middle section of society. It would seem imperative that the schools become more aggressive in establishing rapport with their constituencies.

The public schools have in fact a considerable advantage in the staff of teachers and administrators. These people come out of the communities in which they teach. They are often active in community organizations, such as the churches, Scouting, bowling leagues and dozens of other community groups. Nyla Ahrens' study showed that teachers who had a longer tenure in a school system were less likely to have their book selections challenged than was the case for younger teachers. Parents who become acquainted with teachers in community activities are not very likely to believe that the teachers have horns and a tail and are trying to win the students to the devilish activities that the critics charge.

Given the seriousness of the current critical pressures on the schools it would seem imperative that the schools enter into positive and well-planned activities to capitalize on their advantages. Both schools and libraries presently carry out some activities to establish better rapport with their communities, but in many schools these are rather routine and unimaginative, with limited effectiveness. An example of an extraordinarily effective program was developed in a rural southeastern Ohio school district. The Fort Frye Consolidated School District of Beverly, Ohio, a school district not far from Kanawa County, West Virginia, has similar socioeconomic characteristics with Kanawa County. Yet the English department at Fort Frye has been able quite successfully to teach a number of the books that have aroused controversy elsewhere, including A Day No Pigs Would Die, Lord of the Flies, the Diary of Anne Frank, To Kill a Mockingbird, and Hiroshima, among others.

In the 1970s rumors came to the teachers at Fort Frye that "there was a dirty book in junior high English," a reference to A Day No Pigs Would Die. In considering what to do about it the teachers decided to invite the parents to come and discuss "Books Our Children Read." There were no funds available to support this project; the teachers did it on their own. They announced that each department member would discuss one book used in the curriculum. Parents would be invited to suggest titles. Announcements were put in the daily and weekly newspapers; typed notes were sent home with each student in the junior and senior high schools.

A cross section of community members attended the first session. Some had students in college, some had students in the high school, one woman came because she loved books and had no one to talk to about them. The group met every week on Tuesday nights. The teachers commented briefly on their reasons for choosing the books and showed how the books that were chosen lent themselves to lessons on writing, usage, mechanics, and vocabulary. They then encouraged discussion of the book chosen for that evening.

A documentary film has been made of this activity by Michelle Marder Kamhi entitled "Books Our Children Read."[1]

June Berkley, who played a key role in carrying out this activity, described it in a report at the meeting of NCTE November 23, 1985. Two written reports are also available.[2] These various sources strongly suggest that the success of this activity lay in the excellent teaching skills of the people involved. They did not lecture to the parents; they made clear that they were interested in what the parents thought about the books. Thus the parents learned a number of important lessons about literature. They learned that there are individual and differing responses to a literary work and that good teaching does not impose a single "correct" interpretation of a given book. Since the teachers made clear that they were genuinely interested in the response of the parents to the books, the parents were able to conclude that the teachers were equally responsive to the interpretations and values that their children, the students, brought to the books. Thus without arguing and without any confrontation, a substantial message was communicated to a cross section of the public.

Criticism of the books ceased and there was no pressure on the schools to abandon the various titles listed above. A touching anecdote was the report that one parent asked at the end of a series of discussions, "Can we talk about Shakespeare now?"

A different method was adopted in the early 1970s in Stevens Point, Wisconsin. A committee of 35 persons broadly representative of the community was appointed by the school board to study the curriculum of the public schools. This committee held public hearings for two years on each aspect of the curriculum. Public announcements were made concerning the subject of each public hearing. In some cases, e.g., sex education, two or three sessions were held. At the end of the two years the committee wrote a report which the school board adopted and which it used in its considerations of curricular change.

One result was the addition of what appeared to be a well-designed program of sex education in the junior high. When a few parents complained about that program, it was pointed out that public hearings had been held and it was quite evident in the hearings and in the school board's consideration of the committee report that there was substantial community support for sex education. No candidate has run for the school board on a platform opposing sex education in Stevens Point.

Recent polls suggest that a high proportion of citizens across the nation support sex education in the public schools. In October 1985 an Associated Press-NBC news poll reported that 75 percent of the 1601 respondents approved of schools giving courses in sex education. Nineteen percent disapproved and six percent were unsure. A majority of respondents agreed that sex education gives students a healthy view of sex, and does not encourage sexual behavior. Twelve percent of the respondents, however, believed that sex education would encourage sexual behavior. A Louis Harris and Associates poll, based on interviews with 2510 adults in August 1985, revealed similar conclusions. Over 80 percent indicated approval of sex education in the schools. However, translating reports of this sort into support for sex education in a given community is not necessarily automatic. Positive efforts will have to be made, if support is to be achieved.

An effective method of dealing with a challenge to a single book—*The Adventures of Huckleberry Finn*—was developed at State College, Pennsylvania.[3] It was then required reading in the ninth grade English curriculum of the State College Area School District. A parent filed a written objection to the novel, listing seven grounds for discontinuing the use of the novel. The parent asserted that it had racially potent language, presented a negative stereotyped image of Jim and Blacks in general, contained condescending allusions toward Blacks, used dialects of doubtful authenticity, showed disrespect for longstanding social values, used much non-standard English, and was sexist in its treatment of Aunt Sally and Aunt Polly.

I heard the parent who filed these charges describe them in a session of the 1983 annual meeting of NCTE. The presentation was articulate, civilized, and persuasive. As a result of the challenge a committee was formed to attempt to measure the effect of teaching the novel on the students involved. The committee included equal numbers of members of the Forum on Black Affairs of Pennsylvania State University, and various persons from the public schools; several members of the committee had expertise in testing and measurement.

A carefully worked out system of pre- and post-testing was developed, using both nationally normed tests and locally developed tests. Three hundred ninth grade students were the subjects; one third were taught the novel; one third were asked to read it on their own; one third did not read the novel. The results were complex. As a group those who read the novel were shown to be more accepting of Blacks, were more sensitive to the moral issues involved, and were able to interpret the novel with more literary sophistication.

Younger students were more accepting of Blacks than older students. Students with a religious background were more accepting than those without a religious background. Male students were less accepting than female students. Positive attitudes toward Blacks were associated with higher levels of education on the part of parents.

However, the committee recommended that the novel be discontinued at the ninth grade and be used when appropriate with 11th or 12th graders. The justification for this recommendation was that a substantial proportion of 9th grade students did not understand satire as a literary device. They saw the story only as an adventure story; the regular and continuing use that Mark Twain makes of satire was really over their heads. Satire is a subtle and demanding literary device, probably only learned in the later stages of literary understanding.

The willingness of the parent who challenged the book to cooperate in the study, along with the openness of the State College Area School District to this study was essential to this positive way of dealing with book battles.

Occasionally both school critics and school staff members express cynicism concerning the use of school review policies. Agnes D. Stahlschmidt made a study of the effect of review procedures over a 10-year period in the Cedar Rapids, Iowa public schools.[4] The study revealed that there were 110 challenges filed concerning books used in the Cedar Rapids school during that period. Twenty-two books, or 20 percent of the challenged books were withdrawn from use; 16 books were restricted to one or another grade level. The largest category of books subjected to withdrawal or grade restriction was contemporary realistic fiction. Clearly both at Cedar Rapids, at State College, Pennsylvania, and at Montello, Wisconsin, (as noted in Chapter 1), citizen's challenges are taken seriously by the public schools.

There is increasing reason to believe that the schools have much support from the general public although this is frequently unexpressed and not well-organized. The school critics sometimes acknowledge this opinion. The leader of a Minneapolis right wing organization has said several times that the schools pay little attention to her complaints, and continue to teach views of which she disapproves. Recent changes in textbook selection in Texas and in California offer support for the belief that the general public does not wish a minority of school critics to control the teaching of biology, for example. The changes in Texas came as a result of aggressive, organized efforts by People For the American Way, The National Council of Teachers of English, and other groups in Texas.

I have had several experiences that suggest the general public is amenable to persuasion by supporters of intellectual freedom for the schools. In 1967 a bill was proposed to the Wisconsin legislature to prohibit obscenity; the bill was passed, but ultimately declared unconstitutional by the Wisconsin Supreme Court. I was one of four persons who testified against the bill. Five busloads of persons were brought by a coalition of women's groups in this state to support the bill.

There were newspaper reports that I had testified against the bill and shortly afterwards I received a very intemperate letter from a Sunday school class in Kenosha, Wisconsin. I was labelled a corruptor of youth among other invidious terms. I answered the letter, which was signed; not all such letters are signed. I replied explaining my grounds for opposing such legislation, and alluded to the parable in the New Testament in which Jesus described the situation of the man who had an unclean spirit removed from his soul. (Luke 11:24) The unclean spirit roamed around awhile, then came back to find the man's soul swept clean and empty; it was "put in order," said Jesus. So the unclean spirit moved back in with several other unclean spirits leaving, said Jesus, the final state of that man worse off than before.

I argued that instead of negative, punitive social actions, relying on laws, the police, the courts and jail, we should rely on more positive methods to instill within each person a sense of the best that has been written so that external censors would not be needed. Positive methods would entail better families, better schools, better libraries, better community institutions.

The class wrote back, surprisingly, to ask where that parable could be found. I answered at some length, since my letters were being read to a whole class. There were four exchanges of lengthy letters. In the last letter, the class explained that they had changed their minds; they agreed with me. The exchange of letters was therefore quite worthwhile.

That experience, along with other similar experiences, led me to believe that the public is open to conviction that the First Amendment is practical and is necessary, for both the public schools and the general society, if our democracy is to survive. I must add that not all such activities have had successful outcomes. Nevertheless the frequency of success gives hope to an ultimately successful outcome for the present conflict over the right of students, teachers and citizens to have maximum access to books and to information.

We have, however, a long way to go to accomplish the task of convincing the general public of the importance of the First Amendment. We sometimes forget that a culture cannot be inherited, as a farm, or house or money in the bank can be inherited. Each new generation must make the culture its own by a lengthy process of growth. If our children are not persuaded that the various demands democracy makes are worthwhile, democracy will not survive. Our democracy is after all in process. It is not a stable, fixed, permanent condition of humankind.

The issue of community control is a difficult one. In the Island Trees case two incumbent school board members who supported removing eleven books from the school library were handily re-elected. It is likely that there was substantial community support for the removal of those books. Yet ultimately the books were returned as a result of a Supreme Court decision, *Pico v. Island Trees*. The legal action was supported by the American Civil Liberties Union, the American Library Association, and the National Council of Teachers of English, among others.

Several school critics have argued that the principle stated in the Supreme Court decision of 1973, that community standards should be used to determine obscenity, requires community control of the school curriculum. The minority decision of the Supreme Court in the Pico case offered some support for that view. However, one member of the minority in that decision, Justice Rehnquist, supported the principle that there can be no official suppression of ideas in the schools or libraries, though he disagreed on its application to the Island Trees case.

It would appear that a strong majority of the Supreme Court

would not support action by which a school board suppressed ideas opposing the dominant viewpoint of a given community. However, the circumstances in a given case would greatly influence a decision as to whether the removal of a book or the removal of a course from the curriculum did in fact amount to the suppression of ideas.

Though community control has been upheld in various cases, it is clearly subordinated to constitutional provisions—i.e., segregation could not be re-instated by community control, nor can religious exercises be part of the school curriculum. State control of the curriculum and of textbooks in the public schools is constitutional, as demonstrated by state-mandated requirements for high school graduation, and recently by the state of California's rejecting certain biology textbooks because they paid inadequate atter. tion to evolution. In the fall of 1985 the Wisconsin legislature considered mandating sex education as part of the high school curriculum, but finally dropped the idea. However, the state clearly has the power to establish such a mandate, regardless of a particular community's feelings concerning that subject. The public schools are agencies of the various states; community control is subject to constitutional and state requirements.

Nevertheless, it would seem best, within the parameters of state and constitutional guidelines, that the issues be settled locally. If the community perceives that the books or curriculum are being imposed on it from without, there are likely to be many forms of resistance. In 1962 at Twin Lakes, Wisconsin a newly elected school board adopted McGuffey's *Readers*, in the edition of 1874, for use in the elementary schools.

The ensuing controversy resulted in lawsuits, in six teachers leaving the system, and in the re-election of board members who supported the McGuffey *Readers*. The election was quite close; only a few votes separated winners from the losers who opposed the *Readers*. The election was probably influenced by the belief that outsiders, wh ii ved in Illinois, but who had summer homes on the lakes, were trying to control the local community. Thus voting for McGuffey *Readers* was voting for local control.

In organizing for local community support, teachers and librarians should approach the mainstream churches, the local labor unions, local business organizations such as the chamber of commerce and the local news media. Probably the teachers and librarians should do the organizing rather than the principals or school superintendents.

A successful example of community organization to meet a First Amendment challenge occurred in Davis County, Utah, in 1979. The public library there is controlled by the county commissioners. They ordered Jeanne Layton, the librarian, to remove a book, *Americana*, by Don DeLillo. She refused and was fired. The librarians of the area organized a vigorous campaign using the various media with great skill. Layton was re-instated, and the key county commissioner was ultimately defeated for re-election.

Much of the reason for the librarians' success lay with the skill with which they planned and carried out a campaign to get public support. An illustration of their attention to detail was their effort to make sure that librarians attended a local TV talk show, discussing intellectual freedom in the Davis County Library, in sufficient numbers, and in addition, arrived early enough to get seats that would permit them to be heard and seen. In describing the Davis County controversy Peter Giacoma wrote, "To counter . . . attacks, the library community must direct its efforts to the public, the electorate. The mass media can be utilized effectively for this purpose. . . . But it must be realized that the media is subject to other messages. . . . The media is not immune to the political, religious and social forces of a community, and a library public relations effort must encompass all these forces to be effective. . . ."[5]

School libraries should provide material representative of all points of view concerning the problems and issues of our time.

In addition to the necessity of establishing rapport with the community a second important principle is the importance of librarians and the school living up to the spirit of the Bill of Rights of the American Library Association. This asserts that the library "should provide books and other materials presenting all points of view concerning the problems and issues of our time." Cal Thomas in *Book Burning* has argued that the real book burners are the librarians and teachers who refuse to buy or use the books of the religious right wing. Michael Farris, Moral Majority official from the state of Washington, made the same point in a speech to the annual meeting of the American Library Association in 1981, and in a TV debate over station KOMO, in Seattle Washington in January, 1982.

There is a modest degree of accuracy in this charge if the reader ignores Thomas' metaphorical use of the term book burning. Thomas himself ignores the many examples of actual book burning that have occurred in the United States during the last twenty years, including the event at Warsaw, Indiana, pictured in the front of this book. Nevertheless, it is probably true that public schools and public school libraries tend not to have representative selections from the publications of Jerry Falwell, Tim LaHaye, Phyllis Schlafly or other right-wing writers. Tim LaHaye has some twenty titles in English listed in *Books in Print*, with other titles translated into Spanish, as well as various Spanish versions of his books. The university library at Stevens Point has no books by LaHaye. The public library at Stevens Point has four titles by LaHaye. Phyllis Schlafly has some 13 titles in print; there are two in the Stevens Point university library and one in the public library. Falwell has four titles in print; none appears in either the university library or the public library.

Questions have been raised about LaHaye's scholarship. At a conference on the public schools and the First Amendment April 20, 1982 at Indianapolis, a political science professor alleged in debate that LaHaye's book *The Battle for the Mind* contained many errors of fact. That, however, is irrelevant so far as selecting the book for the library collection is concerned. Readers should be able to decide for themselves about the quality of LaHaye's scholarship. Some years ago the book *Calories Don't Count* was purchased for the public library at Madison, Wisconsin. Dietitians at the University of Wisconsin said that the book was not accurate and urged the library to remove it. That would have been inconsistent with the Library Bill of Rights. There was public protest and the book remained in the library's collection, thus allowing the general public to decide for itself about the merits of that book, as should be the case with LaHaye's *The Battle for the Mind*.

In defense of librarians it should be noted that books dealing with religion published by denominational publishing houses are usually not reviewed in the standard selection aids. That is as true for the mainstream churches as it is for the right wing fundamentalist churches. Abingdon Press, publishing house for the United Methodist Church, has published thousands of titles, most of which are not reviewed in the standard selection aids. One of Falwell's titles is a 13-week Sunday school curriculum. Material of this sort is highly ephemeral, is published by Abingdon Press and by almost every church, and would only be found in highly specialized libraries.

However, such books as LaHaye's *The Battle for the Mind* ought to be in libraries so that the general public will be able to read LaHaye's ideas at first hand. In addition, for historic reasons, and in order that in later years students of our time can more fully understand the present controversies, the libraries should collect the publications of the leading figures among the school critics—the Falwells, Gablers, McGraws, Schlaflys, LaHayes—among others.

A serious deficiency in most libraries probably lies in the area of literature by and about minority life in the United States. To defend the librarians, it should be pointed out that relatively little demand exists in some communities for such books as *Black Elk Speaks* or *American Negro Folktales*. The proportion of such titles among the 40,000 titles published every year is small. The Council For Interracial Books For Children does a useful service in encouraging minority group members to write books, and in encouraging libraries to buy them. However librarians are undoubtedly inhibited by school board members such as the one previously described at Loyal, Wisconsin who approved removing *Saturday Night Fever* from the school library because it contained "four letter words" and because life in a poor Italian section of New York does not "pertain to our style of life at all."

If libraries are to defend their book choices successfully they must consistently collect and circulate books that do indeed represent all points of view concerning the problems and issues of our time.

Frequently encountered arguments for censorship

In dealing with the larger public, certain arguments seem to reoccur as a justification for censorship. Several of those arguments have been dealt with previously and will not be repeated here. Defenders of intellectual freedom will need to do their homework well concerning these arguments. Much material is available beyond this report, as the bibliography suggests.

The *Areopagitica* should be required reading for all who would defend freedom of thought. Milton's insights remain as valid today as when he wrote them. Some years ago, the University of Kansas library bought a copy of the *Areopagitica* for $40,000. It is rather ironic that we enshrine this essay in libraries but ignore its wisdom. The school critics claim that the schools have abandoned the traditional values of this culture.

In making this charge, the school critics frequently do not define the values which they say have been abandoned. This book has attempted to demonstrate that the schools do teach values, and that those values are derived from our basic Judeo-Christian tradition, expressed for example in the *Areopagitica*.

The argument that obscenity or pornography can be defined was discussed previously (pp. 4–5, 49), as was the argument that selection by teachers or librarians is really censorship (p. 10ff). The belief that books are a cause of bad behavior was discussed on pages 125–127. There is a substantial body of literature dealing with these arguments, as the bibliography indicates and librarians and English teachers need to acquaint themselves with it.

While I was collecting Wisconsin folklore, an informant, an elderly woman, told me: "A poor book had best be burned to give place to a better, or even to an empty shelf for the fire destroys the poison and puts it out of the way of doing harm." Another informant told me: "Books are food for the mind, or books are poison for the mind." These statements seem to have a literary quality, though I know of no exact literary source for them. But the ideas expressed in these sayings seem to be strongly embedded in the folk mind, and frequently occur in criticism of schools and libraries. The sayings amount to an argument that if good literature can be expected to be a morally uplifting force, then bad literature must be a morally degrading force. The argument is sometimes supported by an explicit or implicit metaphor as those above that compares good literature to food and compares bad literature to poison. This argument has little scholarly or scientific evidence to support it. While it appears on the surface to be a matter of common sense, it is well established that so-

called common sense conclusions about reality on examination
often turn out not to be supported by scientific evidence. This
argument is on the whole a gross over-simplication of a very
complex matter.

One of the first problems with the argument is the difficulty
of distinguishing between good literature and bad literature. It is
quite ironic in this connection that, insofar as the schools are
concerned, it appears that the forces that act toward limiting or
censoring school materials are most likely to object to the books
that in all probability would be listed among the best of books.
Notice the discussion on page 37 of the books that have appeared
most often on studies of censorship made between 1965 and
1982; the list is repeated below. These books would probably be
regarded as good books by much of the general public; they are
regarded as bad books by would-be censors. I made a large poster
listing the most frequently attacked books and I show it on every
possible occasion. On TV shows, the list produces telephone calls
from viewers who say, "I read three or five or seven of these
books; what is wrong with them?" The poster is one of the most
effective devices I have used, for public understanding of the
problem.

The poster illustrates vividly to audiences that censorship
attacks the best of books, not the worst. Note the 30 most frequently attacked books since 1965, according to 6 surveys:

The Adventures of Huckleberry Finn
The Diary of a Young Girl (Anne Frank)
Black Like Me
Brave New World
The Catcher in the Rye
Deliverance
The Electric Kool-Aid Acid Test
A Farewell to Arms
Go Ask Alice
The Good Earth
The Grapes of Wrath
A Hero Ain't Nothin' But a Sandwich
If Beale Street Could Talk
I Know Why the Caged Bird Sings
Johnny Got His Gun
The Learning Tree

Lord of the Flies
Love Story
Manchild in the Promised Land
My Darling, My Hamburger
Nineteen Eighty-Four
Of Mice and Men
One Day in the Life of Ivan Denisovich
One Flew Over the Cuckoo's Nest
Ordinary People
Our Bodies, Ourselves
The Scarlet Letter
A Separate Peace
Slaughterhouse-Five
To Kill a Mockingbird

The 25 authors objected to by the Gablers include some of the most distinguished American writers; see the list on page 100.

One of the great achievements of American society is its literature. It seems likely that in the far future there will be people who will learn English just to read the books that have been written by American writers. The attractiveness of our literature to people all over the world is well demonstrated by the extent to which it is translated into other languages. The principles of literary criticism strongly suggest that our literature will take its place as a worthy and permanent part of the literature in English. Undoubtedly, the deep commitment of teachers and librarians to American literature is a continuing cause of the tension between the schools and those parents who apparently do not regard American literature of the twentieth century as worth teaching in the schools.

If there is no social agreement as to what books are bad and what books are good, how can we test the proposition that bad books cause bad behavior?

The metaphor that good books are like food and bad books are like poison is clearly a mistaken comparison. In the first place, metaphors are not logical demonstrations of truth. Metaphors are suggestive, illustrative, but not grounds for establishing the truth of a proposition. In the second place, this particular metaphor clearly suggests similarities that do not exist. Reading and eating are not fundamentally comparable activities.

Eating is an activity that enables the energies of a foreign substance to influence the body in a variety of ways, depending on the nature of the substance that is put into the body. The most distinctly human characteristics—freedom of choice and rationality—are called into play only prior to the act of ingesting something. A person may decide to eat a nourishing substance, or a destructive substance, but after the decision is made and carried out, the results of the eating are out of the control of the eater. Good food may be nourishing, bad food may be poison, but the human mind plays no role in the actual working out in the body of the effect of the substances that were ingested. No strength of will, no rational decision, can keep alcohol or drugs, or calories, or poison from affecting the body. A student at the University of Wisconsin, Stevens Point, in a state of depression after failing a test, swallowed lye. In the several hours that elapsed before he died, he bitterly regretted swallowing the poison, but within his body, the poison was no longer under his control.

Reading is quite different. The reader decides during every moment of the reading activity whether to continue reading, how to interpret what is read, how to respond to what is read, and what action, if any, to take, with regard to what is read. In short, with regard to reading, the reader's most human characteristics— freedom of choice and rationality—are constantly in play. In fact, unless these activities continue, no reading occurs. Reading is energized by the human mind, not by the print, and the results of the reading grow out of an activity that we call rational, even though we might differ with one another concerning the meaning of any particular act of reading.

There is, therefore, no valid comparison between eating and reading. They are fundamentally different kinds of activities, and the frequently used metaphor that compares them is simply wrong, realistic as it may seem.

Milton discusses this question in the *Areopagitica*. He argued that the nature of literature makes censorship unnecessary and evil, no matter what sort of literature is under discussion. Let us examine his argument. Milton believed that writing is a moral enterprise. He contradicts the Puritan notion that authors live a gay, Bohemian life, devoted to degrading mankind. We laugh now at the Puritan letter cited above that charged Shakespeare and his fellow actors with being "fiends that are crept into the world by stealth, sent from their great Captain Satan to deceive

the world, to lead the people with enticing shows to the Devil."
Their plays would persuade men and women into the "filthy lusts
of wicked whoredom."

The notion that the artist is dissolute is very old and is still
with us. But, in fact, most writers live disciplined, hardworking
lives. If they did not, they would get no writing done. Writing is
one of mankind's hardest tasks, requiring severe self-discipline
and regular devotion to the desk. We should be wary, said
Milton, of "what persecution we raise against the living labors of
public men, how we spill that seasoned life of man preserved and
stored up in books," for a "good book is the precious lifeblood of
a master spirit, embalmed and treasured up on purpose to a life
beyond life. Revolutions of ages do not oft recover the loss of a
rejected truth, for the want of which whole nations fare the
worse." Writing is, in short, a moral and worthwhile enterprise.

Not only is the enterprise a moral one, the very nature of
literature makes censorship both unnecessary and impossible.
What the censor attempts to do is impossible because the best of
books can be turned to the worst of purposes. "A wise man," said
Milton, "like a good refiner can gather good out of the drossiest
volume . . . and a fool will be a fool with the best book." The
truth of this observation came home to me some years ago, when
I received through the mail an anonymous little tract consisting
of all the explicitly sexual and erotic passages from the Bible,
together with an anonymous letter asking if I was not ashamed to
attend a church which used such a book. Clearly someone with
an obscene mind looked for obscenities and found them, but it
was the mind, not the Book, that was obscene.

A more recent illustration was reported in August 1985. A
deputy sheriff was bitten by a poisonous snake in North Carolina,
while attempting to arrest the man who had brought the snake to
church. Almost every year there are newspaper reports of a death
by snakebite in fundamentalist churches that take literally the
passage in the gospel of Mark which asserts that those who believe
can "pick up serpents and . . . it will not hurt them." (16:18) To
take that passage literally seems irrational; to do so demonstrates
Milton's point that a "fool will be a fool with the best book."

The linguists have made clear to us why it is possible for a
reader to get out of a book what is being looked for. A book,
literally, consists only of black marks on white paper. If you

cannot read, the marks have no effect upon you. If they have any effect, you create that effect by the act of reading. Reading is not passive, as in taking a drug and allowing it to work. Reading is an active engagement of the mind with the symbols on the page. Whatever meaning occurs, occurs in the mind and is the product of the reader's mind based on previous experience.

This process, however, comes to be so automatic that we forget its nature. Language is symbolic; the symbols are arbitrary and conventional. Moreover, while each symbol has some common element, or it would be private, and noncommunicable, each reader brings to the symbol his or her own personal experience. Thus, you cannot learn profanity or erotic terms from a book; unless you know the word in life, it will mean nothing on the page. What is new in a work of literature is the combinations of already known experiences, which is to say, in a sense, that there can be nothing new at all in a work of literature.

This is to repeat that literature communicates by symbols, not signs. A sign is direct and immediate evidence of the reality indicated by the sign. If your child breaks out with a red rash, the doctor knows that the rash is a sign of a disease, measles perhaps. If your child has a high temperature, it is a sign of something wrong. If a hunter sees tracks in the snow, he knows they are a sign that deer have been there. Conceivably a joker might have made the tracks with deer hoofs, but ordinarily deer tracks are a sign of deer. In short, a sign indicates the presence of whatever aspect of reality is associated with the sign—tracks with deer, symptoms with a disease, the sound of squealing tires with a car, barking with a dog, and so on.

But symbols are not direct and immediate evidence of reality. They stand for reality but do not indicate reality. I can say red rash or measles, but no one would expect to get the disease because I mention the words. I can say deer while hunting, but that does not produce a deer. The value of symbols lies in the possibility of using them in the absence of the reality they stand for. In *Gulliver's Travels* the people carried around in a sack everything they wished to talk about. Language makes this unnecessary. You can discuss whatever you please, if your vocabulary is sufficiently well developed, or if not, new words can be learned or created.

Much of the use of euphemisms or circumlocutions and

much of the desire to censor literature is based on a failure to distinguish between sign and symbol. We say venereal disease for fear that using the right words might cause someone to get the disease, just as we refuse to say cancer or tuberculosis. We silence someone riding in a car who mentions a flat. But words are not signs; they are symbols.

Because it uses symbols, art is neither history nor a direct report of reality. Unfortunately, much of our literature teaching does not recognize or enforce the distinction between art and reality, so we sometimes encourage students to identify the two. We interpret novels and short stories as exercises in autobiography. We take students to Hannibal to see the house where Samuel Langhorne Clemens lived and where Laura Hawkins lived under the assumption that something there will explain Tom Sawyer and Becky Thatcher. In fact, the relationship between Hannibal and the book *Tom Sawyer* is of no importance. It is the imaginative creation of the mind of Samuel Clemens. As such Becky Thatcher has a kind of immortality that will long survive Laura Hawkins; Becky Thatcher is known to the world by the public processes of print in contrast to the private and mysterious nature of the actual life lived by Laura Hawkins, of Hannibal, Missouri.

Our tendency to confuse the world of art and reality sometimes reaches such ridiculous extremes that we all notice it, as in the report of a Montana cowboy seeing his first film, who pulled his forty-five and shot the villain on the screen. There is a recent report of Africans who were shown their first film and insisted on going behind the screen to meet the actors. But they were not more primitive than the woman in the audience in New York who watching the play *Othello* sprang up screaming to warn Desdemona that Othello was about to kill her. All three of these cases are further illustrations of an ignorance concerning the way art works and which contributes to censorship. We notice the extreme cases I have cited but do not notice that the same logical fallacies exist in the assumption that censorship will prevent the undesirable realities presented in a work of art.

Since the world of literary art makes use of abstractions, symbolic language which does not call into existence the realities it refers to is therefore a safe way of dealing with dangerous aspects of life. We may, in fact, be greatly stirred by allusions to the dangers of life, as in the Greek play *Oedipus*. But since the allusions are make believe, in pretense, not really in existence on the stage, we are able to endure these references and indeed find ourselves at the end of the play somehow enlightened and made better able to endure the dangers of reality. This therapeutic process we may not be able to explain, but it does occur to many readers or viewers of tragic plays.

It is possible, therefore, to deal with tragedy or evil in literature in ways that enlighten the reader and teach moral lessons. In fact, literature that did not deal with the complete range of human good and evil would seem unrealistic and stilted. Great literature seems convincing to us precisely because it presents mankind in three dimensional reality. This requires frank presentations of evil in its tempting forms; if they were not thus presented, the reader would find unbelievable the characters who fall into sin as a result of the temptation. But since the pictured temptations are only symbolic, the reader is not really endangered. As Milton said, "In literature we may safely scout into the regions of sin and evil."

I referred previously to the Wisconsin father who wrote to me that he objected to the bad books being read in the high schools. "There are enough taverns around," he wrote, "my children don't have to learn about evil from books." But a Wisconsin mother was far wiser, I think, when she thanked a teacher for recommending Nelson Algren's books to her son, for she thought they caused him to lose his interest in taverns and strip tease joints, by revealing the tawdriness and life-destroying traps behind the sleazy, neon-lighted fronts. But if Algren had not presented a realistic picture of the fronts, the alluring attractive side of evil, no one would have believed his picture of the life-destroying quality of the reality behind the attractive facade.

That we may safely scout into the regions of sin and evil by the use of literature is shown by the studies of delinquency. So far as I can discover, there is no substantial evidence that bad literature is an important or significant cause of delinquency. Although many persons have offered their opinion that literature causes delinquency, there is little evidence that is acceptable by legal or medical standards that literature contributes to juvenile delinquency. In fact, delinquents tend to be non-readers. They are rarely found in libraries as they tend to be school dropouts, little acquainted with libraries and books.

If we are to risk the dangers of censorship, we should be sure that evidence is shown to us that it is necessary. As long ago as 1913, Judge Curtis Bok wrote in the case of *Pennsylvania vs. Five Book Sellers* that legal censorship may be applied "only where there is reasonable and demonstrable cause to believe that a crime or misdemeanor has been committed or is about to be committed as the perceptible result of the publication and distribution of the writing in question: the opinion of anyone that a tendency thereto exists or that such a result is self-evident is insufficient and irrelevant. The causal connection between the book and the criminal behavior must appear beyond the shadow of a doubt."

Such evidence has not been shown; the nature of literature and language suggests that the evidence will not be forthcoming.

E. Spencer Parsons, recently retired professor of theology at the University of Chicago, discussed the effect of the Moral Majority movement on the public schools at the 1981 annual conference of NCTE. He compared the movement to remove allegedly pornographic or obscene books from the public schools to the prohibition movement, which began in the 1880's, culminated in the prohibition amendment and did not come to an end until 1933. He suggested that in both movements a minority of passionate people, deeply committed to a belief in their moral superiority, have attempted to impose their own moral standards on the larger society.

If Professor Parsons is correct, we may expect that the current battle of the books may go on for two or three decades. Those persons interested in protecting the right to read in public libraries or school libraries need to gird up their loins for a protracted struggle.

REFERENCES

INTRODUCTION

1. Report of the Select Committee on Pornographic Materials, House of Representatives, 82nd Congress, Union Calendar No. 797, House Report No. 2510, p. 75. Hereafter referred to as the Gathings Committee Report.
2. *Ibid.*, p. 29.
3. Edward B. Jenkinson, *Censors In the Classroom: The Mind Benders*, p. 108.
4. Gathings, p. 64.
5. Joseph E. Bryson and Elizabeth W. Detty, *Censorship of Public School Library and Instructional Material*, p. 49.
6. Gathings, p. 34.
7. Nyla Ahrens, "Censorship and the Teacher of English: A Questionnaire Survey of a Selected Sample of Secondary School Teachers of English." Ph.D. dissertation, Columbia University, 1965. Rozanne Knudson, "Censorship in English Programs of California's Junior Colleges." Ph.D. dissertation, Stanford University, 1967.
8. James Davis, ed., *Dealing with Censorship.* Urbana, Ill., NCTE, 1979.
9. *Bulletin*, Council on Interracial Books For Children, 11 (1980), p. 13.
10. Jenkinson, p. 67.
11. Bryson and Detty, p. 10.
12. Carolyn Peterson, "A Study of Censorship Affecting the Secondary-School English Literature Teachers." Ed.D. dissertation, Temple University, 1975, p. 4.
13. Lester Asheim, "Not Censorship But Selection," *Wilson Library Bulletin*, 28 (Sept. 1953) 67. See also "Selection and Censorship; A Reappraisal," *Wilson Library Bulletin*, 58 (November 1983), pp. 180–184.
14. Edwin Castagna, "Censorship, Intellectual Freedom, and Libraries," in *Advances in Librarianship*, ed. Melvin J. Voigt, Vol. II, New York: Seminar Press, 1971, p. 205ff.
15. *Slaughterhouse-Five:* see Jenkinson, p. 37; *Of Mice and Men*, Jenkinson, p. 57; *Values Clarification*, Warsaw *Times-Union*, December 15, 1977; A pile of books at Omaha, Nebraska, Associated Press report, January 30, 1981; *The Living Bible*, The Charlotte *Observer*, May 9, 1981.
16. Jenkinson, p. 115.

17. Julia T. Bradley, "Censoring the School Library: Do Students Have the Right to Read?" *Connecticut Law Review*, 10:3 (Spring 1978) 747–771.

CHAPTER 1

1. *Madison State Journal*, February 10, 1981.
2. *The Marquette County Educator*, Volume I, March 1981. This was an ephemeral publication of the group that supported removing the books.
3. When Howard Fast's novels were attacked at Scarsdale, New York in the early 1950's, there was a run on the books in libraries and bookstores. See *The Censors and the Schools*, Jack Nelson and Gene Roberts, Jr., p. 50. There are a number of such reports in the literature concerning censorship. When *Slaughterhouse-Five* was challenged in Rochester, Michigan, "Not one bookstore in the town was able to keep it because of the rush of people anxious to buy it, or read the dirty words. . . ." Woodworth, *The Young Adult and Intellectual Freedom*. Publications Committee, Library School, University of Wisconsin, 1977, p. 146.
4. *A Textbook Study In Cultural Conflict, An Inquiry Report*. NEA, 1975. See also Jenkinson, p. 17ff. Don J. Goode, "A Study of Values and Attitudes in a Textbook Controversy in Kanawha County, West Virginia In an Overt Act of Opposition to Schools." Ph.D. dissertation, Michigan State University, 1984.
5. Carolyn Peterson, "A Study of Censorship Affecting The Secondary School English Literature Teacher, 1968–1974." Ed.D. dissertation, Temple University, 1975.
6. See page 172 of this book for the study of books challenged at Cedar Rapids, Iowa over a ten-year period.

CHAPTER 2

1. Marjorie Fiske, *Book Selection and Censorship*, pp. 69–70.
2. L. B. Woods, *A Decade of Censorship in America: The Threat To Classrooms and Libraries*. 1966–1975. Metuchen, New Jersey, Scarecrow Press, 1979.
3. Keith Torke, "Sex Education Books, Censorship and Colorado High School Libraries: A Survey." Ed.D. dissertation, University of Northern Colorado, 1975.
4. James F. Symula, "Censorship of High School Literature." Ed.D. dissertation, State University of New York, 1969.
5. Dorothy Thompson Weathersby, "Censorship of Literature Textbooks in Tennessee; A Study of the Commission, Publishers, Teachers, and Textbooks." Ed.D. dissertation, University of Tennessee, 1975.
6. Ellen Last, "Textbook Selection or Censorship: An Analysis of the Complaints filed in Relation to Three Major Literature Series Proposed for Adoption in Texas in 1978." Ph.D. dissertation University of Texas, 1984.

7. See *The American School Board Journal*, 166 (June 1979) 21.
8. Ahrens, p. 70.
9. See John J. Farley, "Book Censorship in the Senior High School Libraries of Nassau County, New York." Ph.D. dissertation, New York University, 1964, p. 236.
10. Fiske, p. 70.
11. Peterson, p. 70.
12. Fiske, p. 36.
13. Peterson, p. 70.
14. Peterson, p. 74.
15. Jenkinson, "Tell City Rejects the Secular Humanism Charge," *Focus: Teaching English Language Arts*, 11 (Fall 1984) 35–42.
16. Ahrens, p. 94.
17. Burress, Chapter 2, *Dealing With Censorship*, J. E. Davis, ed., p. 22.
18. Previously unpublished Burress survey.
19. Kenneth L. Donelson, "What to Do When The Censor Comes," *Elementary English*, 51 (March 1974) 403.
20. N. Karolides and Burress, *Celebrating Censored Books*; see the introduction.
21. Arlen H. Mitchell, "Historical Perspective of the *Huck Finn* Challenge," *Celebrating Censored Books*, p. 10.
22. Jenkinson, *Censors in the Classroom*, p. 77.
23. L. B. Woods, p. 121.
24. Peterson, p. 85.
25. James E. Baxter, "Selection and Censorship of Public School Textbooks: A Descriptive Study." Ed.D. dissertation, University of Southern Mississippi, 1964, p. 157.
26. Burress survey, 1982; not previously published; see p. 6 of this book.
27. Marshfield, Wisconsin, *News-Herald*, March 20, 1981.
28. *Chicago Tribune*, June 26, 1982.
29. *Des Moines Register*, February 12, 1980.
30. *Wall Street Journal*, October 6, 1981.
31. Last, "Attacks on the content of stories and poems imply a belief that content equals advocacy," p. 146.
32. Avon, 1973, p. 95.
33. Nat Hentoff, *The First Freedom: The Tumultuous History of Free Speech in America*, p. 31.
34. *Ibid.*
35. Bryson and Detty, p. 13.
36. Jack Nelson and Gene Roberts, Jr. *The Censors and the Schools*. Boston: Little, Brown, 1963, p. 4.
37. Burress, "How Censorship Affects the School," Special Bulletin #8. Racine, Wis., Wisconsin Council of Teachers of English, Oct. 1963, pp. 1–23.
38. See page 6 of this book.
39. Woods, p. 57.
40. Bryson and Detty, p. 198.
41. James Edward Baxter, "Selection and Censorship of Public School Text-

books: A Descriptive Study." Ed.D. dissertation, University of Southern Mississippi, 1964, p. 152.

42. Peterson, pp. 83, 85. Peterson also estimated that news accounts represent from 1% to 24% of total censorship cases, based on a comparison of news accounts with state surveys.

CHAPTER 3

1. Woods, pp. 41–53.
2. *Ibid.*, pp. 56–57.
3. August B. Hollingshead, *Elmtown's Youth: The Impact of Social Class on Adolescence.* New York, J. Wiley, 1949, pp. 9, 439–453.
4. Bryson and Detty, p. 85.
5. William Lloyd Warner, *Democracy in Jonesville*, with Wilfred C. Bailey and others. New York, Harper and Row, 1964, pp. 293–298.
6. Vergilius Ferm, ed., *An Encyclopedia of Religion*, p. 699.
7. Cal Thomas, *Book Burning*, Westchester, IL, Crossway Books, 1983, p. 89.
8. Last, p. 136. See also p. 19.
9. Woods, p. 90.
10. Burress, 1966, unpublished study; see page 6 of this book.
11. Burress, in *Dealing With Censorship*, p. 20.
12. Burress, 1966; see page 6 of this book.
13. Hentoff, p. 37.
14. Unpublished graduate student's research paper. The paper was written at the University of Minn. The source wished to remain confidential.
15. Nelson and Roberts, p. 182.
16. *Ibid*, p. 182.
17. From various news reports in scrapbook kept by a teacher who remained in the system.
18. Bryson and Detty, p. 57.
19. *Ibid.*, p. 59.
20. *Ibid.*, p. 47.
21. *Ibid.*, p. 118.
22. Robert M. O'Neil, *Classrooms in the Crossfire*, pp. 9–12.

CHAPTER 4

1. W. Wilbur Hatfield, *An Experience Curriculum in English.* NCTE, 1935, pp. 43–69.
2. Dora Smith, *Evaluating Instruction in Secondary School English*, p. 123.
3. *Ibid.*, p. 125.
4. Robert C. Pooley and R. D. Williams, *The Teaching of English in Wisconsin.* Madison, University of Wisconsin Press, 1948.
5. Gathings Committee Report, p. 103.

6. *Reading Explosion*, New York, International Paper, 1962 (a pamphlet), p. 1.

7. G. Robert Carlsen, "The Magic of Bringing Young People to Books." *Wilson Library Bulletin*, 33 (Oct. 1958) 134–137.

8. Lou LaBrant, "The Use of the Communication Media," *The Guinea Pigs After Twenty Years*, Chapter 8, ed. Margaret Willis. Columbus, Ohio State University Press, 1961.

9. Daniel Fader and Morton H. Shaevitz, *Hooked on Books*. New York, Berkley Medallion Books, 1966.

10. Robert A. Marshall, *The History of Our Schools*. National Council For the Social Studies, Washington, D.C., 1962, pp. 17–19.

11. Chrissie Bamber, *Student and Teacher Absenteeism*. Indiana, Phi Delta Kappa Educational Foundation, 1979, p. 17.

12. R. Mosier, "Profile of the Freshman Class of the University of Wisconsin, Stevens Point." Unpublished report, UWSP, 1981, pp. 6, 7, 24.

13. B. W. Kreitlow, C. Martin, and M. A. Gustrom, "Adults Without Diplomas," *The Wisconsin Vocational Educator*, 5 (Summer 1981) 12–13.

14. *Slate* Report [NCTE] (November, 1977) 1–4. See also Eugenia Kemble, "The Test Score Decline: Much More Than Meets the Eye," *American Educator* 1 (Oct. 1977) 26–27.

15. J. Egerton, "Can We Save Our Schools? Yes, But There Isn't Much Time," *The Progressive*, 46 (March 1982) 26.

16. *Reading Explosion*, p. 1.

17. D. Gray, "Books: A Review Essay, The 1978 Consumer Research Study on Reading and Book Purchasing," *College English*, 42 (November 1980) 283–292.

18. *Ibid.*

19. *Book Research Quarterly*, 1 (Spring 1985) 103.

20. Eleanor Francis Brown, *Library Services To The Disadvantaged*, Metuchen, N.J., Scarecrow Press, 1971, pp. 80–82. See also E. F. Brown, *Bookmobiles*, Metuchen, N.J., Scarecrow Press, 1967, pp. 42–43.

21. *State of Wisconsin Blue Book*, 1985–86, Wisconsin Legislative Reference Bureau, Madison, WI, p. 467. Only Florence County with a population of 4100 lacked library services in 1980.

22. *Ibid.*, p. 694.

23. *Ibid.*, p. 819.

24. Cal Thomas, *Book Burning*, Westchester, IL: Good News Publishers, 1983, pp. 14 & 15.

25. Reported in *Harper's*, 270 (June 1985) 13, from *Growth at Adolescence*, by J. M. Tanner. Springfield, IL: Charles Thomas. See also K. L. Freiburg, *Human Development: A Life Span Approach*. Belmont, California, Duxbury Press, 1979.

26. Vern L. Bullough, "Myths About Teenage Pregnancy," *Free Inquiry*, 1 (Summer 1981) 12, 13. Data from National Center For Health Statistics, report #61, Sept. 26, 1980.

27. J. E. Lancourt, *Confront or Concede: The Alinsky Citizen-Action Organization*. Lexington, Mass., Lexington Books, 1979.

CHAPTER 5

1. E. K. Chambers, *The Elizabethan Stage*. London, Oxford University Press, 1923, Vol. IV, pp. 323–324.
2. The material above is from various sections of Noel Perrin, *Dr. Bowdler's Legacy*. New York: Atheneum, 1969.
3. Reported at the 1985 annual conference of NCTE.
4. Weathersby, p. 142.
5. *The United States in Literature*, Scott, Foresman, 1968.
6. Weathersby, p. iv.
7. Maureen F. Logan, "Star-Crossed Platonic Lovers, or Bowdler Redux," *English Journal*, 74 (Jan. 1985) 53–55.
8. Weathersby, p. 163.
9. *Ibid.* p. 163.
10. Weathersby discusses the problem of ethnic language in some detail, pp. 135–140.
11. *American Literature*. Ginn and Company, 1964, p. 509.
12. Weathersby, p. 192, footnote 10.
13. *Ibid.*, pp. 154ff.
14. *Ibid.*, p. 198, see also p. 184.
15. *Ibid.*, p. 208.
16. Last, p. 145.
17. Last, pp. 137–138.
18. Kenneth Taylor, "Are School Censorship Cases Really Increasing?" In *Library Lit. 14, The Best of 1983*, p. 360. Reprinted from *School Library Media Quarterly*, 11 (Fall, 1982), 26–34.
19. Last, p. 81.
20. Last, p. 147.
21. Weathersby, see pages 135–140; 143–153.
22. Weathersby, p. 184.
23. Last, p. 147.
24. Joseph Blotner, *Faulkner: A Biography*, p. 1181.
25. Weathersby, p. 139.
26. Ray Bradbury, in Author's Afterword to *Fahrenheit 451*, Ballantine Books, 1979.
27. *Ibid.*
28. James J. Lynch and Bertrand Evans, *High School English Textbooks: A Critical Examination*. Boston: Little, Brown, 1963; pp. 46, 106, 133.
29. Reported by James Squire at 1985 annual conference of NCTE.
30. Nelson and Roberts, p. 181.
31. At a conference on Intellectual Freedom sponsored by the American Library Association, Washington, D.C., Jan. 23, 1965.
32. Dora Smith, *Evaluating Instruction in Secondary School English*. Appleton, WI: 1941, pp. 124–125.
33. Wilbur J. Cash, *The Mind of the South*. New York: Knopf, 1980, p. 303.
34. *Ibid.*, p. 414.
35. *Ibid.*, p. 80.
36. *Ibid.*, pp. 328–329.

37. *Ibid.*, p. 319.
38. Robert H. Knapp and H. B. Goodrich, *Origins of American Scientists*, Chicago, The University of Chicago Press, 1952, pp. 325–327.
39. Wayne A. Moyer, and William U. Mayer, *A Consumer's Guide To Biology Textbooks, 1985.* Washington, D.C., People For The American Way, 1985, pp. 9–125. See also the article by Wayne A. Moyer, "How Texas Rewrote Your Textbooks," *The Science Teacher*, 52, no. 1 (January 1985), 23–27.

CHAPTER 6

1. Howard Meyer, "Neutralism Isn't Neutral," CIBC *Bulletin*, 11, No. 6 (1980) 12–13.
2. Moore, CIBC *Bulletin*, 8, No. 2 (1977) 4–5.
3. CIBC *Bulletin*, 8, No. 2 (1977) 20.
4. *Ibid.*, "From Rags to Witches: Stereotypes, Distortions and Anti-Humanism in Fairy Tales," 6, No. 1, 2 (1975) 1.
5. *Ibid.*, 9, No. 2 (1978) 3.
6. Jenkinson, pp. 55–56.
7. *Ibid.*, p. 157.
8. *Ibid.*, p. 77.
9. CIBC *Bulletin*, 11, No. 6 (1980) 3.
10. Richard Beach, "Issues of Censorship and Research on Effects of and Responses to Reading," in *Dealing With Censorship*, ed. by James E. Davis. Urbana, IL: National Council of Teachers of English, 1979, p. 131.
11. CIBC *Bulletin*, 7, No. 2, 3 (1976) 2–29.
12. *Ibid.*, p. 5.
13. B. L. Whorf, *Language, Thought and Reality: Selected Writings of Benjamin Lee Whorf*, Cambridge, MA: M.I.T. Press, 1956, pp. 160–172.
14. Casey Miller and Kate Swift, *The Handbook of Nonsexist Writing for Writers, Editors and Speakers*, New York, Barnes and Noble, 1981.
15. Joshua Whatmough, *Language, A Modern Synthesis*, New York, St. Martin, 1956, p. 187.
16. L. E. Bourne, et al., *The Psychology of Thinking*, Englewood Cliffs, NJ, Prentice-Hall, 1971, p. 298.
17. Insup Taylor, *Introduction to Psycholinguistics*, New York, Holt, Rinehart, and Winston, 1976, p. 303.
18. *Ibid.*, p. 301.
19. Ernest Simmel, ed., *Anti-Semitism*, New York, International Universities Press, 1946, pp. 1–10, 97–124, et. al.

CHAPTER 7

1. School District of Abington Township v. Schemp, 374 v.s. 203, 225, (1963).

2. *Encyclopedia of Philosophy.* N.Y., The Macmillan Company, 1967, vol. 4, p. 72.
3. *New Catholic Encyclopedia*, vol. 7, p. 224 (1967).
4. *Encyclopedia of Philosophy*, p. 70.
5. *Ibid.*
6. *Ibid.*, p. 77.
7. *New Catholic Encyclopedia*, vol. 7, p. 233.
8. *Encyclopedia of the Lutheran Church*, Augsburg Publishing House, 1965, vol. 2, p. 1057.
9. Albert C. Baugh, *et al.*, eds., *A Literary History of England*, New York, Appleton-Century-Crofts, 1948, p. 329. For a fuller account of humanism in English literature see Joanna Martindale, ed., *English Humanism: Wyatt to Cowley.* London, Croom Helm, 1985.
10. Perry Miller, *The American Puritans*, New York, Doubleday, 1956, p. 21.
11. *Ibid.*, p. 20.
12. *Ibid.*, p. 29.
13. *Ibid.*, pp. 121–136.
14. *Ibid.*, p. 123.
15. *Ibid.*, p. 125.
16. *Ibid.*, p. 126.
17. *Ibid.*, p. 128–129.
18. Onalee McGraw, *Secular Humanism and The Schools: The Issue Whose Time Has Come*, Washington, D.C., Heritage Foundation, 1976, pp. 7–8.
19. Mel and Norma Gabler, *What They Are Teaching Our Children*, Wheaton, IL, Victor Books, 1985, p. 141.
20. Seattle *Post-Intelligencer*, Jan. 3, 1981.
21. Leanne Katz, ed., *Censorship News:* A Newsletter of the National Coalition Against Censorship, Summer 1985, Issue No. 21, p. 1.
22. Henry Steele Commager, *The American Mind*, New Haven, Yale University Press, 1950, p. 165.

CHAPTER 8

1. Available through Films Incorporated care of M. M. Kamhi; P.O. Box 20084, Cathedral Finance Station, New York, N.Y. 10025, or Ohio Humanities Council, (614) 231–6879.
2. Michelle Marder Kamhi, "Building Bridges Instead of Walls: An Anti-censorship effort that Worked," *Education Week*, Sept. 29, 1982, also in *Publishers and English Teachers*, NCTE, 1982, pp. 20ff; see also June Berkley, "Teach the Parents Well: An Anti-censorship experiment in Adult Education," in *Dealing With Censorship*, pp. 180–187.
3. See the mimeographed report entitled, "The Effects of Reading *Huckleberry Finn* on the Racial Attitudes of Ninth Grade Students," a cooperative study of the State College, Pa. Area School District and The Forum on Black Affairs of the Pennsylvania State University, Fall, 1983.

4. "The Iowa Plan Revisited: Ten Years Later," a presentation at the 71st Annual Convention, NCTE, Boston, Nov. 20, 1981.
5. Peter Giacoma, "When Librarians Fight, The Media Responds," mimeo report, n.d.

APPENDIX A: TITLES OBJECTED TO, 1982 SURVEY

(Further information about these titles may be found in Appendix B)

The Adventures of Augie March
The Adventures of Huckleberry Finn
Alas, Babylon
Alive: The Story of the Andes Survivors
All Quiet on the Western Front
All You Wanted to Know About Sex
Almost Grown
The American Dream
America in Legend
The Angel Inside Went Sour
Animal Factories: The Mass Production
  of Food and How it Affects the Lives
  of Consumers, Farmers, and Animals
  Themselves
Anne of the Thousand Days
Anthology of New York Poets
Are You in the House Alone?
Are You There God? It's Me, Margaret

Bad: the Autobiography of James Carr
Ball Four
Banquet at Dawn
The Battered Woman
Being a Man in a Woman's World
Bellevue is a State of Mind
Beulah Land
Bible
The Bible Tells Me So: Studies in
  Abundant Living
Bill and Pete

Billy Jack
Biology, Living Systems
Black Boy
Black Fire
Black Like Me
Black Sunday
Bless the Beasts and the Children
Blood Line
Blubber
Blueschild Baby
Blues for Mister Charlie
Bonnie Jo, Go Home
The Book of Lists
The Book of the Zodiac
Born on the Fourth of July
Born to Win
Boss: Richard J. Daley of Chicago
A Boy and His Dog (short story)
Boys and Sex
Boys from Brazil
Brave New World
Breakfast of Champions
The Bridge
Bridge to Terabithia
Butterfly Revolution

The Car Thief
Cat Ballou
Catch-22
Catcher in the Rye

199

The Cheerleader
A Child is Born
Child of our Time
The Chinese Visitor
The Chocolate War
Class Reunion
Cold Feet
Come Alive at 505
Conrack
The Contender
The Crucible
Cruisin' for a Bruisin'
The Cult

Daddy Was a Number Runner
Daughters of Eve
A Day No Pigs Would Die
Day of the Jackal
Dear Bill, Remember Me?
Death of a Salesman
The Deep
Deliverance
The Devil's Storybook
Diary of a Frantic Kid Sister
Dibs: In Search of Self
Dictionary of American Slang
Dog Crisis
Don't Play Dead Before You Have To
The Doomsday Gang
The Double Image

Electric Kool-Aid Acid Test
Elmer Gantry
The Ewings of Dallas
Expectant Fathers
The Exorcist

The Facts of Love: Living, Loving and
    Growing
Farewell to Arms
Flowers for Algernon
For All the Wrong Reasons
For Whom the Bell Tolls
Forever
Forty-four Caliber
Friends
Future Shock

The Game Players of Titan
Gateway
Gaudy Place
Gay Mystique
Gay: What You Should Know About
    Homosexuality
The Geranium on the Windowsill Just
    Died, but Teacher You Went Right
    On
Getting Your Own Way: A Guide to
    Growing Up Assertively
Ghost Fox
A Girl Named Sooner
Girls and Sex
The Glass Inferno
Go Ask Alice
Goodbye Columbus
The Good Earth
The Grapes of Wrath
Grease (the play)
Great Expectations
Great Themes in Lit: Crime and
    Criminals
Great Train Robbery
Great Trials: Pro & Con
Greek Gods and Heroes
Greengage Summer
Growing Up at Thirty-Seven

Happy Endings are All Alike
Hard Feelings
The Hard Life of a Teenager
Harry and Tonto
Haunted Houses
Headman
A Hero Ain't Nothing But a Sandwich
The Heroship
Hey, Dollface
Homosexual Matrix
A House with a Clock in Its Walls
How to Select, Train and Breed Your
    Dog
The Human Body
Human Sexuality

I Am a Man
I Hate to Talk About Your Mother

I Know Why the Caged Bird Sings
I Never Loved Your Mind
I, Pig
I was a Black Panther
If Beale Street Could Talk
In Love
In the Country of Ourselves
In the Night Kitchen
It's O.K. If You Don't Love Me

Jack the Bear
Jambeaux
Janis Joplin
Jaws
Johnny Got His Gun

Key to Rebecca
Killing Mr. Griffin
King, Stephen, various titles
Kramer vs Kramer

The Learning Tree
Life and Health (textbook)
Light in August
Listen to the Silence
Lord of the Flies
The Lottery
Love is One of the Choices
Love and Sex and Growing Up
Love Story

Macbeth
Macos series in Junior High
Man, Myth and Magic (Set of
    Encyclopedias)
Manchild in the Promised Land
Manwatching
The Man Who Liked Slow Tomatoes
Martian Chronicles
Mash
Me and Jim Luke
Memories of An Ex-Prom Queen
Men's Bodies, Men's Selves
The Merchant of Venice
The Miernik Dossier
Mr. and Mrs. Bo Jo Jones
Modern Biology (a textbook)

Modern English in Action
My Darling, My Hamburger
My First Love and Other Disasters
My Sweet Charlie

Naked Came the Stranger
Nam
Native Son
The Negro Revolution
Never On a Broomstick
The New Dynamic Church
The New Journalism
New Whole Earth Catalog
Nigger
Night
Night and Fog
Nineteen Eighty-Four
None of the Above

Occult, all Books on
Of Mice and Men
Oh Boy! Babies!
Oh, God!
Ohio Revised Criminal Law Code
Oliver's Story
The Once and Future King
One Day in the Life of Ivan Denisovich
One Flew over the Cuckoo's Nest
Open Season
Ordinary People
Our Bodies, Ourselves
Our Time Is Now
Outside Over There
The Outsiders

Poseidon Adventure
Portnoy's Complaint
Princess Daisy
Professor of Desire
The Promise

The Quartzite Trip
Questions about Love and Sex
Quizzes, Tricks, Puzzles and Brain
    Teasers

Radical Right: The New American Right
Recreational Drugs

Red Sky at Morning
Remove Protective Coating a Little at a
   Time
Richie
Romeo and Juliet
Rosemary's Baby
Rumble Fish
Run, Shelley, Run
Run Softly, Go Fast

Second Lady
Secret Societies
Sensuous Couple
Sensuous Man
Sensuous Woman
A Separate Peace
Sex: Telling it Straight
Sexually Transmitted Diseases
Sexual Revolution
Six Weeks
The Shining
Shuckin' and Jivin': Folklore from
   Contemporary Black Americans
Slaughterhouse-Five
Something Wicked This Way Comes
Sooner or Later
Soul on Ice
Soup
Speaking for Ourselves
Special Olympics
Sticks and Stones
Strawberry Statement
Street Kids
A Streetcar Named Desire
Summer of Forty-Two
The Sun Also Rises

Teen Angel
Tell Me That You Love Me, Junie
   Moon
Terminal Men

Testament
Them
Then Again, Maybe I Won't
Time Machine
Tisha
To Kill A Mockingbird
Tom Sawyer
Trinity
Turkey Legs Thompson
Two Gentlemen of Verona
True Confessions

Uncle
Understanding Sex
Up In Seth's Room
Upstairs Room

Venereal Disease: The Hidden Epidemic
Voices Text
The Vulgarians

Walls
War on Villa Street
The Warriors
War Year
A Way of Love, A Way of Life
Way to Womanhood
West Side Story
Where the Bright Lights Shone
Who's Afraid of Virginia Woolf?
Winning
Witchcraft and Occult: any books
Work Hard and You Shall be Rewarded
Working
Worlds in the Making
World's Number One Flat-out All Time
   Great Stock Car Racing Book

You
You and the Law
You and Your Child
You Never Knew Her as I Did

PERIODICALS

There were two major objections to the periodicals: an objection to sexual frankness or to nudity, and an objection to presentations of the grimy, gritty realities of today's world in such news magazines as *Time* or *Newsweek*.

American Photographer
American Photography
The Atlas
Bride's
Christian Century
Christianity Today
Der Spiegel
Ebony
Esquire
Essence
Family Health
Glamour
Harper's Bazaar
Home Video
Hot Rod
Human Events
Humanist
Ingenue
Japanese
Jet
Ladies Home Journal
Life
Mad
Mademoiselle
Modern Photography
Mother Jones
Mother Nature
Ms. Magazine

New Ingenue
New Republic
Newsweek
Parents Magazine
Paris-Match
People
Photography
Plain Truth
Popular Photography
Psychology Today
Redbook
Review of the News
Rolling Stone
Science Digest
Seventeen
Shooting Times
Soldier of Fortune
South Africa Panorama
Soviet Life
Sport
Sports Illustrated (Swimsuit issue)
Tampa Bay Life
'Teen
Time
Transaction
True Confessions
Vogue

FILMS

Violence was stated most often as the objection to films, followed closely by objections to sexual frankness or nudity.

Abortion film (from Planned Parenthood)
The Ascent of Man
Assembly Line
The Birds and The Bees: One Hour of "Remember When"
The Birth of a Baby
Birth of a Nation
Bless the Beasts and the Children
Brave New World
Childbirth
Films about China and Russia

Conrade
The Displaced Person
Draft: Yes or No
Excalibur
Family Next Door
Future Shock
The Garden Party
The Green Machine
Halloween
Homosexuality
How to Have a Healthy Baby

Human Reproduction 100 (slides)
I'm 16, Pregnant Parent and Don't know
What to Do
Johnny Got His Gun
La Raza
Let's Learn About the Library
The Lottery
Night and Fog
People
People Soup
Prophesies of Nostradamus (video)
Right to Life films

Romeo and Juliet
Several Health-Sex ed films
Silent Snow, Secret Snow
Film used in *Social Studies* (Boy-Girl
relations)
Teenage Pregnancy and Prevention
The Telltale Heart
This Land
Time Piece
Values
Film on Women Alcholics
You're Single and Pregnant

APPENDIX B: TITLES OBJECTED TO, 17 SURVEYS

The approximately 900 titles below come from 17 surveys carried out by various individuals or groups between 1965 and 1985. I am grateful to the persons and organizations involved as is noted under acknowledgments for permission to use the material. The sources are identified in the chart by numbers as follows:

1. Lee Burress and David Burress surveyed a national sample of librarians in 1982.
2. Lee Burress surveyed a national sample of English department chairpersons in 1977.
3. Lee Burress surveyed a national sample of English department chairpersons in 1973.
4. Lee Burress surveyed a national sample for opinions concerning school censorship problems in 1966. Half the questionnaires went to high school librarians, half went to English department chairpersons.
5. Lee Burress surveyed problems of school censorship in Wisconsin in 1963. Half the questionnaires went to English department chairpersons, half went to school administrators.
6. James Davis surveyed a sample of English department chairpersons in Ohio in 1982.
7. David Madden reported a list of sixty-five titles published by the Concerned Citizens and Taxpayers for Decent Books at Baton Rouge, LA, as reported in *The Daily Reveille*, September 25, 1975.
8. A survey of censorship in Arizona high schools was conducted by Kenneth Donelson and Retha K. Foster, 1967.
9. Edward Jenkinson reported a number of censorship or attempted censorship events in his book *The Censors in the Classroom: The Mindbenders*, 1979.
10. From a report on Book Censorship Litigation in Public Schools by the National Coalition Against Censorship, directed by Leanne Katz, 1983.
11. From titles cited in "Attack on the Freedom to Learn," 1983–1984, by People For The American Way.
12. Titles cited in "Attacks on Freedom to Learn: New York, 1980–1983." A Report by The New York Regional Office of People for the American Way, November 1983.
13. From Dorothy Weathersby's study of the censorship of literature in Tennessee, 1975.

14. From a master's thesis by Susan Ann Frisque Vandertie based on a survey of censorship problems in the elementary schools of northeastern Wisconsin, 1980.
15. "Limiting What Students Shall Read: Books and Other Learning Materials in Our Public Schools: How They Are Selected and How They Are Removed," 1981. Sponsored by the Association of American Publishers, the American Library Association, and the Association for Supervision and Curriculum Development.
16. From *Censorship Of Public School Library and Instructional Material* by Joseph E. Bryson and Elizabeth W. Detty, 1982.
17. From *The Censors and the Schools* by Jack Nelson and Gene Roberts, Jr., 1963.

Persons interested in legal cases involving the books listed below should consult the following sources: *Book Censorship Litigation in Public Schools*, the National Coalition Against Censorship, directed by Leanne Katz, 1983, and later reports, 132 West 43rd Street, New York, NY 10036. See also various reports from People For The American Way, 1015 18th Street N.W., Suite 300, Washington, D.C. 20036; Bryson and Detty's *Censorship Of Public School Library And Instructional Material*; and O'Neil's *Classrooms In The Crossfire*.

Note

An effort was made to check correctness of spelling for title and author and correct date of publication for the titles below. An asterisk in front of the title indicates that it cannot be located in the bibliographic aids available to me. As the different dates indicate, it's unlikely that there is any duplication of reports of the same censorship event, with the exception of the Island Trees case which is reported in several sources, although repetition of the books removed from the Island Trees school has been avoided in the list.

Unfortunately not all sources report as much information as would be desirable and as will be noted there are gaps in the information available. Strikingly enough, some knowledgeable persons on school censorship pressures refuse to make any data public, even the titles of books for which assistance might be requested by persons under censorship pressures. Hospitals are able to report the incidence of various diseases along with mortality rates for each disease without violating the confidentiality of each individual patient. Those agencies concerned with protecting intellectual freedom ought to follow the same practices, instead of practising a quiet censorship of information concerning censorship pressures.

As the reader will note, the nearly 900 titles come from a miscellaneous variety of sources. Eight of the sources are national in nature. Seven of the sources are regional; there are sources from Wisconsin, Ohio, Louisiana, Arizona, New York, and Tennessee.

I was unable to locate Nyla Ahrens and so could not get permission to include the data from her doctoral dissertation in the list of titles. If Nyla Ahrens' list had been included, twenty-four additional titles would have been added to the list, titles that did not show up on the several other sources included. That is a vigorous illustration of the principle that the objects of the censor's attack are quite unpredictable. I have no doubt that every future effort to study this problem will elicit titles not previously challenged.

A striking feature of the following body of material is the similarity of the information. The same group of titles shows up most often, the objections are similar and the results are similar. While frequency of attack may differ by regions, the differences are statistical. The differences afford little comfort to a teacher or librarian just as reported improvement in the cure rate for cancer offers little comfort to a person who suffers from cancer.

If the fifty most frequently attacked books based on the list were removed from the library there still would be hundreds of books left to attract the censor's attention. In short, censors cannot be appeased by agreeing to remove one or two or five or thirty-three or fifty-five books, as the censors wished to do in various places in the United States.

A careful study of the list will be quite rewarding to people interested in the attitude of some Americans toward literature across the last thirty-five years. For example, there are many reports of parents stating that they did not want their daughter reading a given book; there are only three reports of parents stating that they did not want their son to read a given book. William Dean Howell's famous article "What Should Girls Read?" was written in 1902 but describes an attitude still current in 1985. The many objections to books on the (usually mistaken) grounds that they reflect communism suggests the degree to which Americans are ignorant of communism and suffer from a phobia about it. The objection to *The Heart Is A Lonely Hunter* on the grounds that the author was Russian is another example. One person objected to Thomas More's *Utopia*, alleging that it reflected communism and leftism. No person objected to a book in this list because it reflected "right wing views" or "rightism." The height of ignorance about communism may be indicated by objections to *The Red Badge of Courage*, by Crane, or to *The Red Pony* by Steinbeck, because they are allegedly communist or leftist books.

Many other interesting insights concerning the battle of the books may be drawn from this list of challenged books.

Arrangement

The arrangement is alphabetically by title except in the cases of authors G. Cain, A. Hitchcock, and L. Hughes and in the cases of occult and witchcraft as subjects. These exceptions are included with the titles to form one alphabetical sequence.

Title, author, publication date	Objector	Objection	Results	Place	Source, date of objection	Legal Case (if any)
The Abortion: An Historical Romance R. Brautigan, 1971	School board principal, students, teachers	Obscenities and sexual references not socially acceptable	All Brautigan books removed; trial judge ruled books not legally obscene: school board appealed to state court of appeals; Decision not reported in sources	CA	9, 10	Wexner V. Anderson Union High School District
The Adventures of Augie March, S. Bellow, 1953	Parent	Language and Sex	Denied	SC	1	—
The Adventures of Huckleberry Finn, M. Twain, 1884	Member of the Brooklyn Branch of NAACP	A central character in the classic is Miss Watson's big nigger, named Jim	Banished	—	17	—
—	Student	—	Denied	South	3	—
—	Another teacher	Characterization and language offensive to blacks	Decision to use the book was left to the teacher	—	2	—
—	School board, group of black parents	Contains racially derogatory remarks	Book removed from required reading list in Am. Lit. class	New Trier High School, Winnetka, IL.	9	—
—	Parent	The use of the word "orgy," belittling of Jim, racial put down, taking the name of the Lord in vain	Denied	OH	6	—
—	Student	Use of the word "nigger"	Denied	WI	1	—

—		Parent	Use of profane language, racial slurs	Still pending	TX	1
—		Parent	Objectionable language ("nigger" in Huckleberry Finn)	X Material removed from classroom use	TX	1
—		Parent	Racial (reference to blacks)	Denied	CA	1
—		Parent	Promoted discrimination	Denied—parent satisfied after a teacher conference	PA	1
—		Parent	Racist language	Not resolved	PA	1
—		Parent	—	—	NC	1
—		Parent	Racial	X Material removed from classroom use	TX	1
—		Waukegan alderman	Racism and language	Removed from the required reading list	NY	12
—					Waukegan Public Schools, IL	11
—		Teacher	Alleged racism	A guidebook to aid teachers in their presentation of the novel	Springfield High School, IL	11
—	*The Adventures of Tom Sawyer*, M. Twain, 1876	Parent	Racial (reference to blacks)	Denied	CA	1
—	*Advice to Boys on Marriage*, Duprey	Principal	Too frank or revealing	Removal		4
—	*African Images*, H. Scheub, 1972	Concerned Citizens	Pornography and filth		LA	7

continued

Title, author, publication date	Objector	Objection	Results	Place	Source, date of objection	Legal Case (if any)
Again, Dangerous Visions; 46 Original Stories, H. Ellison, 1972	Parents Superintendent	Obscene	Censored	Bloomington, MN	9	—
The Age of Reason, T. Paine, 1794	Clergyman	Anti-religious statement	Denied	—	4	—
The Age of Rock, J. Eisen, 1969	Parent	Bad language	Book placed on closed shelf	—	6	—
Alas, Babylon, P. Frank, 1959		—	—	NJ	1	—
Alive, The Story of the Andes Survivors, P. Read, 1974	Parent	Parent felt moral issues inappropriate for discussion	Alternative book offered	TX	2	—
	Teacher	Contents were grotesque referring to the true story of men eating human flesh to survive an airplane crash in the Andes Mts.	Material removed from classroom use by that teacher	MO	1	
All Quiet on the Western Front, E. Remarque, 1929	Parent	Too violent for the child	Child was told not to read this book	West	3	—
	Parent	War was depicted as brutal and dehumanizing	Denied	CA	1	—
All the King's Men, R. Warren, 1971		—	—	WI	5	—

Title/Author	Initiator	Objection	Action	State		
*All You Wanted to Know About Sex	Teacher	—	Material placed on closed shelf	CA	1	—
Almost Crown, J. Szabo, 1978	School librarian	Photos of young children and teenagers in undesirable situation, some almost sexual	Material placed on closed shelf	TN	1	—
American Argument, P. Buck, E. Robeson, 1949	Concerned citizen	Pornography and filth	—	LA	7	—
American Civics, W. H. Hartley, 1979	—	—	Censored	Mahwah, NJ	9	—
The American Dream, E. Albee, 1961	Parent	Too mature for high school students	—	WI	1	—
American English Today—12, H. Guth; E. Schuster, 1970	English Department Chairman	Incoherent organization	Denied	TX	2	—
The American Heritage Dictionary of the English Language, W. Morris, 1969	People for Better Education	Certain definitions offensive	Censored	Anchorage, AK	9	—
—	Parent, Principal	Slang definitions of words with vulgar connotations	Book removed from classroom use, put in office to be burned	OH	6	—
America in Legend, R. Dorson, 1973	School board	Concones draft dodging	Censored	Cobb County, GA	9	—
—	Parent	—	Material placed on closed shelf	VA	1	—
An American Tragedy, T. Dreiser, 1925	Parent	Too much sex	Closed shelf	—	4	—

continued

211

Title, author, publication date	Objector	Objection	Results	Place	Source, date of objection	Legal Case (if any)
And Then There Were None, A. Christie, 1940	Clergyman, Student	Language—the word damn was used twice and the clergyman and the boy felt this was an unChristian book and we shouldn't be reading such material	Student given alternative assignment and book removed from classroom use	NM	2	—
Andersonville, M. Kantor, 1955	Student, Parent	Too realistic for high school, reference to sex and language and filth	Removed	WI	5	—
—	—	Obscenity, political ideas, author cited by HUAC	Removed	Four Amarillo High Schools, TX	17	—
—	Parent, Librarian	Not "fit" for students, bad language	Removed or put on closed shelf	—	4	—
—	Parent	Coarse language and actions	Denied	IA	2	—
—	School board member	Contains objectionable words	Censored	Asheville, NC	9	—
Androcles and the Lion, Shaw, G. Bernard, 1913	Clergyman	Shaw was an atheist	—	WI	5	—
The Andromeda Strain, M. Crichton, 1969	Parent	Too much attention to sex	Denied	TX	2	—

					Middle West	
The Angel Inside Went Sour, E. Rothman, 1970	Parent	Immoral language	Book removed from classroom use and library	—		3
	Parent	—	Removed from library	IN		1
Animal Factories: The Mass Production of Animals for Food and How It Affects the Lives of Consumers, Farmers, and Animals Themselves, J. Mason and P. Singer, 1980	Member of the Board of Education	The book supposedly presented an untruthful picture of some types of farmers	Denied	WI		1
Animal Farm, G. Orwell, 1945	John Birch Society	Objection to "masses will revolt"	—	WI		5
	Parent, Principal	Sex and vulgarity	No action	—		4
Anne of the Thousand Days, M. Anderson, 1948	—	—	—	—		1
An Anthology of N.Y. Poets, R. Padgett, R. Camp, 1970	Another teacher	Objectionable material	Placed on restricted shelf	PA		1
	Teacher	So-called poetry was vulgar and certainly in poor taste	Material removed from library	OH		1
Are You in the House Alone?, R. Peck, 1976	Parent	Not appropriate for grade level—brutal rape	Material removed from library	WA		1
	Parent	Description of rape	Material placed on closed shelf	—		1

continued

213

Title, author, publication date	Objector	Objection	Results	Place	Source, date of objection	Legal Case (if any)
—	Parent	—	Material placed on closed shelf	VA	1	—
Are You There, God? It's Me, Margaret, J. Blume, 1970	See *Deenie* entry				10, 11	See *Deenie* entry
—	Parents	Don't think their children should be reading this book	—	—	9	—
—	Teacher	"I wouldn't let anybody read that, it's smut"	Material removed from library	MN	1	—
Afive, A. Guthrie, 1970	Library supervisor	Placed teachers in a bad light, foul language	—	Southwest	3	—
The Art of Narration: The Short Story, A. Day, 1971	Concerned Citizens	Pornography and filth	—	LA	7	—
Ask Me If I Love You Now, F. Laing, 1968	—	—	Course was cancelled	OH	6	—
The Assistant, B. Malamud, 1957	Parent	Sex oriented, rape scene	Book removed from classroom use and from recommended list	South	3	—
Auntie Mame, P. Dennis, 1959	Parent	—	—	WI	5	—
Autobiography, B. Devlin	Parent	Promoting immorality of Bernadette Devlin	Student was assigned another work	West	3	—
Autobiography of Malcolm X,	Concerned Citizens	Pornography and filth	—	LA	7	—
Awakened China: Country Americans Don't Know, F. Greene, 1961	The Principal	Shows communist country in favorable light	Not purchased	—	4	—

Title	Initiator	Complaint	Action	State	No.	
Awakenings, M. Sacks, 1973	Gablers	—	—	—	9	—
Babbitt, S. Lewis, 1922	Librarian	—	Placed on closed shelf	—	4	—
Back to School with Betsy, C. Haywood, 1943	CURE, Parents who care, NOW	—	—	Rockville, MD	9	—
Bad: An Autobiography, J. Carr, D. Hammer, I. Cronin, 1975	Parent	Did not like the "deviant sexual material" in book	Denied	—	1	—
The Bad Seed, W. Campbell, 1954	Local citizens, Gillette High School library	They are "anti-Christian and demonic"	Reconsideration committee voted to retain the book but to restrict books to high school students	WY	11	—
Ball Four, J. Bouton, 1970	Principal	Too graphic—too much cussing. Boys were passing it around cafeteria	Material removed from library	KY	1	—
	Parent	Disillusioning for youngsters	Denied	NJ	1	—
*Banquet at Dawn, Abel	Parent	Explicit sex, racial slurs	Removed from the library	—	1	—
Barefoot Boy with Cheek, M. Shulman, 1943	Parent	—	Temporary removal	WI	5	—
*The Bastard, W. Jenks	—	—	—	NY	12	—
*The Battered Woman, L. Walker, 1979	Parent	Chapter on sexual abuse was too strong for teenage reader	Placed on closed shelf	—	1	—

continued

215

Title, author, publication date	Objector	Objection	Results	Place	Source, date of objection	Legal Case (if any)
Battle Cry, L. Uris, 1953	Superintendent	—	Removal	—	4	—
The Beast, A. Van Vogt, 1963	Parent, Clergyman	Graphic sex scenes	Book removed from library	West	3	—
Been Down So Long It Looks Like Up To Me, R. Farina, 1966	Parent, Principal	Objectionable material, in particular sections in last chapter	Book removed from reading list	Northeast	3	—
Before You Marry: Questions to ask and answer, S.M. Duvall, 1964	—	—	Reserve shelf	—	4	—
Being a Man In a Woman's World, D.H. Bell, 1982	—	—	—	—	1	—
Being There, J. Kosinski, 1970	Parent	Sex oriented	Denied	Northeast	3	—
—	Student, Parent	Sexual content suitability for high school, use of suggestive language, description of homosexuality and sexual content	Book removed from recommended list and teacher reconsidered use	IL, NJ	2	—
Bellevue is a State of Mind, A. Barry, 1971	Parent	Sex scenes	Denied	PA	1	—
—	Community resident	Sex scenes	Material placed on closed shelf	—	1	—
A Bell for Adano, J. Hersey, 1944	Parent	Russian author [sic]	—	WI	5	—

Title	Initiator	Objection	Action	State	Grade	Court case
	Parent, Librarian	Objectionable sentence, gross language	Removal of material, placed on closed shelf	—	4	—
	Principal	Use of language	Book removed from classroom use, removed from recommended list and library	South	3	—
	—	Profanity—vulgar words and deeds	Censorship	TN	13	—
The Bell Jar, S. Plath, 1971	Principal	Language too strong for class rooms	Book temporarily removed from classroom use	IN	2	—
	Principal	Sex scenes too explicit	Book removed from classroom use	South	3	—
	School board		Book removed from classroom use; removal upheld by District Court and Appellate Court	Warsaw	9, 10	*Zyken v. Warsaw Community School Board* 631 F 2d 1300 (7th Cir. 1980)
Belly Button Defense	—			—	9	—
Ben Bryan: Morgan Rifleman, J. Brick, 1963	—	Bad language	Destroyed	—	4	—
Best American Humorous Short Stories, R. Linscott, 1971	Parent	Vulgar language	Book placed on closed shelf	South	3	—
	Clergyman			—		—
The Best Plays of 1972–73, M. Dodd, 1973	Concerned Citizens	Against pornography and filth		LA	7	—
The Best Short Stories by Negro Writers, L. Hughes, 1967	Concerned Citizens	Against pornography and filth		LA	7	—

continued

217

Title, author, publication date	Objector	Objection	Results	Place	Source, date of objection	Legal Case (if any)
—	School board	Anti-American, anti-Christian, anti-Semetic [sic] and just plain filthy	This book and ten others removed, student sued, lower Court dismissed the case, Appellate Court ordered a trial, board appealed to Supreme Court which ordered a trial, board then returned books to library	Island Trees, NY	9, 10	Board of Education Island Trees v. Pico 457 U.S. 853 (1982)
Best Wishes, Amen, L. Morrison, 1974	Teacher	Language	Left on open shelves and open access	—	14	—
The Bible	Student	Person is not allowed to read it	—	—	4	—
	Parent	It's teaching religion	—	South	3	—
	Parent	Non-fundamental preaching	Denied	NJ	2	—
	Kanawha County			—	9	—
	Student	The student thought it was illegal to use the Bible in school, she wrote ACLU	Assigned another book "of equal value" [sic]	CA	1	—
	Another teacher	Bible was sacred material to be studied only under auspices of those qualified to reveal its truth	Class continued to be taught—Bible taught as literature	OH	6	—
	Parents	Using the Bible as part of a religious ceremony in the public schools	Bible may not be used for a religious ceremony; may be used for objective study in comparative religion or history or literature	PA	16	School District of Abington Township v. Schempp. 374 U.S. 203, 83 S. Ct. 1560, 10 L. Ed. 2d 844 (1963).

Title	Initiator	Complaint	Action	State	No.	
The Bible Tells Me So: Studies in Abundant Living, V.P. Wierwille, 1971	Student	Material put out by organization called "The Way"	No formal request was ever made	OH	1	—
The Big Sky, A. Guthrie, 1964	—	Charges of obscenity, political ideas	Withdrawn from four libraries	Amarillo High Schools	17	—
	Superintendent	—	Removal	—	4	—
	Parent	Profanity and moral aspects, strong language	—	—	4	—
	Parent	Sexual activities between mountain men and Indian women too explicit, author's excessive use of profanity	Denied	MT	2	—
The Big Sleep, R. Chandler, 1939	Parent	Brutality and abnormality of characters	Book placed on closed shelf	—	4	—
Bill and Pete, T. De Paolo, 1978	Clergyman	*Bill and Pete* showed a little boy who was without clothing on his behind. This was evidence of "secular humanism." Also the book seemed to indicate you should not hunt alligators	Removed from the library	AR	1	—

continued

219

Title, author, publication date	Objector	Objection	Results	Place	Source, date of objection	Legal Case (if any)
A Billion For Boris, M. Rogers, 1974	—	—	—	NY	12	—
Billy Jack, E. Christina, 1973	Student	Sexual rape in Billy Jack—didn't want younger (family) kids to see and read	Material placed on closed shelf	IA	1	—
Biology: Living Systems, R. Oram, 1983	Parent	Taught evolution as fact rather than theory and should have creationism presented as a balance	Denied	WA	1	—
Black Africa On the Move, L. Laccy	Concerned Citizens	Pornography and filth	—	LA	7	—
Black Boy, R. Wright, 1963	See entry for Best Short Stories by Negro Writers			Island Trees, NY	9, 10	See entry for Best Short Stories by Negro Writers
—	Librarian, Principal	Unsuitable for high school students	Removal	—	4	—
—	Parent	Obscenity, book teaches blacks to hate whites	Matter may end up in court	Midwest	3	—
—	—	Obscene literature, hatred between black and white—immorality	Censorship	TN	13	—
—	Concerned Citizens	They are against pornography and filth	—	LA	7	—

Title / Author		Initiator	Objection	Action	Place	No.	
—	—	Parent	Objection to sexual overtones; unsuitable for impressionable sophomores	Removed from classroom use	MI	2	—
—			—	Removed in Anaheim, CA, and removed in Island Trees, NY	—	9	—
—		Parent	Language	Denied	CA	1	—
—					OH	1	—
—		Parents	"Objectionable language"	School board voted to retain books	NY	6	—
Black Fire, I.A. Baraka, 1968		Principal	Repulsive, obscene language	Book placed on closed shelf	Middlewest	12	—
—		Parent	"Dirty words"	Denied	KS	3	—
Black Like Me, J. Griffin, 1960		Parent, Principal	Obscene language, filthy, integration centered, unsuitable for age level, vulgar	—	—	1	—
—		Parent	Language, situations	Removed	AZ	4	—
—		Parent, Teacher	Poor language, dirty, nasty book. In a rural community people don't care to have their children read about Negroes	Book removed from classroom use, not required to read it, denied	Middle West	8	—
—		Parent, Clergyman	Language (four letter words)	Denied	PA	3	—
—		Parent	Objectionable subject matter	Denied	IL	2	—
—						1	—

continued

221

Title, author, publication date	Objector	Objection	Results	Place	Source, date of objection	Legal Case (if any)
—	Parent	Obscene, vulgar; "in my opinion the objections in most cases were because of black people being in the book"	Material placed on closed shelf	MO	1	—
*Black Muslims, J. Clark	Concerned Citizens	They are against pornography and filth	—	LA	7	—
The Black Poets, D. Randall, 1971	Parent	Language offensive to minority groups	Denied	South	3	—
Black Rage, W. Grier and P. Cobbs, 1968	Concerned Citizens	They are against pornography and filth	—	LA	7	—
Black Sunday, T. Harris, 1975	—	—	—	—	1	—
Black Voices Anthology, A. Chapman, 1968	Parent	Offensive to minority groups	Denied	South	3	—
Blackboard Jungle, E. Hunter	Parent	Objectionable language	—	WI	5	—
Bless the Beasts and Children, G. Swarthout, 1970	Parent	Book is critical of parents, schools corrupt youth into rebelling against parents and parent values by encouraging critical attitudes	Book removed from classroom use and recommended list	NY	2	—
—	School board	—	—	Waukesha, WI	9	—
—	Parent, Clergyman	Questionable subject matter, language	The book is read—an assistant principal read and approved it	OH	6	—

—		Swear words	Other titles were assigned to student	IA	1	—
Blood-and-Guts Patton, J. Pearl, 1961	Parent	Language, scenes	Not reordered	—	4	—
Blood Line, W. James, 1976	Parent	Language and sex	Material placed on closed shelf	IA	1	—
Blubber, J. Blume, 1974	Another teacher	The book has no redeemable values, complainant felt it encouraged anti-social behavior	Denied	OH	1	—
—	Parent	Offensive language throughout the book	Denied	OH	6	—
—	Parent	—		NY	12	—
Blue Trees, Red Sky, N. Klein, 1975	Teacher	Language	Left on open shelves and open access	WI	14	—
Blues for Mr. Charlie, J. Baldwin, 1964	Parent, Student	"The language is obscene"	Book removed from library	TX	2	—
Blueschild Baby, G. Cain, 1970	Parent	Language used—swearing	New selection policies for school and libraries	SD	1	—
Body Language, J. Fast, 1970	Parent	Language	Material removed from classroom use	NY	1	—
—	Concerned Citizens	They are against pornography and filth		LA	7	—
Bonnie Jo, Go Home, J. Eyerly, 1972	School Board and parents	Complimented the book but said it must be banned because it condoned abortion	Destroyed the book	Line Mountain School District, Red Cross, PA	9	—

continued

223

Title, author, publication date	Objector	Objection	Results	Place	Source, date of objection	Legal Case (if any)
—	Teacher	In both book titles the use of vulgar language and profanity was questionable	Material removed from library	VA	1	—
The Book of Lists, D. Wallenchinsky and I. Wallace and A. Wallace, 1977	Superintendent	Sexual lists	Material placed on closed shelf	TN	1	—
The Book of the Zodiac, F. Gettings, 1972	Another teacher	Nude pictures were inappropriate for Jr. high students	Denied	ME	1	—
Born on the Fourth of July, R. Kovic, 1976	Parent	Un-American, language, sex	Placed on closed shelf	MD	1	—
Born to Win, W. Guthrie, 1965	Clergyman	Chapter—"Dear Prostitute"	Material placed on closed shelf	VA	1	—
Boss: Richard J. Daley of Chicago, M. Royko, 1971	—	—	—	CT	1	—
—	—	—	—	NY	12	—
A Boy and His Dog, H. Ellison, 1974	Parent	Language and sex	Denied	SC	1	—
The Boy Upstairs, A. Wamlof, 1963	—	—	—	—	4	—
Boys and Sex, W.B. Pomeroy, 1968	—	—	—	—	1	—
The Boys from Brazil, I. Levin, 1976	Parent	Vulgar language	Denied	MI	1	—
—	—	Too dirty	Denied	OH	6	—

Title	Initiator	Objection	Action	Location	No.	Court case
Brave New World, A. Huxley, 1932	—	Charges of obscenity, political ideas	Withdrawn from libraries at four Amarillo high schools	TX	17	—
—	—	—	Denied	Miami, FL	17	—
—	Parent	Too frequent sex passages, objected to test tube babies	—	—	4	—
—	—	—	Teacher asserted that he was dismissed because he taught the book; Board denied the charge, Court upheld the Board	MD	16	Parker v. Board of Educ., 237 F. Supp. 222 (D.Md.), aff'd. 348 F.2d 464 (4th Cir. 1965), cert. denied. 382 U.S. 1030 (1966).
—	Faculty	Sordidness, sex	—	AZ	8	—
—	PTA, Parent, Church, School board, Librarian	Profanity, sex reference, immoral, not suitable for high school students, students not mature enough to understand it	—	—	4	—
—	Parent	Promiscuous, sex and drug advocacy	Students given an option of an independent unit, letter of teacher intent sent to parents to be returned	Middlewest	3	—
—	Parent	Too much attention to sex, immoral, immorality of baby factory	Denied; Student allowed new selection for assignment	CT	2	—
—	Substitute teacher, Student	Unsuitable for students, satanic literature	Denied	OH	6	—

continued

Title, author, publication date	Objector	Objection	Results	Place	Source, date of objection	Legal Case (if any)
—	Parent	Encourage drug use, sex	Denied	WA	1	—
—	Parent	Profanity, explicit sexual discussion	Denied, used alternative book	CA	1	—
—	Parent	Said book encourages drug use	Removed from classroom use for freshman	CA	1	—
Breakfast of Champions, K. Vonnegut, 1973	Another teacher	Questionable language	Book removed from library	SC	2	—
—	School counselor	Inappropriate	Material placed on closed shelf	TX	1	—
Breaking Up, N. Klein, 1980	Parent	"Trash"	Still in progress	MT	11	—
Brian Piccolo: A Short Season, J. Morris, 1971	—	—	—	NY	12	—
The Bridge, a Book for Christian Scientists, I.S. Moore, 1971	Another teacher	Shock at conclusion—religious implications	Removed from classroom use	—	1	—
Bridge to Terabithia, K. Patterson, 1977	Parent	Language	Removed from recommended lists	IN	1	—
Buried Alive: The Biography of Janis Joplin, M. Friedman, 1973	Parent	Student told guidance counselor of his parents' objections—no specific reasons given	Alternate selection given to student	IL	2	—
Janis Joplin, J. Joplin	Teacher	The material was too sensational, the reported incidents could not be proven	Material removed from library	—	1	—

Title/Author	Initiator	Objection	Action Taken	Location	No.
Butterfly Revolution, W. Butler, 1961	Student, Parent	Language	Book removed from classroom use	South	3
—	Parent	Objected to "farting scene" in book	Parent burned book; book was re-ordered	WI	2
—	Parent	Profane language	Material removed from classroom use	WI	1
—	Parents	Offensive language	Review of book still in progress	Norwood Jr. High class—NJ	11
Cain, G., Any book	Concerned Citizens	Pornography and filth	—	LA	7
Call of the Wild, J. London, 1963	Student	Language	Teacher talked to the student about the book	LA	2
Calm Down Mother, M. Terry, 1966	—	—	Censored	New Lisbon, ME	9
Calories Don't Count, H. Taller, 1961	Librarian, Teacher	Not medically accurate	Removal	—	4
Canterbury Tales, G. Chaucer, 1478	Principal	Risque language in some tales	Denied	—	4
—	Parent	Unhealthy characters and nasty words	Book put back on library shelf	South	3
—	Parent	"We don't read things like this in my house and I don't expect my daughter to be subjected to that at school."	Student assigned a ternate selection	OH	2
—	Parents, citizens, clergyman	—	—	—	8

continued

227

Title, author, publication date	Objector	Objection	Results	Place	Source, date of objection	Legal Case (if any)
—	Parent	"Unhealthy" characters and "nasty" words	Book put back on library shelf, no further complaint made	South	3	—
—	—		Students read if they desire	—	1	—
The Car Thief, T. Weesner, 1972	Parent	Offensive language	Denied	IA	1	—
Cat Ballou, W. Neuman	Parent	"I don't want my daughter exposed to such books."	Denied	CA	1	—
Cat On A Hot Tin Roof, T. Williams, 1975	Principal	Sexual perversion, foul language	Book removed from classroom use	VA	2	—
Catch-22, J. Heller, 1961	Member Board of Education	"Garbage"	Book removed from classroom use and library; District Court upheld board, Appellate Court ordered the book returned to the library	Strongsville, OH	9, 10, 16	Minarcini v. Strongsville City School Dist., 384 F. Supp. 698 (N. D. Ohio 1974), aff'd in part, rev'd in part, 541 F. 2d 577 (6th Cir. 1976)
	Concerned Citizens	Pornography and filth	—	LA	7	—
	Parent	Pornography	Book removed from library, classroom use and recommended list	LA	2	—
	Parent	Objected to sex in novel.	Alternate book allowed.	MD	2	—
	Parent	Language	—	NY	2	—
	Clergy	"Dirty words"	Denied	IL	1	—

Title/Author	Initiator	Objection	Action	Location	No.	Legal Case/Notes
Catcher in the Rye, J. Salinger, 1951	Parents	Presented women in a negative way. Book should be removed from the library	Denied	WA	1	—
	Parents	Not proper for teenagers, dirty words, writing, talk, profanity, sex, and immoral	Teacher dismissed for insubordination; dismissal upheld by Court	NY	16	Harris v. Mechanicville Cent. School Dist., 408 N.Y.S.2d 384 (1978).
	Parent	Bad language, bad example for adolescents, negative in impact	Denied—court case supported plaintiff; appeals court reversed	MI	1	Legal case not reported by informant
	—	—	—	San Jose, CA	17	—
	—	—	Dismissal of teacher in 1960	Louisville, KY	17	—
	Superintendent	Book is shocking	Teacher resigned because the school administrator had not supported her choice of book	Tulsa, OK	17	—
	Parent, Librarian, Teacher	Too sophisticated, gross, shocking vulgarity in profusion, bad language, lack of plot	Not Recommended	—	4	—
	Teacher, Superintendent, Parents, School board member	Vulgarity, sacrilegious, unsuitable	Removed	AZ	8	—
	Concerned Citizens	Pornography and filth	—	LA	7	—

continued

229

Title, author, publication date	Objector	Objection	Results	Place	Source, date of objection	Legal Case (if any)
—	Parents, Administration	Language obscenities, sexual account with prostitution	Denied and child allowed to read another selection	ND	2	—
—	—		Removed and returned to reading list	Issaquah, WA	9	—
—	Librarian, Parent, Member of Board of Education, Principal	Unsuitable for children, language, objectionable references to homosexuality, not a positive examination of youth	Denied and alternative selections chosen	—	1	—
—	Parents, Citizens	Language and theme	At first placed on closed shelf and then returned to regular circulation	SC	1	—
—	Parent	Daughter should not read such filth	Censorship	TN	13	
—	Clergyman, Parent	Obscene language, detrimental to moral growth, blasphemy, profanity	Alternative novel assigned	Middle West	3	
—	Administration	Language, obscenities	Book placed on closed shelf		2	
—	Parent	Vulgar language	Request denied		2	
—	Parent	Bad language; sexual account with prostitution	Request denied		2	

230

—	Parent	Parents had heard there were four letter words in the book	Another book choice required	2
—	Parent	Language	—	2
—	Parent	Language—four letter words; some situations sexual or homosexual overtones	Request denied	2
—	Parent	Language	Request denied	2
—	Parent	Language	Book was read aloud to class; students could read own selection	2
—	Parent	Language reference to sex	Child allowed a different book selection	2
—	Parent	Language used	Book removed from curriculum temporarily, students choose courses from class outlines; child made wrong selection	2
—	Clergyman	Vulgar language	Request denied; individual child given alternate assignment	2
—	Parent	Bad language	Student was allowed to read alternate book for assignment	2
—	Parent	"Language is unfit for teens to read" (Sophomores)	Student given alternate book; we teachers each still use the book each year	2

continued

Title, author, publication date	Objector	Objection	Results	Place	Source, date of objection	Legal Case (if any)
—	Parent, Student	Generally all the reasons for all objections are either: 1. The language in the book 2. Religious principles of the students and/or the parents	When a student and/or a parent reject a book, the student is assigned another book to read. First, a parent must complete a form stating his reasons for objections. If the parent will not complete the form, the student is expected to read the book		2	
—	Another teacher	The filthy language	Book removed from library		2	
—	Parent	The profanity used in the novel was offensive to the complainant. She said, "How can you teach such a dirty book?"	Request denied		2	
—	Parent	Language (4-letter words)	Book placed on closed shelf		2	
—	Student	Objected to portrayal of characters—language especially	Student allowed new selection		2	
—	Parent, Student	Language	Request denied		2	
—	Parent	"Foul language"	Book not used by student involved		2	
—	Parent, Clergyman	Profane language Questionable sexual reference	Request denied		2	

continued

Initiator	Reason	Disposition	WI	No.
Parent, Principal	"Foul language, poor example for students"	Book removed from classroom use		2
Parent	Parent objected to description of young people's approach to sex; "Bad example"	Student allowed to read another selection		2
Parent	Adults only	Removal	WI	5
Band Member	Not proper for teenagers		WI	5
Parent	Dirty words, writing, talk	Removal	WI	5
Principal	Profanity and sex reference		WI	5
PTA	Language		WI	5
Citizen & Parent	Dirty		WI	5
Church & Parent	Immoral	Removal	WI	5
School			WI	5
Teacher	Book for adults	Restricted	WI	5
Parents			WI	5
Principal			WI	5
Administrator	Filthy language—sexy		WI	5
Church	Sex, language		WI	5
Parent	Too old for students		WI	5
Teacher			WI	5
Librarian	Because of publicity	Removal	WI	5

Title, author, publication date	Objector	Objection	Results	Place	Source, date of objection	Legal Case (if any)
	Supt.	Don't put on reading list.	—	WI	5	
	Librarian	—	Not put on shelves.	WI	5	—
—	Parent	Objectionable	Denied	CT	1	—
—	Parent	Profanity, explicit sexual discussion	Denied and used alternative book	CA	1	—
—	Parent	Language	Denied	CA	1	—
—	Parent	Obscene language—use of God's name	Still pending	IL	1	—
—	Parent	Language	Denied	MA	1	—
—				NY	1	—
—	Student	"Dirty" book	Replace with other material	MA	1	—
	Parent	Obscene objectionable language, no use for book, no "redeeming social value"	Denied	MI	1	—
	Parent	Remove title from recommending list	Material removed from recommending list	MT		—
	Parent	Strong language, loose morals of hero, lack of direction of character, not typical of adolescent boy	Material removed from classroom use as required novel	IL	1	—
—	Parent	Obscene	Denied	—	1	—
—	Parent	Language—hell	Alternate book read	OH	1	—

School librarian	Not suitable for 9th grade students	Material placed on closed shelf	LA	1
Parent	Language	Material placed on closed shelf	PA	1
Parent	Language and attitude of protagonist	Denied	MO	1
Parent	—	Material removed from classroom use	WI	1
Teacher	Bad language	Denied	NC	1
Parent	Language, sex, etc., objected to entire content	Denied	PA	1
Parent	Objectionable literature language level for student maturity, profanity, corruption of morals	Individual student was not required to study the material—but the rest of the class did	Middle West	3
Parent, Palm Harbor Parents' League	Too many curse words	Book removed from classroom use; from recommended list	South	3
Parent, a "missionary for fundamentalist sect"	Objected to author's use of profanity throughout the novel	Classroom teacher assigned alternate novel	Northeast	3
Parent, Clergyman	Offensive to minority groups.	Request denied	South	3
Parent	Not appropriate for world studies.	Request denied	West	3
Parent	Poor language	Book removed from classroom use.	Rural	3

continued

Title, author, publication date	Objector	Objection	Results	Place	Source, date of objection	Legal Case (if any)
—	Parent	"Dirty book"	Request denied	Rural	3	
—	Parent	Language	Student was excused from reading the book for class	Middlewest	3	
—	Parent	Language	Met with the Board of Education for decision; optimistic	Northeast	3	
—	Parent	Language	Substitution made	South	3	
—	Parent	Language profanity	Student allowed to leave course.	Middlewest	3	
—	Parent	—	Request denied	South	3	
—	Parent	Suggestive book	Request denied	Middlewest	3	
—	Parent	Foul language	Alternate choice	Middlewest	3	
—	Parent	Language	—	South	3	
—	Parent	Use of language not suitable for child	Discussing and explaining book with parent along with study questions	Southwest	3	
—	Parent	Vocabulary	Told to read another book	Middlewest	3	
—	Parent	"A dirty book read by children behind the woodshed."	Request denied	South	3	
—	Parent	The book was dirty and he didn't want his 15-yr.-old son exposed to such trash.	Request denied—his son was not required to read the book. Another book was provided.	Northeast	3	
Cat's Cradle, K. Vonnegut, 1963		See *Catch-22* entry at Strongsville, OH		—	10,16	Strongsville, OH

236

continued

Title, author, date	Initiated by	Objection	Action taken	State	10,16	Island Trees, New York
See The Best Short Stories by Negro Writers	Principal	The use of four letter words or similar sounding words.	Book removed from classroom use	NY	2	—
	Parent, teacher, Principal	Profanity, illicit sex, ridiculous convention	Book removed from classroom use and recommended list		2	—
Challenge and Change: A History of the National Intramural Assn., J.S. Clarke, 1978	Clergyman		Alternate book assigned	OH	6	—
	—			—	9	—
Changing Bodies, Changing Lives, R. Bell, 1980	Parents	"Gives little attention to the moral and financial consequences of abortion and sex."	Book transferred from the school library to the administration office	OR	11	—
The Charge of the Light Brigade, C.B. Woodham, 1953	Student	Book is boring	Book placed on closed shelf	Midwest	3	—
Chariots of the Gods, F. Von Daniken, 1968	—	Offensive language, too much violence, against religion, subversive	—			—
Cheaper by the Dozen, F. Gilbreth Jr. and E. Carey, 1948	Parents	Theme of book was objectionable, objectionable language	Another book substituted and censored copies were prepared	—	6	—

Title, author, publication date	Objector	Objection	Results	Place	Source, date of objection	Legal Case (if any)
The Cheerleader, R. MacDougall, 1973	School librarian	The book seemed to condone sexual permissiveness	Book removed from library	LA	2	—
—	Parent	Material was too explicit about teenage sexual encounters	Denied	IA	1	—
The Cheese Stands Alone, M. Prince, 1973	Parents and school board	Shocking language	Removed from library and destroyed	Line Mountain School District, Red Cross PA	9	—
The Child Buyer, J. Hersey	—	—	Restricted list	WI	5	—
A Child is Born: The Drama of Life Before Birth, L. Nilson 1977	Teacher	Picture showing childbirth, disruptive use in classroom, "My kids aren't ready for this."	Request denied	KY	1	—
Child of Our Time, M. Del Castillo, 1958	Parent	Language	—	AZ	8	—
China: the Country Americans are not Allowed to Know, F. Greene, 1961	Principal	Shows communist country in favorable light	Not purchased	—	4	—
The Children of Sanchez, W. Lewis, 1961	Teacher	For mature students	Available for mature students	WI	5	—
—	Parent	Unsuitable	Removed	AZ	8	—
The Chinese Visitor: A novel of Espionage, J. Eastwood, 1965	School librarian	Sexual scenes, cursing, adult situations	Material removed from library	TX	1	—

Title, Author, Year	Initiator	Objection	Action	Location	No.	
The Chocolate War, R. Cormier, 1974	Parent	Didn't want her daughter to read swear words or be exposed to other elements in the book	Student given alternate book	MA	2	—
—	Parent	Objection to vocabulary	Denied	TX	1	—
—	—	Vulgar language	Denied	TX	1	—
—	Teacher	Unnecessary to risk the trust of the community	Removed from paperback stand	—	6	—
—	—	"Pervasive vulgarity"	Book used on restricted basis, for eighth graders only	Richland School District—SC	11	—
The Choirboys, J. Wambaugh, 1975	School librarian	Obscene material	Removed from library	SD	2	—
Christy, C. Marshall, 1968	Board of Education	Prevented teaching grammar	Removed	Anaheim, CA	9	—
—	—	Not included in approved list	—	—	—	
Class Reunion, R. Jaffe, 1979	—	—	—	NJ	1	—
Claudelle Inglish, E. Caldwell, 1958	Parent	Language, situation	Remained	AZ	8	—
Clock Without Hands, C. McCullers, 1961	Superintendent	Sex, language	Removed	AZ	8	—
A Clockwork Orange, A. Burgess, 1962	Clergyman's wife	Obscene and violent language	Denied	Middlewest	3	—

continued

Title, author, publication date	Objector	Objection	Results	Place	Source, date of objection	Legal Case (if any)
—	Board of Education	Several books not recommended by faculty committee were not adopted by school board	Decision upheld by Court	Aurora, CO	9, 10	Cary v. Board of Education of Adams-Arapahoe School District, 427 F. Supp. 945 (D. Colo. 1978), affirmed, 598 F.2d 535 (10th Cir. 1979).
Cold Feet, G. LeRoy, 1979	—	The use of vulgar language and profanity	—	VA	1	—
Collected Poems, P. Goodman, 1973	School board		Book remained in library	Wauzeka, WI	9	—
Color Blind, M. Halsey, 1946	Concerned Citizens	Pornography and filth	—	LA	7	—
Color, Communism and Common Sense, M. Johnson, 1958	Concerned Parents and Taxpayers for Better Education	—	—	Nashua, NH	9	—
The Color Purple, A. Walker, 1982	Parent	Inappropriate portrayal of religion, sexually explicit and excessive violence	Still pending	Oaklands Far West High School—CA	11	—
Come Alive at 505, R. Brancato, 1980	Parent	Language	Temporarily removed from library	VA	1	—
Come Back, Little Sheba, a drama in two acts, W. Inge, 1951	Parent	Naughty language	Denied	—	4	—
Coming of Age in Mississippi, A. Moody, 1968	District Curriculum Committee	Black issues	Had a hearing	West	3	—

	Concerned Citizens	Pornography and filth				
*Communicating	—	—	—	LA	7	—
				Kanawha County, WV	9	—
Communism: An American's View, G. Johnson, 1964	Teacher	Thought certain parents would object	Denied	—	4	—
A Coney Island of the Mind, L. Ferlinghetti, 1955	School board	Several books not recommended by faculty committee were not accepted by school board	Decision upheld by Court	Aurora, CO	9, 10	Cary v. Board of Education, Arapahoe School District 598 F 2d 535 (19th Cir. 1979)
A Confederate General From Big Sur, R. Brautigan, 1964	School board	See The Abortion entry		Anderson, CA	9, 10	See The Abortion entry
*Conflicts	Gablers	Invasion of Privacy		TX	9	—
Conrack, P. Conroy	Parent	Language	English teacher quit using Conrack	—	1	—
Contemporary American Short Stories, Ed. by D. Angus and S. Angus, 1967	School board after one parent complained	Several sentences in first chapter of R. Ellison's The Invisible Man	Censored	Butler, PA	9	—
The Contender, R. Lipsyte, 1967	—	—	—	—	1	—
Cowboy Songs, and Other Frontier Ballads, J. Lomax, 1910	Parent, Principal	Words as "hell" and "damn," suggestive songs	Removal	—	4	—
Cow People, J. Dobie, 1964	Parent	Vulgar language, profanity	Removal	—	4	—
A Crack in the Sidewalk, R. Wolff, 1965	—	Unsuitable for some lower grade levels	—	OH	6	—

continued

241

Title, author, publication date	Objector	Objection	Results	Place	Source, date of objection	Legal Case (if any)
Cress Delahanty, J. West, 1965	Parent	Situations	—	AZ	8	—
Crime and Punishment, F. Dostoyevsky, 1866	Parent	Too much profanity	—	WI	5	—
The Crucible, A. Miller, 1953	—	Language throughout book, no historical benefit	Censored	TN	13	—
—	Parent	Unacceptable language and plot was objectionable	Student assigned alternate book	MI	2	—
—	Principal	The sexual implications might be misunderstood and resented by the people viewing it	Play was not done	AR	2	—
—	Parent	Objected that *The Crucible* "taught" witchcraft	Parent's child exempt	CT	1	—
—	Parents	Morally corrupting child, Satan figures in work	Denied and alternate selection chosen as per board policy	OH	6	—
The Cruel Sea, N. Monsarrat, 1951	Parent	—	Removed	—	5	—
Cruisin' For a Bruisin', W. Casey, 1976	Parent	No social value—too many sexual implications	Book was lost and never reordered	MI	1	—
The Crying of Lot 49, T. Pynchon, 1966	Student	Objected to entire book—character, dialogue, situation on basis that book was vulgar	Student offered new selection	VA	2	—

Title, Author, Date	Initiator	Objection	Action	Location	No.	
Cujo, S. King, 1981	Thirty parents urged removal	Considered "profane, sexually objectionable"	Book is in restricted area	Rankin County School—MS	11	—
The Cult, M. Ehrlich, 1973	Parent	Offensive language	Denied	IA	1	—
The Curious Eye, V. Huntington, 1974	A Student said: I find the poverty, despair described in the book obscene, not the words.	Obscene stories and words	Book retained	New Hanover County, Wilmington, NC	9	—
The Curse of Jezebel, R. Slaughter, 1961	Superintendent	Sex, language	Removed	AZ	8	—
Daddy Was a Number Runner, L. Meriwether, 1970	Parents	Insults Blacks	Removed	Oakland, CA	9	—
—	Clergyman	—	Placed on closed shelf	IN	1	—
—	Another teacher	The girl "damned" her father—[Only one bad word]—also explicit sex		OR	1	—
—	Superintendent	The book was under attack in a neighboring district, with much publicity, and had been removed from library shelves in that district	Material removed from library	CA	1	—
Daughters of Eve, L. Duncan, 1979	Parent	Language, the way one of the female character was treated by one of the male characters	Denied	OH	1	—

continued

243

Title, author, publication date	Objector	Objection	Results	Place	Source, date of objection	Legal Case (if any)
Dawn, E. Wiesel, 1961	Teacher	Suggestive words	Closed shelf	—	4	—
The Day of the Jackal, F. Forsyth, 1971	Parent	Obscene	Denied	—	1	—
A Day No Pigs Would Die, R. Peck, 1972	Student	Language	New choice offered	NY	2	—
			—	TX	1	—
Dear Bill, Remember Me?, N. Mazer, 1976			—	MO	1	—
Death of a Salesman, A. Miller, 1949	Principal	Language	Destroyed	AZ	8	—
	Parent, Clergyman	Had never read it, just heard it was bad	Denied	FL	2	—
	Parent	The word "whore"	Denied	IL	2	—
	Principal	Blasphemy	—	MO	1	—
			—	—	1	—
	Clergyman	Too many "God damn" plus other objectionable parts	Another play was read	OH	6	—
A Death in the Family, J. Agee, 1957	Parent	Irreverent, vulgar language	Denied, individual students read alternate works	Middle West	3	—
Deenie, J. Blume, 1973	School board, parent	Vulgar and obscene language, sexually explicit, anti-religious sentiment	Book removed; after lawsuit was filed, book returned	Elk River, MN	10	Antoinnette R. Maris v. Independent School District #728 Elk River, MN
	Parent	Sexual behavior	Restricted shelves	WI	14	—

Title / Author	Challenger	Objection	Action	State	No.	
The Deep, P. Benchley, 1976	—	—	—	NY	12	—
	—	—	—	—	1	—
*Deep Valley	Parent	Sociological descriptions of sexual mores and practices among early tribes of California Indians	Denied	CA	2	—
Delinquency: Sickness or Sin?. R. McCann, 1957	Teacher	Chapter on gangs	Removal	WI	5	—
Deliverance, J. Dickey, 1970	Concerned Citizens	Pornography and filth	—	LA	7	—
	Parents	Language, unacceptable sexual references, vulgar language, sex scenes	Another selection offered and book removed from library and later returned	VA	2	—
	Parent	Subject matter inappropriate for use in school; anti-religious matters	Denied	OH	6	—
	Parent, Student, Another teacher, English supervisor	Homosexuality promoted in book, questioned sodomy scene	Denied, book allowed to be used by certain teachers	Middle West	3	—
	Parent	Parent had seen film of book—objected to homosexuality portrayed in film	Denied	—	1	—
	Parent	Homosexuality promoted in book	Parent was to read entire book and make decision later	Middle West	3	—

continued

245

Title, author, publication date	Objector	Objection	Results	Place	Source, date of objection	Legal Case (if any)
—	Parent, Student, Another teacher, English supervisor	Questioned sodomy scene	Request denied, book allowed to be used by certain teachers	Middle West	3	—
—	School Board objected to three books: *Slaughterhouse-Five*; *Deliverance*; a collection of short stories, including Hemingway, Conrad, Steinbeck, Faulkner, et al.	None of the five school board members had read any of the books but decided they were "dirty," they ordered the books burned	Only *Slaughterhouse-Five* burned, much publicity and law suit by teacher	Drake, ND	9	Out of court settlement; *Slaughterhouse-Five* and *Deliverance* may be used in Jr.-Sr. high school classes; the teacher's performance could not be denigrated; teacher awarded $5,000
Demian, H. Hesse, 1919	Parent, Clergyman	Book was not Christian	Denied	Middle West	3	—
The Devil and Daniel Webster, S. Benét, 1937	Parent	"I don't want my daughter learning nothing about the devil"	Denied	FL	2	—
Devil at 4 O'clock, M. Catto, 1958	Parents		—	WI	5	—
Devils and Demons, N. Garden, 1976	Parent	Religious belief	Removed	WI	14	—
The Devil's Storybook, N. Babbitt, 1974	Parent	"Children should not read stories about the Devil, other than in the Bible"	Material removed from library	—	1	—
The Dharma Bums, J. Kerouac, 1959	Parent	Book was used by student teacher, parents	Student teachers must stick to textbook list	Northeast	3	—

		...were aroused by the language, and general worthlessness of the book	Material placed on closed shelf	—	1	—
Diary of a Frantic Kid Sister, H. Colman, 1973		Foul language and immoral thoughts; *Sister* was both criticized for foul language and immoral thoughts	Denied	—	1	—
Diary of a Young Girl, A. Frank, 1952	Parent	E. Roosevelt's prejudiced introduction	Denied	—	4	—
	Parent	Sex	Remained	AZ	8	—
	Parent	Parent was an Arab, objected to portrayal of Jewish girl	Student assigned other work	West	3	—
	Parent	Parent felt there was an objectionable passage with strong sexual connotations	Denied	NE	2	—
	Parent	Objected to the discussion of the mistreatment of the Jewish people	Parent was satisfied when explanation for its use was given	OH	6	—
Dibs: In Search of Self, V. Axline, 1964		—	—	MI	1	—
Dictionary of American Slang, H. Wentworth and S. Flexner, 1960		—	Removed	WI	5	—

continued

Title, author, publication date	Objector	Objection	Results	Place	Source, date of objection	Legal Case (if any)
—	Principal	Objectionable words listed	Removal	—	4	—
—	Parents, Members of John Birch Society, Administrators	Obscene	Removed	AZ	8	—
—	Principal	"No reason given, just a dictational principal who is narrow minded"	Material placed on closed shelf	NC	1	—
Dictionary of Slang and Unconventional English, E. Partridge, 1970	Chairman of the Citizens Commission on Education	Linked the book to suspension of 696 students for using profanity	—	Pinellas County, FL	9	—
Diversity, Houghton Mifflin	Gablers	See Jenkinson		TX	9	—
Dog Crisis, I. Nowell, 1978	Principal	Presented a negative aspect of school, reference made in book to sexual intercourse between humans and dogs	Parent had conference with principal	IL	1	—
Dog Day Afternoon, P. Mann, 1974	School board	Vulgarity and obscenity	Book removed; insufficient evidence of First Amendment violation; no political motivation involved	Vergennes, VT	10	*Bicknell v. Vergennes High School Board* 475 F. Supp 615 (D. Vt. 1979) 638 F. 2nd 438 (2nd Cir 1980)
The Dog Next Door and Other Stories, T. Clymen, 1969	NOW	—	Censored	Montgomery County, MD	9	

248

Title	Initiator	Objection	Action	State	No.	Notes
Dogs: Selection, Care and Training, W. Boorer, 1971	Parent	Sexual behavior	Book removed	WI	14	—
Don't Play Dead Before You Have To, M. Wojciechowska, 1970	Clergyman	Not indicated	Denied	West	3	—
—	Parent	Language of book made it "trash"	Request denied; student given alternate book to read	West	3	—
—	Parent	Objected to language	Book removed from library	OH	6	—
—	Parent	Poor choice of words (swearing)	Denied	CA	1	—
The Doomsday Gang, K. Platt, 1978		—	—	—	1	—
Dorothea, M. Elwood, 1962		—	—	AZ	8	—
Dorp Dead, J. Cunningham, 1965	Teacher	Would frighten children	Removal		4	—
*The Doubleday Dictionary [sic]	Commissioner of Education	Offensive language; greatly embarrassing situation in class	Not purchased	TX	9	—
The Double Image, H. MacInnes, 1970	Parent	Foul language	Material placed on closed shelf	PA	1	—
Down These Mean Streets, P. Thomas, 1967	See entry for Best Short Stories by Negro Writers			Island Trees, NY	10	See entry for Best Short Stories by Negro Writers
—	Parent	Both language and situation	Book removed from recommended list	Northeast	3	—

continued

249

Title, author, publication date	Objector	Objection	Results	Place	Source, date of objection	Legal Case (if any)
—	Concerned Citizens	Pornography and filth	—	LA	7	—
—	School board		Book withdrawn from junior high libraries; later made available to students by direct loan to parents; Board's action upheld by Court	NY	16	Presidents Council, Dist. 25 v. Community School Bd. No. 25, 457 F.2d 289, 292 (2d Cir.), cert. denied, 409 U.S. 998 (1972).
—	Parent	Words considered obscene	Book removed from classroom use	NY	2	—
—	School librarian, another teacher	Younger students were poring over the hot spots	Book removed from library	IA	2	—
Drawing People for Fun, R. Vernam, 1943			Removed	WI	5	—
The Drug Scene, D.B. Louria, 1968	School librarian	Vulgar and irreverent language	Denied	South	3	—
Drums, J. Boyd, 1925	Parent		Denied	—	4	—
Drums Along the Mohawk, W. Edmonds, 1936	School board members, clergyman	Obscene words: "damn" and "hell"	Removed	Coffee County, TN	9	—
East of Eden, J. Steinbeck, 1952	Parent	Against teachings of church	Removed	AZ	8	—
	See Christy entry		Censored	Anaheim, CA	9	—
	See Black Boy entry					
Edith Jackson, R. Guy, 1978	Superintendent, School officials	Pervasively vulgar	Removed from school library and then returned 3 months later	St. Tammany Parish—LA	11	—

Title/Author	Initiator	Objection	Action taken	State	No.
Electric Kool-Aid Acid Test, T. Wolfe, 1968	Parent	Language, explicit rape scene	Book removed from library	West	3
—	Parent	Concepts of explicit sex and language	Material placed on closed shelf	CA	1
—	Parent	"Graphic" description of gang-rape	Removed from library	WA	1
—	Teacher	There was too much sex and violence	Material removed from library	OK	1
—	Another teacher	Sex perversion	Placed on closed shelf	OH	1
Elmer Gantry, S. Lewis, 1927	Parent	—	—	WI	5
—	Student	Sexual and religious—too controversial if not handled correctly	Particular student given alternative reading material	WA	1
Emotional Problems of Living, O. English, 1955	Concerned Citizens	Pornography and filth	—	LA	7
*Engine House #5.	Parent	A misunderstanding over the fact that the book was a choice, not required reading	Alternative book selected	OH	6
Eric, D. Lund, 1974	Parents	"Objectionable language"	School board voted to retain books	NY	11
"Everyday Life in Ancient Times," National Geographic Magazine, 1951	—	—	Removed	WI	5

continued

Title, author, publication date	Objector	Objection	Results	Place	Source, date of objection	Legal Case (if any)
The Ewings of Dallas, B. Hirshfeld, 1980	Principal	"We'll get rid of this trash" (he threw the book in the trash can)	Material removed from library	TX	1	—
°*Examination Day*, H. Slezer	Concerned Citizens	Pornography and filth	—	LA	7	—
Exodus, L. Uris, 1958	Clergyman	Fornication	—	WI	5	—
	Parent	Unapproved by church, unsuitable	Denied	—	4	—
The Exorcist, W. Blatty, 1971	Parent, Principal	No redeeming qualities in this literature, inappropriate for underclassmen	Book removed from library but was returned to shelf later	Middle West	3	—
	Parent	Crudity of language	Optional book offered	IL	2	—
	Parent	—	Denied	AR	2	—
	Parent	Profanity, explicit sexual discussion	Denied, alternative book used	CA	1	—
	Parent	Too violent and nauseating for young high school girls to handle	Formal objection not filed	IL	1	—
	Parent	Teachers are causing students to have nightmares and predicting the end of the world	Material removed from library	IN	1	—
	Parent	Sexual matter	Material removed from classroom use	NY	1	—

continued

	See entry for A Coney Island of the Mind for Aurora, CO				9, 10	See Coney Island entry
Expectant Fathers, S. Bittman and S. Zalk, 1978	Counselor	"I wouldn't want my 14 year old daughter to see these drawings"	Material removed from library	—	1	—
Experiences in Biology, P.H. Bauer, 1981	—	The publisher omitted the word in order to "avoid the publicity that would surround a controversy," the word omitted was evolution	Adopted for statewide use	NM	11	—
The Explorer, F. Keyes, 1964	Teacher	Unsuitable	Closed shelf	—	4	—
Eye of the Needle, K. Follett, 1978	Parent	"Four etter words and sex"	Removed from library shelf	UT	11	—
Factories in the Field, C. McWilliams, 1939	Concerned Citizens	Pornography and filth	—	LA	7	—
Facts About Sex, S. Gordon, 1969	Principal	Too explicit: pictures, too realistic, "street words is used."	Book was torn up by superintendent	Middle West	3	—
Facts of Life and Love, for Teenagers, E.M. Duvall, 1950	Concerned Citizens	Pornography and filth	—	LA	7	—
	Parent	Too explicit	Removed	AZ	8	—
The Facts of Love: Living, Loving and Growing, A. Comfort, 1979	Superintendent	Content too explicit for children in this school	Material placed on closed shelf	MN	1	—
Fahrenheit 451, R. Bradbury, 1969	—	Use of phrase "queer-duck"	Denied; not required for the student's reading	—	1	—

253

Title, author, publication date	Objector	Objection	Results	Place	Source, date of objection	Legal Case (if any)
Fail-safe, E. Burdick and J. Wheeler, 1962	Librarian	Undermine America's confidence in their defense system	—	WI	5	—
Failures	Gablers	See Jenkinson		TX	9	—
The Family, E. Sanders, 1972	Parent	Language used, "would you like to see your 13-year-old daughter reading this?"	Board of Education has formed a censorship committee and code	NY	2	—
Fandango Rock, J. Masters, 1959	Student, Clergyman	Obscene passage, immoral	Removed until student graduated	WI	5	—
A Farewell to Arms, E. Hemingway, 1929	Teacher	—	—	WI	5	—
	Parent	Glorifies unmarried sex	Remained	AZ	8	—
	Parent, Principal	Procreation without marriage; desertion of duty; profanity; negative portrayal of military personnel	Book removed from classroom use and recommended list	OH	2	—
	Parent	—	—	OH	1	—
The Far Side of Home, M. Davis, 1963	Parent	Reference to sex	Removal	—	4	—
The Feather Merchants, M. Shulman, 1944	Teacher	Too much sex	Removal	—	4	—
The Female Eunuch, G. Greer, 1970	Parent, Clergyman, English dept. chairman	Unsuitable in content and expression to high school age	Voluntarily eliminated by the teacher	West	3	—

Title	Initiator	Objection	Action	State	No.
Feminine Plural: Stories by Women about Growing Up, S. Spinner, ed., 1972	Principal	See Jenkinson		Warsaw, IN	9
The Fiction of Experience, M. Lesser and J. Morris, 1962	Another teacher	—	Ten books were replaced with material more in keeping with the students' abilities	OH	2
A Field of Broken Stones. L. Naeve, 1950	Concerned Citizens	Pornography and filth	—	LA	7
The Final Diagnosis, A. Hailey, 1959	Parent	Sex passages	Closed shelf	—	4
Final Score, W. Beck, 1944	Librarian	—	Available	WI	5
The Fire Next Time, J. Baldwin, 1963	Principal	Too controversial	Removal	—	4
Firestarter, S. King, 1980	Local citizens	They are "anti-Christian and demonic"	Restrict King's books to high school students	Gillette High School, WY	11
*First Blood	Superintendent, Member of Board of Education	Objectionable material, language, and incidents in the book	Book removed from recommended list	OH	6
My First Love and Other Disasters, F. Pascal, 1979	Parent	Not appropriate material for high school students	Material removed from classroom use	—	1
The First People in the World, G. Ames and R. Wyler, 1958	Parent	Dealt more with theory of evolution than divine creation	Removal	—	4
The First Sip of Wine, J.G. Pattison, 1960	Student	Outspoken about extramarital sex		WI	5

continued

255

Title, author, publication date	Objector	Objection	Results	Place	Source, date of objection	Legal Case (if any)
Five Smooth Stones, A. Fairbairn, 1966	Parent	Parent told daughter that the picture on the front was vulgar (Black-white couple)	Alternate selection was given to student	IL	2	—
The Fixer, B. Malamud, 1966	See entry for *Best Short Stories by Negro Writers*			Island Trees, NY	9, 10	See entry for *Best Short Stories by Negro Writers*
—	Member of Board of Education, English Supervisor, Parent	Vivid grossness of scenes of immature juniors and seniors, the end of chapter 8, "she stood naked"	Denied, book allowed to be used by certain teachers	Middle West	3	—
—	Parent	Language (four letter words)	Book removed from classroom use and child given alternate selection	PA	2	—
—	Concerned Citizens	Against pornography and filth	—	LA	7	—
Flowers for Algernon, D. Keyes, 1970	Another teacher	Subject matter related to sex	Book removed from classroom	PA	2	—
—	Parent	Included profanity and explicit sex acts.	Book removed from classroom	IN	2	—
—	Parent	Sexually oriented	Book removed from classroom	PA	2	—
—	Parent	The book was dirty—parent lifted certain sections, lines, words out of context and never did read the book.	Request denied	MO	2	—

Book / Author	Initiator	Objection	Disposition	State	Emporium, PA
Cameron County School District					9
	Parent	Sex presented in a distorted view	Removed from library		1
	Parent				1
For All the Wrong Reasons, J. Neufeld, 1982		Unsuitability	Book retained	WY	12
	Parent	Pages with sexual mention—bad words	Denied	NY	11
	Parent, Superintendent	The first twenty pages are terrible, otherwise the book is O.K.	Material placed on closed shelf	AR	1
	Member of Board of Education	Obscenities, profanity	Book placed on closed shelf	OH	6
				NY	12
Forever, J. Blume, 1975	Principal	Obscene language	Book removed from library	TN	2
		Trash	See Jenkinson		9
	Another teacher, English Dept. Chairman, Principal	Sexual subject treated or presented in objectionable manner	Placed on closed shelf	PA	1
	Parent	Explicit sexual language	Placed on closed shelf	IL	1
	Parent	Represented secular humanism	Denied	MO	1
	Library and A. V. Director	Explicit sex—low readability level—encourage sexual relations in young people	Material removed from library	MI	1

continued

257

Title, author, publication date	Objector	Objection	Results	Place	Source, date of objection	Legal Case (if any)
—	Principal	He asked to see the book because of a news item he read about some controversy over it and never returned the book	Material removed from library	IN	1	—
—	Parent	Sex scenes	Material removed from library	—	1	—
—	Parent	Dirty book, local bookstore did not stock it because it was unfit for young people to read	Material removed from classroom use	IL	1	—
—	Parent	Sex	Material removed from library	MI	1	—
—	Informed Parent Group	Sexual matter	No specific action requested	NY	1	—
—	Parent	Too sexually explicit	Denied	OH	1	—
—	School librarian	Sexual content not suitable for 12 year olds	Removed from library	OK	1	—
—	Another teacher	No material on abortion should be available	Denied	NY	1	—
—	Student, Teacher	Treatment of sexual activity among teens in a way which did not reflect the mores of the community	Book removed from recommended list, library, and classroom use	OH	6	—

Title	Initiator	Objection	Action taken	State/Location	No.
—	Parent	—	Banned book	Green Bay, WI Middle School	11
The Fortunes and Misfortunes of the Famous Moll Flanders, D. Defoe, 1722	Parent, Clergyman	"Dirty book," word "whore"	Denied	—	4
*Forty-Four Caliber, J. Breslin and D. Schaap	Student	The language and the situations portrayed	The book disappeared from the shelf and has not been replaced	KS	1
For Whom the Bell Tolls, E. Hemingway, 1940	Townspeople	—	Principal removed from library; probably will return after controversy dies down	WI	5
—	Student	"Dirty book"	Denied	—	4
—	—	Intimate subjects, relationships between sexes	—	TN	13
—	—	—	—	NY	1
The Fountainhead, A. Rand, 1943	Teacher	—	—	WI	5
—	Parent	Sex description	Continued reading it	West	3
Franny and Zooey, Salinger, J.D. 1961	Parent (1)	Characters too concerned with sex.	Request denied	—	4
—	Principal	Too sophisticated, too frank or revealing.	Removal	—	4
—	Parent	Book uses some objectionable language and is an affront to God	Book put back on shelf, nothing else was said	OH	2

continued

Title, author, publication date	Objector	Objection	Results	Place	Source, date of objection	Legal Case (if any)
Friends, P. Dunn, 1971						—
Fundamentals of English	Parent	Foreword, introduction, poorly written, the parent wanted "back to traditional"	—	—	1	—
Future Shock, A. Toffler, 1970	Parent		—	—	1	—
The Game Players of Titan, P.K. Dick, 1976	Parent		—	PA	1	—
The Gang That Couldn't Shoot Straight, J. Breslin, 1969	Another teacher		Book removed from classroom use	KY	2	—
	Parent	Language	Book removed: under consideration by principal	WI	14	—
Gateway, F. Pohl, 1977	Parent, Local organization	Obscene language, excessive violence	Denied	MD	1	—
Gathering of Ghetto Writers: Irish, Italian, Jewish, Black and Puerto Rican, W.G. Miller, 1972	Superintendent	Language and situations in various situations	Book removed from classroom use	AR	2	—
Gaudy Place, W. Talsman	Parent	Profane language	Removed from library	NC	1	—
Gay Mystique: The Myth and Reality of Male Homosexuality, P. Fisher, 1972	Member of Board of Education	Un-American part of Communist conspiracy "didn't show both sides"	Denied, removed by board, went to court and still waiting		1	—

Title	Initiator	Objection	Action	State	No.	
Gay: What You Should Know About Homosexuality, M. Hunt, 1977	Parent	"Homosexuality is not in our school so why do we have to have a book like that?"	—	IA	1	—
The Genetic Code, I. Asimov, 1962	Parent	"Genetic projection and genetic preorientation is an affront to my religious beliefs"	New selection allowed to student	MA	2	—
The Geranium on the Window-sill Just Died, but Teacher You Went Right On, A. Cullum, 1971	Parent	—	—	PA	1	—
Getting Your Own Way: A Guide to Growing up Assertively, M. Mihaly, 1979	Parent	"Book . . . written by a political scientist drastically espouses the humanist thinking [which] leads to the breaking up of families and worship of self"	Denied	MO	1	—
Ghost Fox, J. Houston, 1976	Parent	Objection to passage in book, "They slept together in their leanto with the warm fire before them"	—	OH	1	—
Ghosts, H. Ibsen, 1890	Parent	Deals with aberrant sex	Book removed from classroom list	NJ	2	—
Gidget, F. Kohner, 1957	Parent	Rough language	Removal	—	4	—
*Ginn 360 Reading Series	Parent	The dialect was demeaning to blacks	Still in use	CT	11	—

continued

261

Title, author, publication date	Objector	Objection	Results	Place	Source, date of objection	Legal Case (if any)
A Girl Named Sooner, S. Clauser, 1972	Parent	Profanity and sex-incest	Material placed on closed shelf	WI	1	—
Girls and Sex, W. Pomeroy, 1969	Concerned Citizens	Pornography and filth	—	LA	7	—
—	Student	Information not suitable for high school girls	Denied	FL	1	—
—	Principal	—	Placed on closed shelf	OK	1	—
The Girls of Huntington House, B. Elfman, 1972	Parent	Profanity	Denied	MN	2	—
Give Me One Good Reason, N. Klein, 1973	Parent	"Immorality, promiscuity, and profanity"	Refused to ban the book	CO	11	—
The Glass Inferno, T. Scortia and F. Robinson, 1974	Principal	—	Material placed on closed shelf	IN	1	—
Glory Road, R. Heinlein, 1963	Parent	Too much discussion of sex, unsuitable language	Removal	—	4	—
Go Ask Alice, Anonymous, 1971	See entry for Best Short Stories by Negro Writers			Island Trees, NY	10	See entry for Best Short Stories by Negro Writers
—	See The Bell Jar entry			Warsaw, IN	9, 10	See The Bell Jar entry
—	Parent	A filthy book, makes drugs sound exciting	Parents tore up book but hard copy remains on the shelf	Midwest	3	—

Complainant	Reason	Action	State	No.
Concerned Citizens	Pornography and filth	—	LA	7
Another teacher	Language used, too many curse words	No action pressed	GA	2
Parent	Filthy language	Book removed from library	MI	2
School board and parents	"a true story and very shocking—language not fit for anyone, let alone children—should be banned and destroyed."	Destroyed	Red Cross, PA	9
			—	
Student	Encourages drug use, sex	Denied	WA	1
Parent	Unsuitable language	Material placed on closed shelf	PA	1
Parent	—	Material removed from library	WI	1
Parent	Language	Denied	WI	1
Superintendent	Surrounding school corporation had "campaign" by parents and wide media coverage on, "Go Ask Alice"	Material removed from library	IN	1
Parent	Dirty language, teaching kids to use drugs	Material placed on closed shelf	VA	1
Parent	Bad language	—	MI	1
School librarian	—	Let children read with parent consent	MI	1

continued

Title, author, publication date	Objector	Objection	Results	Place	Source, date of objection	Legal Case (if any)
—	Parent	Language, drugs, sex	Denied	MD	1	—
—	Parent	Obscene language	Removed from library	TX	1	—
—	Parent, Another teacher	Filthy language	Removed from classroom use	—	1	—
—	Parent	Concern over language	Denied—no real request, just concern	—	1	—
—	Parent	"The obscene language," the complainant indicated the theme was "drugs, sex, and improper language"	Denied	—	1	—
—	Parent	Objectionable language	Denied	—	1	—
—	Parent	Sexual/drug information in book	Denied	—	1	—
—	—	Sisters were both criticized for foul language and immoral thoughts	Denied	—	1	—
—	Parent	Filthy language and promotion of use of drugs	Material removed from library	IN	1	—
—	Parent	Sexual references, objectionable language	Material removed from library	TX	1	—
—	Parent	Too explicit in terms of details and events	Material placed on closed shelf	AR	1	—

Parent	Language vulgar and some passages suggestive to sex	Denied	IN	1	—
Parent	Language and events described	Material placed on closed shelf	IN	1	—
Parent	Use of four letter words, sex, and drugs	Material removed from recommended list	FL	1	—
Parent	Felt subject matter and language was too mature for her 7th-grade daughter, questioned reasons for inclusion in the school's collection	Another outside reading book was selected by student and approved by teacher	IN	1	—
Parent	Vocabulary in book	Material removed from library	NC	1	—
Parent	The terrible language	Material placed on closed shelf	MS	1	—
Clergyman	—	—	—	1	—
Parent	Objectionable language	Denied	IN	1	—
Parent	Foul language and immoral thoughts	Denied	IA	1	—
Superintendent	"This book is not fit for anyone to read, child or adult," obscene language	Removed from library	—	1	—
Parent	"Filthy and immoral book"	Denied	—	1	—

continued

Title, author, publication date	Objector	Objection	Results	Place	Source, date of objection	Legal Case (if any)
—	Parent	Reference to and description of sex act	Denied	—	1	—
—	Principal	Language and topic	Material removed from library	—	1	—
—	Student	Language was too strong and included sexual scenes	Denied	—	1	—
—	Parent	Language	Denied	—	1	—
—	Parent	Too adult subject matter, reference to sex	Material placed on closed shelf	—	1	—
—	—		—	—	1	—
—	—		—	—	12	—
—	Parents	Considered "profane, sexually objectionable"	Removed from library and placed in a restricted area	MS	11	—
—	—		Removed	Adams, WI	9	—
—	—		Removed	Trenton, WI	9	—
—	Parents	"Profanity and sexual references"	School board voted to retain the book	NJ	11	—
—	Parent	Language	School board voted to retain the book	MN	11	—
—	Parents		Placed on "limited access shelves" available only with teacher or parental permission.	KS	11	—

Title/Author	Initiator	Reason	Action	Location	No.	Notes
—	Parent	Content (encourages drug use), language obscene	—	—	6	—
—	Parent	Language too foul; material too mature for jr. high students	—	—	6	—
—	Principal	Not suitable reading. Bad influence on students	—	—	6	—
God Bless You, Mr. Rosewater, K. Vonnegut, 1965	See Cat's Cradle entry	Drugs, abortion	—	—	6	See Cat's Cradle entry
—	See Black Boy		Removed by board; restored by Court	Island Trees, NY	10, 16	
—	Parent, Principal	Inappropriate language	—	NH	10	
—	—		Book removed from classroom use	NY	2	
The Godfather, M. Puzo, 1969	English Dept. Chairman	Sexual scenes and the violence, language	—	West	10	
—	Parent	Vulgarity—lack of Christian sentiment	New choice selections	MO	3	
God's Little Acre, E. Caldwell, 1933	Principal	Language too "raw"	Removed	—	4	
The Golden Book of the Mysterious, J. Watson and S. Schaneles, 1976	Local church	Witchcraft and occult content that is deemed "uneducational"	Book kept	Moscow, ID	11	

continued

Title, author, publication date	Objector	Objection	Results	Place	Source, date of objection	Legal Case (if any)
Gone with the Wind, M. Mitchell, 1936	Clergyman, Parent	Immorality of Scarlett	—	—	5	—
—	Teacher	Could be misunderstood	Closed shelf	—	4	—
—	Alderman	"Racism" and language	—	Waukegan, IL	11	—
The Good Earth, P. Buck, 1944	Parent	Content—"sex lives of old men" and killing of children	Denied	NY	2	—
—	Parent	Sexual objection—concubines and prostitutes	—	WA	1	—
Goodbye, Columbus, P. Roth, 1959	Parent, Clergyman	Language, sexual imagery	Book removed from classroom use	NE	2	—
—	Parent	Language and sex	Material removed from library	WI	1	—
Good Morning, Miss Dove, F. G. Patton, 1954	Parent, who was a Birch society member	Communist propaganda	Remained	AZ	8	—
Go Tell It On The Mountain, J. Baldwin, 1952	Parent, Student	It was "nigger" literature	Allowed to substitute another book	North	3	—
—	—	To fill a child's mind with a trashy idea of sex, cause him to loose [*sic*] confidence in ministers and churches	—	TN	13	—
—	Clergyman	Immoral	Denied	IL	2	—

Title	Initiator	Objection	Action	Location	No.	
The Graduate, C. Webb, 1964	Parents	Subject matter, objections to sexual overtones, unsuitable for impressionable sophomores	Removed from classroom use	—	2	—
Grapes of Wrath, J. Steinbeck, 1939	Parent, Librarian	Immoral and obscene	Refuses to order	—	5	—
	—	Charges of obscenity and political ideas	Withdrawn from 4 libraries	Amarillo, TX	17	—
	Parent	Vulgarity	—	AZ	8	—
	Parents	Objectionable language and sexual activity, against church beliefs	Children of objecting parents given another title and book removed from classroom use	South	3	—
	Parent, Student	Questioned the selection, bad language, depressing story	Book removed from recommended list.	IN	2	—
	Parent	Use of profane language	Denied	TX	1	—
	Student	Language	Student read her choice from several chosen by the teacher of literary value	ME	1	—
	Parent	Bad language	Denied	IN	1	—
	Parent	Profanity	Denied	OR	1	—
	Parent	Profanity	Students removed from class using book	CA	1	—
	Parent	The parent was offended by the language	The teacher and librarian assigned another book of equal value	CA	1	—

continued

Title, author, publication date	Objector	Objection	Results	Place	Source, date of objection	Legal Case (if any)
—	Clergyman		Student was given another book to read	OH	6	—
—	Parent	Religious reasons	The daughter, in the class, was given an alternate selection to read for course credit	OH	6	—
—	Parent	Demeaning to Southerners	Book removed from classroom use	OH	6	—
—	Parent	Language was offensive	Student given option to read another book	OH	6	—
—	Parent	Objectionable language sexual activity; against church beliefs	Children of objecting parents given another title	Midwest	3	—
—	Parent	Curse words & sordidness	Book removed from classroom use and recommended list	South	3	—
—	Parent	Pornography	Request denied	South	3	—
—	Parent	Language, vividness of some scenes	Other title given to student to read	Northeast	3	—
—	Parent	Questioned the selection	Objection dropped	IN	2	—
—	Parent	Bad language, depressing story	Request denied	CA	2	—
—	Parent	Obscene language	The student was allowed to read another book	TX	2	—
—	Parent	Parent objected to language used in book—cursing, etc.	Book removed from recommended list	LA	2	—

—	Student	"Offensive language"	Student read alternate selection	NC	2	—
—	Parent	Language of some characters	I asked the parent to read the book and compare it with others the child reads—never heard any more from parent	UT	2	—
—	Parent	Mockery of religion concerning fornication after a revival meeting—profanity	Request denied	MN	2	—
—	Student	Said the book was full of filth. Also cuts down the ministry in the character of Jim Casey	Student was assigned different novel. Later decided to read original novel	WI	2	—
The Gray Captain, J. Wheelwright, 1954	Teacher	Swearing	Remained	NY	12	—
—		—	—	AZ	8	—
Grease (The Play), R. DeChristoforo, 1978	Parent	Filthy language	The materials were commented on by the parents	—	1	—
—		—	—		1	—
Great Expectations, C. Dickens	Parent	Theme of book was objectionable	Student was given the option of reading another book mutually agreed upon by parent and teacher	—	1	—

continued

Title, author, publication date	Objector	Objection	Results	Place	Source, date of objection	Legal Case (if any)
The Great Gatsby, S. Fitzgerald, 1925	Parent, Student	Parent objected to the "illicit love affair" which is part of the central theme of the book	Student was offered alternate reading choice	CA	2	—
°*Great Themes in Literature: Crime and Criminals*	Parent	Too violent and makes heroes out of criminals	Materials removed from classroom use	IL	1	—
The Great Train Robbery, M. Crichton, 1974	Parent	Bad language in book	Denied	OR	1	—
Great Trials: Pro and Con, Current Affairs, 1977	Member of Board of Education	Un-American, part of Communist conspiracy—"didn't show both sides"	Denied, removed by board, went to court, still waiting	—	1	—
Great Unsolved Mysteries, J. Durvis, 1978	Local minister	Inappropriate biblical references	Remained	FL	11	—
Greeks, Gods, and Heroes, R. Graves, 1967	Parent	Language too graphic	Removed from library	—	1	—
The Greengage Summer, R. Godden, 1958	Student	"People in picture was [sic] not decently dressed"	—	WA	1	—
Grendel, J. Gardner, 1971	—	—	Challenged	Middletown, MD	9	—
The Growing Human Family, M. Masani, 1951	Concerned Citizens	Pornography and filth	—	LA	7	—

Growing Up Absurd—Problems of Youth in the Organized System, P. Goodman, 1960	Concerned Citizens	Pornography and filth	—	LA	7	—
Growing (Up) at Thirty-seven, J. Rubin, 1976	Parent	Inappropriate for 9th-grade reading	Material placed on closed shelf	VA	1	—
Growing Up Female in America, E. Merriam, 1971	School board	—	Removed	WY	9	—
—	See The Bell Jar entry	—	—	Warsaw, IN	9, 10	See The Bell Jar entry
Growing Up Puerto Rican, P. Cooper, ed., 1972	Concerned Citizens	—	—	MA	9	—
Growing up with Sex, R. Hettlinger, 1970	—	Pornography and filth	—	LA	7	—
Hamlet, W. Shakespeare	—	—	—	Anaheim, CA	9	—
A Handful of Dust, E. Waugh, 1945	—	Risk to student's morality	—	—	5	—
The Hangman, P. Geddes, 1977	Member of the Board of Education	Not appropriate for age level of students (9–12)	Denied	MA	1	—
Happy Endings Are All Alike, S. Scoppettone, 1978	School librarian, Counselor	"Presents homosexuality as an acceptable alternative to heterosexual friendship"	Material placed on closed shelf	TX	1	—
—	—	The lesbian acts in the book	—	MS	1	—

continued

Title, author, publication date	Objector	Objection	Results	Place	Source, date of objection	Legal Case (if any)
Hard Feelings, D. Bredes, 1977	School librarian	Subject matter inappropriately presented	Material removed from library	PA	1	—
—	Parent	Explicit sexual descriptions, language	Parent dropped complaint when she was asked to put it in writing	SD	1	—
—	Parent	Language, sexuality—oral, not written	Denied	CA	1	—
The Hard Life of a Teenager, J. Collier, 1972	—	—	—	KS	1	—
Harry and Tonto, J. Greenfield and P. Mazursky, 1974	—	"Language and sexual descriptions but most strongly (objections) to references to God"	Material placed on closed shelf	TX	1	—
Hatter Fox, M. Harris, 1973	Parent, Principal	Objectionable language, great violence and too much sex	Teacher agreed not to use book in future as novel for study	—	1	—
Haunted Houses, R. Winer and N. Osborn, 1979	Library aide	It was not a book children should read, they could not understand what they have not experienced	Material placed on closed shelf	IN	1	—
Have Jumpshot, Will Travel: a novel, C. Rosen, 1975	School board	—	Removed	—	9	—
Hawaii, J. Michener, 1959	Teacher, Administrator	Unsuitable for general use	—	WI	5	—
—	Parents	Immorality	Remained	—	8	—

Title/Author	Initiator	Objection	Action taken	Location	No.	Notes
Headman, K. Platt	Parent	Vulgar language—cursing, "Man all them fucking trees, whatever pisses you off," similar language throughout	Librarian explained to teacher that street language was the nature of the book	SC	1	—
—	Parent	Obscene language	Material removed from library	SD	1	—
—	Parent	The parent objected to the language in the book	Removed from library	CT	1	—
—	Parents	Considered "profane, sexually objectionable"	Placed in a restricted area	MS	11	—
The Heart Is a Lonely Hunter, C. McCullers, 1940	Parent	Not a classic—not enough literary merit	Denied	IL	2	—
Helicopters and Gingerbread, T. Clymer and others, 1969	Gablers	—	—	—	9	—
Hello, Good-bye, L. Klamkin, 1973	Parent	Bad language	Book placed on closed shelf	OH	6	—
A Hero Ain't Nothin' but a Sandwich, A. Childress, 1973	See entry for *Best Short Stories by Negro Writers*	See entry *Best Short Stories by Negro Writers*		Island Trees, NY	10	See entry for *Best Short Stories by Negro Writers*
—	President of school board	Objectionable	Censored	Savannah, GA	9	—
—	Parent	Objected to use of "street language"	Material placed on closed shelf	OK	1	—
—	Parent	Used abusive language	Material placed on closed shelf	AL	1	—

continued

Title, author, publication date	Objector	Objection	Results	Place	Source, date of objection	Legal Case (if any)
—	Parent	Questioned the language and intent	Removed from the junior high library	WI	1	—
—	Parent	Language and situation	Students whose parents objected were given other books to read	NY	1	—
—	Student	Objectional language	Material placed on closed shelf	—	1	—
—	—	Language	—	IA	1	—
—	Parent	Language	Removed from library	MI	1	—
—	Parent	Language and sexual descriptions but most strongly (objections) to references to God	Material placed on closed shelf	TX	1	—
Hero/Anti-Hero, R. Rollin, ed., 1973	Parent	The entire book is obscene	Denied	PA	2	—
*The Heroship	—	—	—	VA	9	—
Hey Dollface, D. Hautzig, 1978	Parent	Felt homosexuality dealt with too explicitly	Denied	ME	1	—
H is for Heroin, D. Hubbard, 1952	Concerned Citizens	Pornography and filth	—	LA	7	—
Any book, A. Hitchcock	Parent	Religious	—	—	1	—
Holt, Rinehart and Winston Reading Series	Citizens Organized for Better Schools	Promotes secular humanism and teaches values contrary to religious beliefs	—	TN	11	—

276

Title	Initiator	Reason	Action	State	No.	
The Homosexual Matrix, C.A. Tripp, 1975	—	—		PA	1	—
The Horse Dealer's Daughter, D. Lawrence, 1922	Parent on school board	Book used in sophomore literature had one story which was immoral	Book removed from classroom use	IL	2	—
The House with a Clock in its Walls, J. Bellairs, 1973	Parent	It could encourage a student's interest in the occult	Denied	WI	1	—
How to Cast a Love Spell, P. Bonewits	Concerned Citizens	Pornography and filth	—	LA	7	—
How to Select, Train and Breed Your Dog, L.F. Whitney, 1969	Parent	Considered the book factually inaccurate	Denied	WA	1	—
Hughes, Langston: Works of	J. Evetts Haley	Hughes had communist front connections; was a "willing tool of this international conspiracy to destroy us"	Hughes' name and works would have to be deleted from books	TX	17	
The Human Body, J. Noel, 1973	Parent	Sexual behavior	Restricted access: censorship committee	—	14	—
Human Comedy, W. Saroyan, 1943	Principal		Placed on closed shelf	OK	1	—
		—	—	CA	5	
The Humanities in Three Cities, E. Fenton, 1969–75		—	No action taken yet	TX	2	—
Human Reproduction, Health and Hygiene, T. Knepp, 1967		—	Placed on reserve	—	5	—

continued

Title, author, publication date	Objector	Objection	Results	Place	Source, date of objection	Legal Case (if any)
Human Sexuality, E. S. Morrison, 1973	Parent	Too graphic	Pending	—	1	—
Hunchback of Notre Dame, V. Hugo, 1941	Teacher	—		—	5	—
Hurry, Sundown, K.B. Gilden, 1964	Teacher	Smut	Remained	TX	8	—
	School librarian	One scene described in graphic detail	Book removed from library	—	2	—
I Am A Man: Ode to Martin Luther King, Jr., E. Merriam, 1971	Florida Action Committee on Education	"Martin Luther King Jr. was a Communist who encouraged revolution and incited people to riot"	Denied—dropped case	FL	1	—
I Can't Wait Until Tomorrow: Cause I Get Better-looking Every Day, J. Namath, 1969	Principal, Teacher	Use of foul language		Southwest	3	—
I Hate to Talk About Your Mother: a novel, H. Jones, 1980	Parent	Objected to language used in the book and use of language in explaining sexual feelings and actions	Placed on closed shelf	WI	1	—
	Teacher	Objected to the gutter language and an explicit sex incident in the book	Denied	NY	1	—

—	School librarian	Language, not a very good book	Material removed from library	OH	1	—
I Know Why the Caged Bird Sings, M. Angelou, 1969	Parent	Sections not suitable for young people to read	Book placed on closed shelf	West	3	—
—	—	A form of pornography, disturbing mind implants	—	TN	13	—
—	Parent, Another teacher	Sex—unfit for high school use, graphic description of young girl raped by her stepfather and of one other sexual encounter	Book not assigned to student	ME	2	—
—	Parent	The language and base way of telling the story are "slurs" to the black race	Material removed from library	FL	1	—
—	Parent	Sex and obscene language	—	TX	1	—
—	Parent, Student	Objected to realism	Denied	NC	1	—
—	Parent	Parent called to tell the superintendent that there was a waiting list to read this book because of the description of rape	Didn't remove book because it is a beautiful book		1	—
If Beale Street Could Talk, J. Baldwin, 1974	Student	"This is the filthiest book I've ever read"	Material removed from library		1	—

continued

Title, author, publication date	Objector	Objection	Results	Place	Source, date of objection	Legal Case (if any)
—	Parent	Language in book—This was 3 years ago	Material removed from classroom use	OH	1	—
—	Parent	Sex descriptions too advanced for 7th graders	Placed on closed shelves	WI	1	—
—	Parent, Student	Explicit sexual events	Book removed from classroom use	—	1	—
If I Love You, Am I Trapped Forever?, M. Kerr, 1973	English Dept. Chairman	—	—	—	1	—
I'll Get There, It Better Be Worth the Trip, J. Donovan, 1969	Parent	—	—	NM	2	—
—	Parents	"Parents prone to censor books do not think their children should be reading" this book	—	—	9	—
I'm Really Dragged But Nothing Gets Me Down, N. Hentoff, 1968	Grandparent	Foul language, range of subject matter	Book placed on closed shelf	Middle West	3	—
Images of Women in Literature, M. Ferguson, 1977	Principal	None—questioned reordering	—	CA	2	—
In Cold Blood, T. Capote, 1965	Parent	Language—too "modern", ungraded structure	Denied	IL	2	—

Title/Author	Complainant	Objection	Action	State		
—	School board	—	—	WI	9	—
I Never Loved Your Mind, P. Zindel, 1970	Student	Objected to some of the vulgarity	Student offered substitute book	WI	2	—
—	Parent	Swearing, sex	Material placed on closed shelf	MI	1	—
Inherit the Wind, J. Lawrence, 1957	Parent	Theory of evolution	Denied	Middle West	3	—
—	Parent	Theme of book was objectionable	Student was given the option of reading another book mutually agreed upon by teacher and parent	—	1	—
In Love, G. Parks, 1971	Principal	There is a phrase that can be misinterpreted by children	—	IN	1	—
Inside: Prison American Style, R. Minton Jr., ed., 1971	Concerned Citizens	Against pornography and filth	—	LA	7	—
*Interaction, H. Mifflin	—	—	Removed	Kanawha County, WV	9	—
In the Country of Ourselves, N. Hentoff, 1971	School librarian	"Dwells overmuch on masturbation and sexual fantasies for no apparent socially redeemable purpose"	Material placed on closed shelf	TX	1	—
In the Night Kitchen, M. Sendak, 1970	Another teacher	—	Book placed on closed shelf	IN	2	—
—	—	—	—	MO	9	—

continued

281

Title, author, publication date	Objector	Objection	Results	Place	Source, date of objection	Legal Case (if any)
—	Teacher	Nudity	Material removed from library, but only temporarily	OR	1	—
—	Parent	Not appropriate for grade level—shows young boy's penis	Material removed from library	WA	1	—
Invasion Diary, R. Tregaskis, 1944	Parents	Language	—	—	5	—
Invisible Man, R. Ellison, 1952	Student, Parent	Scene where Negro boys put on a boxing show for whites; scene where old Negro rapes his daughter, vulgarity of incidents	—	Middle West	3	—
In Watermelon Sugar, R. Brautigan, 1968	—	—	Removed	PA	9	—
—	—	—	—	Anderson, CA	9	—
I, Pig, J. Muller, 1971	Parent	"Foul" language	Denied	IL	1	—
—	School librarian	Vulgar language	Placed on closed shelf	—	1	—
Is There Life After Graduation, Henry Birnbaum?, C. Balducci, 1971	Parent	Book's language was objectionable	Book removed from library	TX	2	—
I, Trissy, N. Mazer, 1971	Parent	Language	Complaint dropped	—	14	—
It's O.K. If You Don't Love Me, N. Klein, 1977	Parent	Sexually explicit	Parent refused to file a formal complaint	SC	1	—

Title	Initiator	Reason	Action	Place	No.	
	Teacher	—	—	MN	1	—
	Parent	—	Material placed on closed shelf	TX	1	—
	Parent	Sexual descriptions in the book	Temporarily removed from library	OH	1	—
	Parent	Language, explicit sexual scenes	Material removed from library	CA	1	—
	Parent	Use of the word "fuck"	Material placed on closed shelf	VA	1	—
	Parent	The word "fuck" used several times; pre-marital [sic] sex which reader felt would lead to "teenage pregnancy and VD"	Material removed from library temporarily until due process is complete	OK	1	—
	Teacher	Unnecessary to risk the trust of the community	Removed from paper back stands	—	1	—
	Parent	Book has sexual passages	Removed from library	WA	11	—
I was a Black Panther, as told to Chuck Moore, W. Stone, 1970	Parent	Subject matter	Temporarily removed from library	VA	1	—
*Jack and the Beanstalk		—	—	Kanawha County, WV	9	—
Jack the Bear, D. McCall, 1974	Concerned Parents	—	Removed	Monticello, IA	9	—
	Parent	—	—	AL	1	—

continued

Title, author, publication date	Objector	Objection	Results	Place	Source, date of objection	Legal Case (if any)
Jambeaux, L. Gonzales, 1979	Parent	Too many "fucks" in it, just the word not the act	Placed on closed shelf	OR	1	—
°James Bond Omnibus, I. Fleming	Parent	Influence on young children	Not sold	—	4	—
J. B., A. MacLeish, 1957	Parent	Sacrilegious	Remained	—	8	—
Jaws, P. Benchley, 1974	Parent, Clergyman	Explicit details about sex	Book removed from recommended list	AL	2	—
—	Antioch School District	—	Removed	Gardner, KS	9	—
—	Parent	Sexual content	Material removed from recommended list and put on closed shelf	CA	1	—
—	Parent	Use of abusive language, sex or violence	Didn't do anything	—	1	—
Jesus Christ Superstar, A.L. Webber, 1971	Parent	Sacrilegious	—	—	1	—
Johnny Got His Gun, D. Trumbo, 1959	Parents	Too much profanity, too gruesome details of a human being, unpatriotic and anti-American, sexual encounter passages	Book removed from classroom use	MI	2	—
—	Parent	Anti-war	Denied	WI	1	—
—	Parent	Too much profanity—would tolerate all but "mother fucker"	Book removed from classroom use	WI	2	—

	Initiator	Objection	Action	State	No.	
—	Parent	Too gruesome details of a human being. Brother was a war veteran in hospital. Too emotionally close to daughter	Another selection required	MI	2	—
—	Parent	Unpatriotic and anti-American	Student was allowed to read another book	TX	2	—
—	Parent	Objection was to the description of the main character after he had been maimed in the war; also the language	Request denied	CO	2	—
—	Parent	Parent objected to several passages describing sexual encounters	Request denied	CA	2	—
—	Parent	Vulgarity of incidents and language	Book removed from classroom use	Midwest	3	—
—	Clergyman	It is too violent	Denied	VT	1	—
—	Parent	"Heard" it was a violent book	Alternative selection provided	IL	1	—
Journey to Ixtlan, C. Castaneda, 1972	Concerned Citizens	Pornography and filth		LA	7	—
Joy in the Morning, B. Smith, 1963	School Librarian	Sexual references	Book removed from library	OK	2	—
Joy of Photography, Addison-Wesley Pub. Co., 1979			—		1	

continued

Title, author, publication date	Objector	Objection	Results	Place	Source, date of objection	Legal Case (if any)
The Joy of Sex, A. Comfort, 1972	Librarian	Inappropriateness for high school students	Removed	NY	11	—
Judas, I. Mossinsohn, 1963	Superintendent	Sex, language	Removed	—	8	—
Jude the Obscure, T. Hardy, 1923	Librarian	—	Available	—	5	—
The Jump Rope Jingles, E. V. Worstell, 1961	Concerned Citizens	Pornography and filth	—	LA	7	—
Junior Miss, S. Benson, 1941	Parent	Father swore in story	Temporary removal	—	4	—
Juvenile Delinquency; Development, Treatment, Control, R. Caver, 1969	Students	Sex and immoral references, not suitable for students	Removal	—	5	—
Kaddish and Other Poems, 1958–1960, A. Ginsberg	Board of Education	See *A Coney Island of the Mind* entry	See *A Coney Island of the Mind* entry	Aurora, CO	9, 10	See *Coney Island* entry
The Key to Rebecca, K. Follett, 1980	Another teacher	Felt scenes were too explicit	Material was re-evaluated	MI	1	—
A Kid Nobody Wants, R. Kost, 1961	Teacher	Described seduction of teacher by one of her students	Removal	—	4	—
Killing Mr. Griffin, L. Duncan, 1979	Parent	Language	Denied	OH	1	—
—	Another teacher	Advocates killing a teacher	Denied	NY	1	—
Knock on Any Door, W. Motley, 1947	Concerned Citizens	Pornography and filth	—	LA	7	—

Title	Complainant	Reason	Action	State	No.	
Kookanoo and the Kangaroo, M. and E. Durack, 1966	—	Racist	Removed	MD	9	—
Kramer versus Kramer: a Novel, A. Corman, 1977	School librarian	Vulgar language	Removed from library	—	1	—
Lady Chatterly's Lover, D.H. Lawrence, 1928	—	—	—	WI	5	—
	Faculty	Immorality	Not ordered	—	4	—
	Student	Immorality	Removed	—	8	—
Lady L., R. Gary, 1958	Parent, Man	Russian author	—	—	8	—
The Lady with the Dog, A. Chekhov					5	—
The Last Butterfly, J. Jacot, 1974	School Committee	—	Removed	New Lisbon, ME	9	—
Last Parallel, M. Russ, 1957	Parent	Swearing	Remained		8	—
The Last Picture Show, L. McMurtry, 1966	Parent	Obscene	Denied	Southwest	3	—
Last Summer, E. Hunter, 1968	Another teacher, Parents	Objectionable content on sex and violence, too explicit in sex scenes—particularly the rape scene	Book removed from recommended list, from classroom at 10th grade level	NY	2	—
Last Whole Earth Catalog, 1974	Principal	Descriptions of female body and functions and considered it a "hippie commune" type book	Book had come apart from use and was not replaced	Middle West	3	—

continued

Title, author, publication date	Objector	Objection	Results	Place	Source, date of objection	Legal Case (if any)
The Lathe of Heaven, U.K. Le Guin, 1971	Parent	"Advocacy of Non-Christian religions," profanity, poor sentence structure	An alternative selection policy was made, book remained	WA	11	—
Laughing Boy, O. LaFarge, 1963	—	Charges of obscenity and political ideas	Withdrawn from libraries	Four Amarillo high schools, TX	17	—
	Concerned Citizens	Pornography and filth		LA	7	—
			Returned	NY	9	—
	See entry for Best Short Stories by Negro Writers	See entry for Best Short Stories by Negro Writers		Island Trees, NY	10	See entry for Best Short Stories by Negro Writers
The Learning Tree, G. Parks, 1963	Parent, Principal	Seduction scene, language too adult and sexually explicit material		—	3	—
	—	Too mature for teenagers; the troubles that blacks encounter in life; the idea that Jesus Christ is portrayed as a white man who loves only white people	Book removed from classroom use and recommended list	TN	13	—
	Parent, Principal, English Specialist	Sex scene in chapter one, inappropriate language	Book removed from classroom use	MA	2	—
	CURE	—	—	Rockville, MD	9	—

Title	Initiator	Complaint	Action	State	No.	Court Case
	Parent	Blacks in book, personal opinion	Material placed on closed shelf	MO	1	—
	Parent	Page 29 or whatever—sexual action	—	IA	1	—
	Parent	Sex scene in chapter one	Child allowed another selection	MA	2	—
	English Specialist	Ungraded structure	Books suggested for older students unless parent permission obtained	VA	2	—
	Parent, Principal	Inappropriate language	Book removed from classroom use	NH	2	—
	School librarian	Not suitable for our use	Material placed on closed shelf	LA	1	—
	Parent	"This is Trash"	No change, material was optional reading	WA	1	—
	Parent	Unsuitable for high school—"sex and foul language"	Denied	CA	1	—
	Parents, Citizens	Language and theme	At first placed on closed shelf and then returned to regular circulation	SC	1	—
	Parent	Swearing, explicit sex, blasphemous, teaches secular humanism	School board defended the book after recommendation of review committee; District Court and Appellate Court upheld School board	Mead, WA	10	Grove v. Mead School District #354 753, F 2nd, 1528
Les Miserables, V. Hugo	Teacher	—		WI	5	—

continued

289

Title, author, publication date	Objector	Objection	Results	Place	Source, date of objection	Legal Case (if any)
Letters to Jane, G. Schultz, 1960	Principal	Didn't agree with philosophy of writer	—	WI	5	—
Let Us Now Praise Famous Men, W. Evans and J. Agee, 1960	Parent	Discussions on sex	Available	WI	5	—
Life and Health/Textbook, R. Crawunder and M. Steinmann, 1980	Parent	Too humanistic; too many values mentioned. Mentioned homosexuality	Removed from classroom use for some students and recommended list for others	—	1	—
Life with Father, Lindsay and Crouse, 1940	Parent	Language	Child was not required to read book	Middle West	3	—
Light in August, W. Faulkner, 1932	Parent	Language used felt to be offensive; book should be removed from library	Material placed on closed shelf	PA	1	—
The Light in the Forest, C. Richter, 1953	Parent	Language	Child was not required to read book, substitution was made	Middle West	3	—
A Lion Is in the Streets, A. Langley, 1946	Visitor from State Dept. of Public Instruction	—	Remained	AZ	8	—
Lisa Bright and Dark, J. Neufeld, 1969	—	"These books contain certain questionable material for use with general student populations as indicated"	Book removed from library	NE	2	—
Listen to the Silence, D. Elliot, 1969	Parent	Unsuitable language	Material removed from classroom use	PA	1	—

Title	Initiator	Objection	Action	Location	No.	
Listen to the Worm, R. McKuen, 1968	Parent	Inappropriate for junior high	Book removed from library	OH	6	—
Literature of the Supernatural, R. Beck, 1974	Parent	Book contained pictures of tarot cards	Parent withdrew complaint	KS	2	—
—	American Christians in Education	—	—	Culver City, CA	9	—
Little Black Sambo, H. Bannerman, 1899	Anti-Defamation League of B'nai B'rith	—	—	—	17	—
The Little Fellow, P. Cotes, 1965	Concerned Citizens	Pornography and filth	—	NY	12	—
—	—	—	—	LA	7	—
The Little Girl Who Lives Down the Lane, L. Koenig, 1974	Student	Objectionable language	Denied	OH	6	—
Little Red Riding Hood	Parent	"Excessive violence"	Remained	NC	11	—
The Loneliness of the Long-Distance Runner, A. Sillitoe, 1967	Parent	Language used was poor, and reference made to adultery was deemed unnecessary	Removed from classroom use	NE	2	—
The Lonely Girl, E. O'Brien, 1962	Student	Language and too vivid sexual descriptions	Removal	—	4	—
Look Homeward, Angel, T. Wolfe, 1934		—	—	San Jose, CA	17	—
Looking Backward, E. Bellamy, 1959	Parent	Socialism	Removed	AZ	8	—
Looking for Mr. Goodbar, J. Rossner, 1975		—	No longer used in classroom	OH	6	—

continued

Title, author, publication date	Objector	Objection	Results	Place	Source, date of objection	Legal Case (if any)
Lord of the Flies, W. Golding, 1954	Teacher	Killing of a pig	—	WI	5	—
	Parent	Violence	Remained	AZ	8	—
	Parent	Distorted view of youth	Removed	AZ	8	—
	Parent, Principal, Teacher	Added nothing to curriculum, too suggestive, too frank, too savage for junior high, undue violence	—	—	4	—
	Parent	Dealt with death, wondered why book was chosen in English class, "sick literature"	Child was permitted to read alternative		3	—
	Parents	Too violent for student to handle, work of the devil, language	Remove from classroom use		2	—
	Parent, Teacher	—	Material removed from library	MS	1	—
	Uncle	"You're teaching cannibalism," "the book is anti-family"	Denied	SC	1	—
	Parents	The parent misunderstood a critic's comment on one episode and decided the book was obscene	Another book was assigned	CA	1	—
	Parent	"Excessive violence and bad language"	Book kept on approved reading list	TX	11	—

Title	Requester	Reason	Resolution	State	Number	Citation
"The Lottery", S. Jackson, 1949	Parent	Book too violent	Still being debated	South	3	
—	Parent	Violence at end	The story is still being taught	OH	6	
—	Parent	"Don't know"	—	PA	1	
—	Parent	Objected on religious grounds, it was paganistic in their viewpoint	Other titles were assigned to student	IN	1	
—	Parent	"Values" shouldn't be taught in school, objection on religious grounds	Material removed from classroom use	NY	1	
"The Lottery", S. Jackson (the film)	Several parents	Questioned family values, accentuated the brutality and senselessness of our times	School board voted removed; court ordered the film returned	MN	16	Pratt v. Independent School District No. 831, 670 F.2d, p. 744, (8th Cir. 1982).
Love and the Facts of Life, E. Duvall, 1963	Student, Teacher, Parent, Principal, English Dept. Chairman	"Dirty" aspect of sex, students shouldn't have these facts, boys looked at pictures and snickered	Denied, Closed shelf	—	4	
Love and Marriage, F.A. Magoun, 1948	—	—	—	—	4	
Love and Sex and Growing Up, E. Johnson, B. Johnson, 1970	Teacher	Sex	Available only to instructors	—	8	
—	Principal	The district will not buy materials with evolution theory in it unless creation theory is given equal time	Material removed from the library pending outcome	CA	1	

continued

Title, author, publication date	Objector	Objection	Results	Place	Source, date of objection	Legal Case (if any)
Love and Sex in Plain Language, E. Johnson, 1977	Principal	Pictures too explicit, too realistic, "street words" used	—	—	3	—
Love Is One of the Choices, N. Klein, 1978	Parent	Obscene language and too much sex	Denied	NY	1	—
Love Story, E. Segal, 1970	Parents	The language and the theme were objectionable, book was "dirty," not consistent with Christian teachings, sexual scenes	Denied, remained on shelf but not in classroom	Middle West	3	—
—	Concerned Citizens	Pornography and filth	—	LA	7	—
—	School librarian, Parent, Teacher, Chairman, Superintendent	Offensive language, filthy terms, implications and words	Book removed	ID	2	—
—	Parent	Language and sexual behavior	Removed from shelves	—	14	—
—	Parent	—	Material removed from library	WI	1	—
—	—	—	—	OR	1	—
—	Principal	Premarital sex was condoned	Removed from library, but put back when new principal started	MD	1	—
—	—	—	—	SC	1	—
—	Parent	Explicit sex, foul language	Book removed from library	—	1	—

Title	Initiator	Reason	Action	Location	No.	Notes
Lunch Poems, F. O'Hara, 1965	See entry for *A Coney Island of the Mind* for Aurora, CO				9, 10	See *Coney Island* entry
Lust for Life, I. Stone, 1934	Librarian, Teacher	Obscene or risqué	Removal	—	4	—
Lysistrata, Trans. by D. Fitts, 1966	Parent	Play was trash	Controversy dissolved	CA	2	—
Macbeth, W. Shakespeare		—	—	NY	12	—
McBroom's Zoo, A.S. Fleischman, 1972	Parent	"Jews portrayed as mcneylendars" [sic]	Denied	MA	1	—
			—	Rockville, MD	9	—
Macos Series in Jr. High	Clergyman	It teaches evolution, euthanasia, inhumanity, and is secular humanist	Denied	VT	1	—
Madame Bovary, G. Flaubert, 1857	Parent	Too mature	Denied		4	—
Magic, W. Goldman, 1976	Parent	Profanity and obscenity	Book removed from library	OH	6	—
Main Street, S. Lewis, 1948	Librarian	—	Closed shelf		4	—
	Townspeople	—	Principal removed book from library, probably will return after controversy dies	WI	5	—
The Major Young Poets, A. Lee, 1971	Another teacher	Book was "shocking, tasteless, obnoxious"	Book removed from library	South	3	—

continued

295

Title, author, publication date	Objector	Objection	Results	Place	Source, date of objection	Legal Case (if any)
Makers of the Red Revolution, O. Coolidge, 1963	Principal	Shows communists in favorable light	Not purchased	—	4	—
Malcolm X, Malcolm X, 1965	Parent	Objectional material for young minds, in a rural community people don't care to have their children read about Negroes	—	—	3	—
Male and Female Under 18, N. Larrick & E. Merriam, 1973	Parents, School board, others	Obscene	Removed by the school board, ordered returned by the Court	Chelsea, MA	16	Right to Read Defense Committee v. School Committee of the City of Chelsea, 454 F. Supp. 703 (D. Mass. 1978).
—	CURE			Montgomery County, MO	9	—
Man: A Course of Study	Gablers			—	9	—
A Man for All Seasons, R. Bolt, 1962	Parent	"Damnit, More, You're dangerous to know"	Denied	OH	6	—
Man in Literature	—	—	—	—	9	—
Man, Myth, and Magic, R. Cavendish, 1970	Principal, Board member	Unfair treatment of Mormons, unchristian	Alternate book required	CA	2	—
—	—	—	—	—	1	—
—	Teacher	Photographs of nudes participating in	Material placed on closed shelf	CA	1	—

Man, the Mythmaker, T. Jewkes, 1973	—	witchcraft—chapter entitled "Fuck Fair" [sic]	—	—	9	—
The Man Who Liked to Look at Himself, K. Constantine, 1982	Another teacher	Language not suitable, book not worth reading	Material removed from library	IL	1	—
Manchild in the Promised Land, C. Brown, 1965	Concerned Citizens	Pornography and filth	—	LA	7	—
—	Parents	Work considered obscene, masturbation scene	Book removed from classroom use	NY	2	—
—	—		Removed	WI	9	—
—	Parent	The swearing was too much	Material removed from recommended shelf	VT	1	—
—	—		Denied	WI	1	—
—	Parent	Trash	Denied	MA	1	—
—	Parent	Objectionable subject matter	Denied	—	1	—
—	Parent	Unsuitable for mandatory class assignment; bad language and graphic sex	Removed from classroom use		1	—
—	—		Removed	Waukesha, WI	9	—
—	Parent	Work considered obscene	Book removed from classroom use	NY	2	—

continued

Title, author, publication date	Objector	Objection	Results	Place	Source, date of objection	Legal Case (if any)
—	Parent	"If my daughter had selected it from the library I wouldn't care, it is just that you suggested it."	Mother was invited to class discussion and didn't show. She never called again	OH	2	—
—	Parent	Obscene language and masturbation scene	Request denied	MA	2	—
—	Teacher	"I returned to my position after a maternity leave and felt that the book which had been brought to my attention was not unsuitable for some more mature, perhaps, students. If I feel a book is not suitable for some grade level, I just tell the student outright that perhaps in a few years, he/she may read this particular book."	Book removed from library	—	2	—
—	Parent, clergyman, student, Member of Board of Education	"Trash like this does not belong in our classrooms. I don't want my child to read such words. We don't say things like this in our home. That hippie English teacher is perverted."	Simply not to force any student to read the book if it is graphically realistic	Northeast	3	—

Title/Author	Challenger	Reason	Action	Location	No.
—	Parent	Language and content	Book placed on closed shelf. District policy not followed in this single instance	West	3
—	Another teacher	"Obscene"	Book removed from classroom use	Middle West	3
—	Parent, Committee of Concerned Parents	Profanity, sex scenes too explicit	Placed on closed shelf	Southwest	3
—	Parent, Clergyman, Student, Member of Board of Education	"Trash like this does not belong in our classrooms," language and content, profanity, sex scenes too explicit	Not to force any student to read the book if it is graphically realistic, book placed on closed shelf, book removed from classroom	Northeast	3
—	—	Unsuitable for grade level	Book removed from library	—	1
The Mansion, W. Faulkner, 1959	Student	"I can't be Christian and read about horrible things and horrible words"	Students were given another book to read	South	3
Manwatching: A Field Guide to Human Behavior, D. Morris, 1977	Teacher	The students should not have those illustrations available to them. They weren't appropriate	Material placed on closed shelf	TX	1
The Marauders, C. Ogburn, 1959	Student	Swearing	No action	—	4
Marjorie Morningstar, H. Wouk, 1955	—	Obscene and political ideas	Withdrawn from library	Four Amarillo High Schools	17
Martian Chronicles, R. Bradbury, 1958	Parent	Vulgar language	Book removed from classroom use	Middle West	3

continued

Title, author, publication date	Objector	Objection	Results	Place	Source, date of objection	Legal Case (if any)
—	Parent	Atheistic, use of blasphemous words	Student was transferred to a different course	NC	2	—
—	Student	The word "nigger" was used in classroom discussion; a black student's sister said of her brother, "No Black student should have to listen to this"	Material removed from class room use and then later was put back in use	PA	1	—
Maryland Folklore and Folklife, C.G. Carey, 1970	Parent	Proverb on page 66: "So foolish he can't pour piss out of a boot with the directions on the heel"	Book removed from class-room use	—	3	—
M*A*S*H, R. Hooker, 1968	Parent	Language and sex references	Book removed from recommended list	IL	2	—
—	Parent	—	Material removed from library	—	1	—
Massacre At Fall Creek, J. West, 1975	School librarian	"Too explicit and frivolous showing of birth control materials, specifically filling a condom with water and waving it in women's faces"	—	OK	1	—
Mass Media and the Popular Arts, F. Rissover and Birch, 1971	Concerned Citizens	Pornography and filth	—	LA	7	—

			Removed	East Baton Rouge, LA	9	
Masters of Deceit, J.E. Hoover, 1958	Parent				9	
Matador, B. Conrad, 1952	Parent	Vulgar terms	Removal		5	
A Measure of Dust, S. Turner, 1970	Another teacher	Graphic sex scene	Principal removed book and threw it away		4	
Me and Jim Luke, R. Branscum, 1971	Parent	Slang referring to boy's penis	Material removed from library	KY	1	
Meat on the Hoof, G. Shaw, 1972	Parent	Language, subject matter	Book removed from recommended list	ME	2	
*Memories of an Ex-Prom Queen, M. Schulman	Parent	Parent felt heroine was not suitable role model and there was too much explicit sex in novel	Substitute reading	IL	1	
Men's Bodies, Men's Selves, S. July, 1979					1	
Mephisto Waltz, F. Stewart, 1969	Parent	"Student would be taught the occult"	Book removed from classroom use	Midwest	3	
The Merchant of Venice, W. Shakespeare, 1600	Parents, Anti-Defamation League of B'nai B'rith	Presents an offensive stereotype of Jews	Book retained by decision of New York Supreme Court		5, 16	See Oliver Twist entry
	Parent	Witches scene—unholy [sic]—see Macbeth entry	Denied		1	
The Miernik Dossier, C. McCarry, 1973					1	

continued

Title, author, publication date	Objector	Objection	Results	Place	Source, date of objection	Legal Case (if any)
Mila 18, L. Uris, 1961	Parent, Student	—	Denied		4	—
Mississippi: Conflict and Change, J. Loewen & C. Sallis, eds., 1974	Lawyers Committee for Civil Rights Under Law	State textbook purchasing board refused to purchase unbiased books about blacks	District Court enjoined State textbook purchasing board from rejecting texts for racial reasons, ordered State to make available a multiracial, multiethnic book	MS	10	*Lowen v. Turnipseed* 488 F Supp 1138 (N.D. Miss 1980)
Mr. and Mrs. Bo Jo Jones, A. Head, 1967	Parent	Too much attention to sex	Request denied	TX	2	—
—	Parent	Subject matter treated (sex)	Book removed from classroom use and recommended list	NM	2	—
—	Parent	Put-down of black readers	Material removed from classroom use	—	1	—
—	Parent	Book's treatment of sex was "most obscene I have ever read"	Denied	—	1	—
—	—	—	—	NY	12	—
Mr. Roberts, T. Heggen, 1946	Parent	—	—	WI	5	—
Mixed Bag, H. Hutchinson, 1970	Another teacher, English Dept. Chairman	Biased articles not suitable to impressionable minds of many high school students	Book removed from classroom use	Northeast	3	—
Moby Dick, H. Melville, 1851	Parent	Homosexuality	Remained	AZ	8	—

Modern Biology, J. Otto and A. Towle, 1965	Local Baptist Church	Wanted "creationism" taught as well as evolution	Denied	—	1	—
A Modest Proposal, J. Swift, 1969	—	—	—	NY	12	—
The Monk, M. Lewis, 1952	Parent	Objections to sexual overtones; unsuitable for impressionable sophomores plus vulgar language	Alternate book offered	MI	2	—
Moonflower Vine, J. Carleton, 1962	Superintendent	Sex, language	Removed	AZ	8	—
The Moon is a Harsh Mistress, R. Heinlein, 1965	Concerned Citizens	Against pornography and filth	—	LA	7	—
More Joy; a Beautiful Lovemaking Sequel to the Joy of Sex, A. Comfort, 1973	High school librarian	"Inappropriateness for high school students"	Removed from display	NY	11	—
Mother Goose Rhymes, F. Muller, 1926	Citizen	Alleged anti-Semitic verse	Remained	—	11	—
The Motorcycle Betrayal Poems, D. Wakoski, 1971	School librarian	Use of objectionable, blunt language	Denied	South	3	—
The Mountain Road, T. White, 1958	Parent	Shocking profanity	Removal	—	4	—
My Darling, My Hamburger, P. Zindel, 1969	Parents	Idea of unwed mother, language was objectionable, dirty book	Removed from classroom use	NE	2	—
—					9	

continued

303

Title, author, publication date	Objector	Objection	Results	Place	Source, date of objection	Legal Case (if any)
—	Parent	Sexual behavior	Left on open shelves	WI	14	—
—	Another teacher, Parents	Some of the language used seemed objectionable, sex, drugs, abortion	Remained, student could read it if desired	OH	6	—
—	Parent	Too much sex for twelve year old reader	Denied	MO	1	—
—	Parent	Teacher was reading book to an entire sixth grade class and parent objected	Material removed from classroom use	PA	1	—
—	Parent	Was inappropriate reading for high school students because it dealt with abortion	Denied	WA	1	—
—	—	—	—	IN	1	—
—	Parent	Abortion	Denied	WI	1	—
—	Student	—	—	IN	1	—
—	—	Objection to language	Denied	NY	1	—
—	—	—	—	IN	1	—
My Shadow Ran Fast, B. Sands, 1964	Principal	Objectionable chapter	Removal	—	4	—
My Sweet Charlie, D. Westheimer, 1965	Parent	Marlene's reference to the penis as "his thing"	Denied	NY	2	—
—	Parent	—	Material placed on closed shelf	MO	1	—

Title, Author, Year	Instigator	Reason	Action	Place	Ref.	Notes
Mythology, E. Hamilton, 1942	Student	Boring, doesn't make any sense, stupid	Denied	Middle West	3	—
The Naked Ape, D. Morris, 1967	Concerned Citizens	Against pornography and filth	—	LA	7, 9	—
—	Another teacher	Not appropriate for persons of high school age	Book placed on closed shelf	OH	6	—
—	See entry for Best Short Stories by Negro Writers	—	—	NY	12	See entry for Best Short Stories by Negro Writers
Naked Came I, D. Wiess, 1963	English Dept. Chairman	Language and scenes too vivid and detailed	Closed shelf	Island Trees, NY	9, 10	—
Nam, M. Baker, 1981	Another teacher	"Too blunt of a description of the war—too realistic and brutal"	Denied	PA	4	—
Naomi in the Middle, N. Klein, 1974	Superintendent	—	—	NY	1	—
Native Son, R. Wright, 1940	Parent	Obscenity	—	WI	9, 15	—
—	Parent	—	Case dropped	—	5	—
—	Parents	Obscene language, book "unfit" for high school students	Removed from library	TN	4	—
—	—	—	—	NJ	2	—
—	Parent	Obscene language	Removed from library	TN	9	—
—	—	—	—	TN	2	—
—	Parent	The book was "unfit" for high school students to read.	Student was allowed to read an alternate book	MO	2	—

continued

Title, author, publication date	Objector	Objection	Results	Place	Source, date of objection	Legal Case (if any)
—	Parent	Inappropriate material	Material removed from classroom use	OR	1	—
—	Parent	Too sophisticated and violent for 15 year old to read	Material removed from classroom use	IN	1	—
The Natural, B. Malamud, 1952	Student	Religious convictions would not permit him to read it	Excused from assignment	Middle West	3	—
The Negro Revolution, R. Goldston, 1968	—		Complaint dropped, when objectors shown reviews	NJ	1	—
Never on a Broomstick, F. R. Donovan, 1971	Parent	Material dealt with controversial subject—witchcraft, anti-Christian book	Material placed on closed shelf	WI	1	—
New American and Canadian Poetry, J.E. Gill, ed., 1971	Another teacher, Principal	Sex and language	Book removed from library	NE	2	—
The New American Poetry, D. Allen, 1960	Principal	He did not like the language in poems of Ginsberg, Corso, etc.	Book removed from library		2	—
—	Board of Education	See *A Coney Island of the Mind* entry	See *A Coney Island of the Mind* entry	Aurora, CO	9, 10	See *Coney Island* entry
—	—			CO	10	—
The New Dynamic Church, V.P. Wierwille, 1971	Student	Material put out by organization called "The Way"	Nothing	OH	1	—
The New Journalism, T. Wolfe, 1973	Parent	Language was objectionable	Denied	FL	1	—

Title	Initiator	Objection	Action	Location	No.	
New Whole Earth Catalog; Living Here and Now, S. French, ed., 1973	Parent	—	Principal tore out pages which a parent had complained about, and destroyed them before consulting librarian or advisory committee	IN	1	—
The New Women: A Motive Anthology of Women's Liberation	Principal	—	—	Warsaw, IN	9	—
Nigger, D. Gregory, 1964	Parents	Rough language of ghetto was deemed unnecessary and harmful to any student reading it	Removed from classroom use	Middle West	3	—
—	Parents	Language, Mormon parent disapproved of Gregory's "black view" and of its alleged "profanity"	Denied, son released from class to read another book	PA	2	—
—	Parent	"I don't want my little girl reading words like 'mother fucker.'"	Denied	IL	1	—
The Nigger of the Narcissus, J. Conrad, 1914	Parent	Negro parent objected to word "nigger" in title	Removal	—	4	—
Night, E. Wiesel, 1960	Parent	One passage had a man's hand on a woman's breast	—	OH	1	—
Night and Fog, P.A. Schrelvogel, 1969	Member of the Board of Education	Not appropriate for age level (9–12)	Denied	MA	1	—

continued

307

Title, author, publication date	Objector	Objection	Results	Place	Source, date of objection	Legal Case (if any)
Night of Fire and Blood, L. Kelley, 1979	Parent	Alleged unsuitability for young readers	Restrict use to middle and high school library.	CO	11	—
Nine Stories, J.D. Salinger, 1953	Parent	—	—	—	4	—
—	Parent	"Gives them wrong idea of proper values . . . undermines parental religious and moral teaching"	Censor book	NY	2	—
Nineteen Eighty-four, G. Orwell, 1949	Parent, PTA, Band member, Citizen, School board, Teacher, Member Birch Society	Immorality, depressing, sexy, profanity, too old for students, study of communism	—	WI	5	—
—	—	Charges of obscenity and political ideas	Withdrawn from four high schools	Amarillo, TX	17	—
—	—	—	—	Miami, FL	17	—
—	—	—	Remained	—	5	—
—	—	Teacher was fired after refusing to remove 1984 from his reading list, but was reinstated	He eventually won reinstatement after arguing that the book illustrates what happens in a totalitarian society	MN	17	Wrenshall, MN
—	Parents, Students	Treatment of marriage and family, too much sex and violence, language, religious principles	Denied, Student read alternate book	NE	2	—

Who complained	Reason	Action taken	Region	No.
Principal	Unsuitable for age group, drug oriented	Material placed on closed shelf	MD	1
Parent	—	Denied	MI	1
Parent	Nothing but pornography	Request denied	South	3
Parent	Mention of female character's breasts	Book placed on closed shelf	South	3
Parent	Vulgar language and reference to sex	Request denied		3
Superintendent	Sex, language	Removed		8
Faculty	Sordidness, sex	—		8
Parent	Sexual episodes	Remained		8
School board member	Moral issue	Not recommended		4
Principal	Shows communism in favorable light	Not purchased		4
Member of the Board of Education	Sexual connotations, mainly a paragraph saying "she unzipped her jeans"	Book placed on closed shelf		1
Parent who is member of Board of Education	Objectionable passages, not fit to read	Book removed from library, removed from classroom use		1
Parent	Obscene sex act	Book removed from classroom use. (I was told that it was because it was a paperback)		1
Parent	Treatment of marriage and family	Request denied	NE	2

continued

309

Title, author, publication date	Objector	Objection	Results	Place	Source, date of objection	Legal Case (if any)
—	Student	Too much sex and violence	Student read alternate book	NC	2	—
—	Parent	Explicit sex	Student assigned other selection	GA	2	—
—	Principal	Not suitable for high school students	Removal	—	4	—
—	Parent	Socialistic state shows utopia which is wrong	Request denied	—	4	—
—	Parent	Too mature, undesirable passages	Closed shelf	—	4	—
—	Librarian	Not suitable	—	—	4	—
—	Superintendent, Faculty, Parent	Sex, language, sordidness	Removed, Remained	—	8	—
—	Member of the Board of Education, Parents	Sexual connotations, mainly a paragraph saying "she unzipped her jeans," objectionable passages not fit to read	Denied, Book placed on closed shelf	—	1	—
95 *Poems*, E. Cummings, 1958	Superintendent	Obscene language	Denied	TN	2	—
None Dare Call It Treason, J. Stormer, 1964	Teacher, Principal	Too biased	Closed shelf	—	4	—
None of the Above, R. Wellis, 1974	Another teacher	Subject matter	Material removed from library	—	1	—
—	Parent	Offensive material	Denied	AL	1	—

Title	Who objected	Objection	Action	State	No.	
Not as a Stranger, M. Thompson, 1954	Parent, Teacher	Unsuitable for school library	Removal	—	4	—
Not Bad for a Girl, I. Taves, 1972	—	—	—	LA	9	—
Not Without Laughter, L. Hughes, 1969	Parent	Language	Denied	AR	2	—
O, Beulah Land, M. Settle, 1956	Parents	Vulgarity	Removed	AZ	8	—
—	Parent	The sexual scenes between plantation owner and slave were not necessary	Material placed on closed shelf	FL	1	—
Occult: all books	Parent, clergyman	Satanic content	Removed from use	WA	1	—
Of Human Bondage, W.S. Maugham, 1956		Immoral and obscene	—	—	5	—
—	Parent	Inappropriate reading material, prostitutes, illicit affairs, alcoholism	Request denied	Middle West	3	—
Of Mice and Men, J. Steinbeck, 1937	Mother, Parent, Teacher	Too much profanity	—	WI	5	—
—	Parents	Bad language, objectionable language	Denied	—	4	—
—	Principal	Language, situations	Removed	AZ	8	—
—	Parents	Rough language, too depressing, sexual activity, against church beliefs	Student not required to read book	Midwest	3	—

continued

Title, author, publication date	Objector	Objection	Results	Place	Source, date of objection	Legal Case (if any)
—	Concerned Citizens	Against pornography and filth	—	LA	7	—
—	Parents	Use of profanity, put down of black people	Substitute reading was given	IL	2	—
—	Parents	Language, distorted view of life	Another book offered to student	VA	2	—
—	School board	—	Removed	PA	9	—
—	Parents, Citizens	Language and theme	At first placed on closed shelf and then returned	SC	1	—
—	Parent	Had a blasphemous statement, "God damn"	Denied	PA	1	—
—	Parent	The language was too realistic—mainly "damn"	Material placed on closed shelf	TX	1	—
—	Parent	Language—God damn	Student given alternate book to read	OH	1	—
—	Parent	Book was filthy	Another book was chosen	KS	1	—
—	Parent	Use of profane language	Denied	TX	1	—
—	Parent	Objectionable language, violence	Material removed from classroom use	SD	1	—
—	Principal	Choice of subject	—	PA	1	—
—	Parent, Clergyman	Language	Denied	SC	1	—
—	Parent	Bad language	Another book assigned	IN	1	—
—	Parent	"Took the name of the Lord in vain"	—	CA	1	—

	Initiator	Reason	Action	State	No.	
—	Parents, Local church group	Foul language, taking the name of the Lord in vain, violence, against religion, subversive	—	OH	6	—
—	School board chairman	Charges of obscenity, vulgarity	Remained	TN	11	—
—	Parents		"Limited access shelves"	Mackville, KS	11	—
—		Obscenity, political ideas	Removed from four high school libraries	Amarillo, TX	17	—
Of Time and the River, T. Wolfe, 1929		Charges of obscenity, political ideas	Withdrawn from four high school libraries	Amarillo, TX	5	—
—	Teacher	Ugliness, loose morals	Removal	—	4	—
Oh Boy! Babies!, J. Mali, 1980			Material removed from library	AR	1	—
Oh, God!, A Novel, A. Corman, 1971	Parent	Do you know about pp. 114–115? Do you allow that in the library?	Denied	MN	1	—
*Ohio Revised Criminal Law Code			—	OH	1	—
The Old Man and the Sea, E. Hemingway, 1952	Librarian		Closed shelf	—	4	—
The Old South; A Summer Tragedy and Other Stories of the Thirties, A. Bontemps, 1973	Parent	It describes death and old age "too vividly"	Book retained	NC	11	—

continued

313

Title, author, publication date	Objector	Objection	Results	Place	Source, date of objection	Legal Case (if any)
Oliver Twist, C. Dickens	Parents, Anti-Defamation League of B'nai B'rith	Presents an offensive stereotype of Jews	Book retained by decision of New York Supreme Court	—	17, 16	Rosenberg v. Board of Educ., 196 Misc. 542, 92 N.Y.S.2d 344 (Sup. Ct. 1949).
Oliver's Story, E. Segal, 1977	School librarian	Objectionable language	Removed from library	OK	1	—
The Once and Future King, T.H. White, 1958	Parent	Objected to relationship between Launcelot and Guinevere	Student was not required to read the book	—	1	—
One Day in the Life of Ivan Denisovich, A. Solzhenitsyn, 1963	Parent	"Filth," not educational	Denied	—	4	—
—	School board	Does not comply with N.Y. Times language guidelines	Removed from class use, not from library	New Lisbon, ME	9	—
—	Parent, Clergyman, Student, Member of Board of Education	"Trash like this does not belong in our classroom," too filthy and unchristian	—	—	3	—
—	Parent	Language	Denied	MI	1	—
—	Parent	"Was communistic," language, too strong for classroom use	—	MI	1	—
—	Superintendent	Possibly about communism	—	—	1	—
—	—	—	—	NY	12	—
—	Parent	Offensive Language	Request denied	ID	2	—

—	Parent	"Filthy language"	Request denied	OK	2	—
—	Parent	Language	Student allowed new book selection for assignment	UT	2	—
—	Parent	Obscene Language	Two students substituted another Russian novel.	MI	2	—
—	Parent	Too many four letter words in evidence	Book placed on closed shelf	IL	2	—
—	Principal, Superintendent	Use of vulgarisms, School board supported teacher's choice	Request denied	NC	2	—
One Flew Over the Cuckoo's Nest, K. Kesey, 1962	Student	Language, profanity	Student was given a substitute book to read	Middle West	3	—
—	Parent	Contained "dirty" language	—	TN	13	—
—	Parents, Principal	Profanity, "We didn't need any trash in our school," parent claimed it was pornography, obscenity, objectionable language	Student chose new selection, Book removed from classroom use	IL	2	—
—	Superintendent	—	Book removed, teacher fired, lawsuit filed, school board established a review policy	St. Anthony, ID	9, 10	Fogarty v. Atchley (filed but not decided)
—	Parent	Profanity	Student chose new selection	IL	2	—
—	Principal	"We didn't need any trash in our school."	Book removed from classroom use	CA	~2	—

continued

Title, author, publication date	Objector	Objection	Results	Place	Source, date of objection	Legal Case (if any)
—	Parent	Parent claimed it was pornography	Substitute book offered to student	WI	2	—
—	Parent	Obscenity	Alternate book required	LA	2	—
—	Another teacher	Objectionable language	Request denied	MA	2	—
—	Principal	Swearing by characters	Removed from classroom use	IA	2	—
—	Parent	Language	Request denied	KS	2	—
—	Parent, Clergyman	"Language is outrageous" (Juniors and seniors reading it.)	Student given another book to read—Kesey's *One Flew Over the Cuckoo's Nest* was never taught again.	MO	2	—
—	Parent	Profanity, explicit sexual discussion	Denied, Used alternate book	CA	1	—
		Prostitutes	—	OH	6	—
			—	NY	12	—
The Onion Field, J. Wambaugh, 1978	Concerned Citizens	Against pornography and filth	—	LA	7	—
On the Beach, N. Shute, 1957	Clergyman	Scene in water when sailing	Denied	OH	0	—
—	Principal	—	—	WI	5	—
—	Librarian	—	Closed shelf	—	4	—
—	Parent	Immorality	Remained	AZ	8	—
—	Parent	Illicit love scenes, (we could find none)	Denied	OH	2	—

On the Edge: a novel, R. Doliner, 1978	—	—	—	—	9	—
Open Season, A Novel, D. Osborn, 1974	—	—	—	—	1	—
The Ordeal of Major Grigsby, J. Sherlock, 1964	Librarian, Principal	"Too Dirty"	Removed	—	4	—
Ordinary People, J. Guest, 1976				NE	1	
—	Parents, Clergyman, Lay minister	The book is morally bad, it contains profanity, sexual innuendos and takes the name of the lord in vain	No action as of yet	TX	1	
				OH	6	
Othello, W. Shakespeare, 1622	—	Sex	Denied	NY	12	—
				OH	6	
The Other, T. Tryon, 1971	Parent	"A very immoral and mixed up view of life," "degrading to the mind, no progression—only retrogression," "blood and gore, bad morals."	Denied	ID	2	—
Our Bodies, Ourselves—A Book By and For Women, The Boston Women's Health Book Collective, 1971	School District Trustees		Removal of book by Trustees was challenged in District court; after suit was filed, book was returned to library	Helena, MT	10	Helena Citizens for Freedom of Expression v. Helena School District #1

continued

Title, author, publication date	Objector	Objection	Results	Place	Source, date of objection	Legal Case (if any)
—	Concerned Citizens	Against pornography and filth	—	LA	7	—
—	Parent	Birth control treatment, too vivid portrayal of homosexuality	Denied	PA	1	—
—	Parent	Sexually stimulating material, pornographic	Material placed on closed shelf	OH	1	—
—	Clergyman	"Was humanistic in nature and against the Bible"	Dropped complaint	ME	1	—
—	Another teacher	Pro-abortion	Placed on closed shelf	NY	1	—
—	Moral Right (local organization)	Explicit sex instructions	Denied	NM	1	—
—	Teacher	Explicitness	Material placed on closed shelf	IL	1	—
—	Parent	Pornographic and obscenity	Material placed on closed shelf	WI	1	—
—	National Organization	—	Denied	WI	1	—
—	Teacher Aide	The book was inappropriate for our students	Denied	WI	1	—
—	Parent	Language too strong	Material placed on closed shelves	AL	1	—
—	Teacher	Students don't need to see those kinds of materials	Denied	OH	1	—

Title/Author	Source	Reason	Action	State	No.	
—	Parent	The book was on a hit list	Denied	CA	1	—
—	Principal		Material removed from library	IN	1	—
—	Parent	Parent stated that it was not necessary to be so graphic to teach about the topic	Denied	AK	1	—
—	Parent	This book is trash—shouldn't be where kids can see it	Material placed on closed shelf	TX	1	—
—	Several parents	Material unsuitable for high school students	Material placed on closed shelf	CA	1	—
Our Sexual Evolution, H. Colton, 1971	Concerned Citizens	Against pornography and filth	—	NY	12	—
Our Time is Now, J. Birmingham, 1970	—		—	LA	7	—
—			—	KS	1	—
Outside Over There, M. Sendak, 1981	School librarian, Teacher	Youngsters couldn't handle the nude goblins, they just laughed, also the story line was not appropriate	Material removed from library	SD	1	—
The Outsiders, S.E. Hinton, 1967	—		Likely to censor	—	9	—
—	Parent	Violence	Dropped the challenge	WI	14	—
—	—			OH	1	—
—	Parent	"Too much violence"	The student was not required to read the book	IN	1	—

continued

Title, author, publication date	Objector	Objection	Results	Place	Source, date of objection	Legal Case (if any)
Ox-Bow Incident, W. Clark, 1940				OH	6	—
	Parent	Language	Removal	WI	5	—
—	Local organization, Parent	Swear words, too many obscene descriptions	Denied	—	4	—
—	Parents	Language	Removed book	AZ	8	—
—	Parents	Language	Book remained	AZ	8	—
The Painted Bird, J. Kosinski, 1966	Student	The book was basically senseless, excessively violent and concentrated too heavily on morbid sex issues	Book removed from class-room list	CT	2	—
The Panther and The Lash; Poems of Our Time, L. Hughes, 1967	Concerned Citizens	Against pornography and filth		LA	7	—
Patch of Blue, G. Hill, 1932	Clergyman	Objected to language and description of scenes of prostitution	Student offered alternate selection	NJ	2	—
—	Parent	Scary situation	Parent only demanded that the book be reconsidered	OH	6	—
Patton, L. Peck, 1970	Parent, Principal	"Foul language"	Book placed on closed list	VA	2	—
The Pearl, J. Steinbeck, 1947				WI	5	—
—	Parent	Use of abusive language, sex, violence	Didn't do anything	—	1	—
Pemberton Ltd., A. Glyn, 1957	Teacher	Ugliness, loose morals	Removal	—	4	—

Title	Initiator	Objection	Action	State	No.	Notes
The People Make a Nation, M.W. Sandler, E.C. Rozwenc and E.C. Martin, 1971	Gablers	—	—	TX	9	—
Peppercorn Days, J. Rose, 1959	Librarian	—	Removal	WI	5	—
Petals in the Wind, V.C. Andrews, 1980	Parent	Language was obscene	Removed from classroom use	OH	6	—
*A Piece of the Action	Parent, Concerned Citizens	Un-American, un-Christian	Book retained	IA	9	—
The Pigman, P. Zindel, 1968	Parent	Did not teach the appropriate behavior	Students allowed to make new selection	NY	2	—
—	—			—	9	—
—	—			—	1	—
Pilgrims in Paradise, F. Slaughter, 1960	Superintendent	Sex, language	Removed		8	—
The Pill Versus the Springhill Mine Disaster, R. Brautigan, 1968	See *The Abortion* entry		Censored	Anderson, CA	9, 10	See *The Abortion* entry
*Poems Over Line and Longer	Parent	Use of four-letter words	No action was taken	MI	2	—
The Poorhouse Fair, J. Updike, 1958	Parent	Language	Remained	AZ	8	—
Poor No More, R. Ruark, 1959	Superintendent	—	Removal	—	4	—
Portnoy's Complaint, P. Roth, 1969	Parent	"Inappropriate reading matter for my son"	Student selected another book	SC	1	—

continued

321

Title, author, publication date	Objector	Objection	Results	Place	Source, date of objection	Legal Case (if any)
The Poseidon Adventure, P. Gallico, 1969	Parent	Language	Material removed from classroom use	WI	1	—
The Power and The Glory, G. Greene, 1940	Parent	Objectionable passage on p. 17	Book removed from classroom use and recommended list	South	3	—
Praise the Human Season, D. Robertson, 1974	—	—	Censored	ME	9	—
Princess Daisy, J. Krantz, 1980	—	—	—	—	1	—
The Professor of Desire, P. Roth, 1977	Parent	"Morally unsuitable for high school students"	Material removed from library, pending hearing	OH	1	—
The Promise, D. Steele, 1978	Parent	—	—	PA	1	—
Property Of: a Novel, A. Hoffman, 1977	School librarian	Violent and foul language	Material removed from library	PA	1	—
Prostitution and Society, F. Henriques, 1962	Parent	Too adult for students	Closed shelf	—	4	—
°Pursuits	Gablers	—	—	TX	9	—
Psychology For You, S. Gordon, 1974	Concerned Citizens	Against pornography and filth	—	LA	7	—
The Quartzsite Trip, W. Hogan, 1980	Parent	"I didn't have contact with the objector but it was probably due to language and sex"	Material placed on closed shelf	TX	1	—
°Questions About Love and Sex, ed. of *Bride's* magazine	Parent	Too detailed about "how-to" for sex	Material removed from library	MO	1	—

322

Title	Challenger	Reason	Action	State	No.	Reference
*Quizzes, Tricks, Puzzles, and Brain Teasers	Parent	Fire hazard for youngsters, encourages playing with matches	Material placed on closed shelf	WI	1	—
Rabbit Redux, J. Updike, 1971	Another teacher	Use of objectionable, blunt language	Denied	South	3	—
Rabbit Run, J. Updike, 1964	—	—	—	ME	9	—
Radical Right: report of the John Birch Society and its Allies, B. Epstein, 1969	Member of Board of Education	Un-American part of communist conspiracy—"Didn't show both sides"	Denied, removed by board, went to court, still waiting	—	1	—
Raisin in the Sun, L. Hansberry, 1966	—	Demeaning to race	Alternate title assigned	OH	6	—
The Random House Dictionary of the English Language, College Edition, S.B. Flexner, 1968	Commissioner of Education	—	Removed from his list of recommended dictionaries	TX	9	—
The Razor's Edge, a Novel, W.S. Maugham, 1944	Church	—	—	WI	5	—
A Reader For Writers; a Critical Anthology of Prose Readings, J. Archer, ed., 1971	Concerned Citizens	Against pornography and filth	—	LA	7	—
—	See entry for Best Short Stories by Negro Writers			Island Trees, NY	9, 10	See entry for Best Short Stories by Negro Writers
Real Magic, P.E. Bonewits, 1971	Concerned Citizens	Against pornography and filth	—	LA	7	—
The Rebels, J. Jakes, 1979	Gablers	—	—	TX	9	—

continued

Title, author, publication date	Objector	Objection	Results	Place	Source, date of objection	Legal Case (if any)
Rebels and Renegades, M. Nomad, 1968	Gablers	—		TX	9	—
Recreational Drugs, L. Young, 1977	Parent	Objected to title, apparently thought we were promoting drug use by having such a book	Book never returned by student	ME	1	—
The Red Badge of Courage, S. Crane, 1895	Parent	Profane language	Denied	—	4	—
The Red Pony, J. Steinbeck, 1933	Parent	Profanity	Denied	—	4	—
Red Sky at Morning, R. Bradford, 1968	Clergyman, Parent	Language	Denied	West	3	—
	Parent	Bad language, poor morals for children	Denied	CA	2	—
	Parent	Used insinuating notes about sex	Material placed on closed shelf	AL	1	—
Reds, J. Thomas, 1970	Parent	Explicit sex, obscene language, discrimination	Book removed from classroom use	MI	2	—
The Reincarnation of Peter Proud, M. Ehrlich, 1974	Parent	—	Removed from recommended list	AR	2	—
	Board of Education	See entry for *A Coney Island of the Mind* for Aurora, CO			9, 10	See *Coney Island* entry
The Re-learning: (poems), J. Humphrey, 1976	—	—	—	RI	9	—

Title	Initiator	Action	State	Ref	Note
Remove Protective Coating a Little at a Time, J. Donovan, 1973	Member of Board of Education	Bad language, content concerning masturbation	ME	1	—
—	Parent, Teachers	Removed from classroom use and recommended list	OH	6	—
Revenge of the Lawn, R. Brautigan, 1971	—	Subject matter and vocabulary	CA	9, 10	*See Abortion* entry
Richie; The Ultimate Tragedy Between one Decent Man and the Son he Loved, T. Thomson, 1973	Parent	See *Abortion* entry	—	1	—
Riders on the Earth, A. MacLeish, 1978	—	Language and violence	Bloomington, MN	9	—
Robin Hood	Member of Indiana Textbook Committee	Denied	IN	9, 17	—
Romeo and Juliet, W. Shakespeare, (film)	Parent, Clergyman	Robin and his "merry men" were following the "straight communist line" while dashing through Sherwood Forest	IN	1	—
—	Parents	Nudity in the filmed version	MN	11	—
Rommel Drives on Deep into Egypt, R. Brautigan, 1970	—	"Sexually explicit material" removed from text; parents wanted complete text	Anderson, CA	9	See entry for *The Abortion*
		Remains part of the curriculum			
		See *Abortion* entry			
		Removed			

continued

Title, author, publication date	Objector	Objection	Results	Place	Source, date of objection	Legal Case (if any)
Rosemary's Baby, I. Levin, 1967	Parent	Immorality	Student allowed to read another book	CA	10	—
	Board of Education	—	Censored	IL	2	—
		The book "glorified the Devil"	Denied	Aurora, CO	9	See The Exorcist entry
Rumblefish, S.E. Hinton, 1975	Parent	Unnecessary language—students too young to hear	Material removed from classroom use	IL	1	—
	Parent	—	—		1	—
Run, Shelley, Run!, G. Samuels, 1974		—	"removed and destroyed"	AR	9	—
	Parent	Profane language	Denied	WI	1	—
	Parent	"Dirty words" on every other page	Material placed on closed shelf		1	—
	Parent	Use of dirty language	Denied	PA	1	—
		—	—		1	—
		—	—		12	—
Run Softly, Go Fast, B. Wersba, 1970		These books contain certain questionable material for use with general student population as indicated by the passages including sex, smoking, foul language	Book removed from library	NE	2	—
	School librarian, Teacher	Language and sex	Material removed from library	WI	1	—

Title	Complainant	Objection	Action	State	No.	
Runaways, E. Swados, 1978	School Board	—	Students requested injunction against the ban; Federal Judge denied it	VT	12	—
The Runaway's Diary, M. Harris, 1971	—	—	Censored	—	9	—
The Sailor Dog, M.W. Brown, 1953	CURE, Parents Who Care, NOW	—	—	MD	9	—
Sarah T., Portrait of a Teenage Alcoholic, R. Wagner, 1975	Parent	"The book was dirty." "I read the book and found nothing objectionable," wrote the librarian	Book placed on closed shelf	MO	2	—
Sartoris, W. Faulkner, 1929	Student	Too difficult to read, irrelevant in terms of life today	Book removed from classroom use	Middle West	3	—
Saturday Night Fever: a Novelization, H.B. Gilmour, 1977	Principal	—	Censored	MI	9	—
The Scarlet Letter, N. Hawthorne	Parent, Principal	Involvement of clergy in fornication—"degrades Christian ministry as a whole."	Book removed from classroom use and recommended list	—	2	—
—	—	Book had "4-letter words" and undesirable content	He was convinced by library that he was wrong	MO	2	—
—	Student	Available for Freshmen	No action	—	4	—
—	Parent	Immoral	Request denied	—	4	—
—	Parent	Adultery	Request denied	—	4	—
—	Principal	Too frank or revealing	Not recommended	—	4	—

continued

Title, author, publication date	Objector	Objection	Results	Place	Source, date of objection	Legal Case (if any)
	Parent	Adultery	Remained	AZ	8	—
					15	—
	Parent	About adultery, womanizing preacher, prostitution	—	OH	6	—
The Sea Around Us, R. Carson, 1958				AZ	8	—
Second Lady, I. Wallace, 1980	Principal		Placed on closed shelf	OK	1	—
Secret Societies, N. MacKenzie, 1968	Parent	Incorrect but secret information	Denied	PA	1	—
Semi-tough, D. Jenkins, 1972	English Dept. Chairman	Obscenity, vulgarity that was the rule, not the exception	Book removed from classroom use	IL	2	—
The Sensuous Couple, R. Chartham, 1971	Parent, School librarian, Teacher, English Dept. Chairman, Principal, Superintendent	Sexually explicit	—	HI	1	—
The Sensuous Man; the first how-to book for the man who wants to be a great lover, L. Stuart, 1971	Parent	Sexual	—	HI	1	—
The Sensuous Woman; the first how-to book for the female who yearns to be all woman, J. Garrity, 1971	Parent	Sexual	—	HI	1	—

Title	Initiator	Objection	Action Taken	State	No.	
A *Separate Peace*, J. Knowles, 1959	Parents	Homosexuality as theme, encouraged homosexuality, there are swear words in the book and our children shouldn't have to be subjected to this	Students offered another selection, Book removed from classroom use	IL	2	—
—	Parent	Strong language	Material removed from classroom use and library	SC	1	—
—	Parent, Student	Language objectionable	—	AL	1	—
—	Parent	Objectionable language	Another book substituted—censored copies prepared	—	6	—
—	Parent, Clergyman	Profane dialogue	Denied	—	4	—
—	Parent, Clergyman	Language, book considered too adult, objection to certain paragraphs	Denied, Student was not required to study the particular book	Northeast	3	—
Seven Contemporary Short Novels, C. Clerc and L. Leiter, 1969	Parent	Language	Removed from classroom use	—	2	—
The 17 Gerbils of Class 4A, W. Hooks, 1976	—	—	—	IA	9	—
Sex: Telling It Straight, E. Johnson, 1970	Principal	Pictures too explicit, too realistic, "street words" used	Book torn up	Middle West	3	—

continued

Title, author, publication date	Objector	Objection	Results	Place	Source, date of objection	Legal Case (if any)
—	Concerned Citizens	Against pornography and filth	—	LA	7	—
—	Another teacher	Book used slang for sex	Material removed from library	IL	1	—
—	Parent	The book DID NOT condemn homosexuality as an offense against God and nature	Denied	CA	1	—
*Sexism In Education, H. Perrault	Concerned Citizens	Against pornography and filth	—	LA	7	—
Sexual Politics, K. Millet, 1970	Concerned Citizens	Against pornography and filth	—	LA	7	—
*Sexual Revolution: Traditional Mores vs. New Values, D. Beuder	Member of Board of Education	Un-American, part of Communist conspiracy—"didn't show both sides"	Denied		1	—
Sexually Transmitted Diseases, G. Hart, 1977	—		—		1	—
The Shining, S. King, 1977	Parent	Obscene language is used in the book	Material removed from library	NY	1	—
—	Local citizens	Because they are "anti-Christian and demonic"	King's books restricted to high school students	WY	11	—
Ship of Fools, K. Porter, 1962	Parent	One big bedroom scene	—		4	—

continued

Title	Initiator	Objection	Disposition	State	No.
*Short Stories For English Courses, F. Jacobs		"humiliating and derogatory references to the Negro"	Replaced the text with a later edition of the same book with no controversial issues	—	5
Shuckin' and Jivin': Folklore From Contemporary Black Americans, D. Dance, 1978	School librarian	Very crude language	Material placed on closed shelf	TN	1
Siddhartha, H. Hesse, 1952	Clergyman	Book is non-Christian in philosophy	—	Northeast	3
The Silver Chalice, T. Costain, 1952	Mother	Brief paragraph describing Helena	—	WI	5
—	Librarian	—	Closed shelf	—	4
Since You Ask Me, A. Landers, 1961	Teacher	—	—	AZ	8
Sister Carrie, T. Dreiser	Parents	Dreary book	—	WI	5
Six Weeks: A Novel, F. Stewart, 1976	Parent	Sexual connotations	Material removed from library	In	1
Slaughterhouse-Five, K. Vonnegut, 1969	Parent	Obscenity, vulgar language, objectionable language	Book removed from classroom use	Northeast	3
—	Parents	The use of vulgar and obscene words and phrases to describe sexual organs, cruelty and violence also, language—too modern	No disposition reached yet, book removed from classroom use	NY	2

331

Title, author, publication date	Objector	Objection	Results	Place	Source, date of objection	Legal Case (if any)
—	Parents	Obscenity; refers to religious matters	School board retained the book, supported by Court	NY	16	Todd v. Rochester Community Schools, 41 Mich. App. 320, 200 N.W.2d 90 (1972).
—	—		The book was burned	Drake, ND	9	—
—	Parent, Student	Language used	Student read her choice from several books chosen by teacher of literary value	ME	1	—
—	School librarian	Inappropriate	Material placed on closed shelf	TX	1	—
—	School librarian	Unnecessary bathroom language	No action as of yet	AR	1	—
—	—		—	—	1	—
—	Parent	"R-rated" language	No written request was ever filed	WA	1	—
—	Parent	Objectionable	Denied	CT	1	—
—	Parent, Clergyman	Ungodly; immoral subject matter; bad language	Material removed from classroom use, no longer required	MI	1	—
—	Parent, Clergyman	Not suitable material for students (9–12)	There is an alternative reading assignment but book remains	CA	1	—
—	Parent, Clergyman	Language used is obscene	Book removed from recommended list	—	6	—

Title	Initiator	Objection	Action	Location	No.	Note
—	See entry for *Best Short Stories* by *Negro Writers*			Island Trees, NY	10	See entry for *Best Short Stories by Negro Writers*
Snowbound, R. Pronzini, 1974	Parent	—	Removed from library	MO	2	—
The Snows of Kilimanjaro, E. Hemingway, 1937	Parent	Profane language	Removal	—	4	—
The Social Rebel in American Literature, R. Woodward and J. Clark, 1968	—	The literature in the text was far too difficult for the students who elected the course	The books were replaced by materials more in keeping with the students' abilities	OH	2	—
Some Other Place, The Right Place, Harrington, 1972	School librarian	Book is bawdy, lacks literary merit	Book placed on closed shelf	South	3	—
Something of Value, R. Ruark, 1957	Superintendent, School librarian	Vivid description of native rituals	—	WI	5	—
Something Wicked This Way Comes, R. Bradbury, 1962	Another teacher	—	—	OH	1	—
Sons and Lovers, D.H. Lawrence, 1913	Parent	Sexual references	Denied	—	4	—
Sooner or Later, B. and C. Hart, 1978	Parent	Explicit sex	No formal objections made	OR	1	—
Soul on Ice, E. Cleaver, 1968	Parent	Dirty book	Denied	Middle West	3	—
—	See entry for *Best Short Stories* by *Negro Writers*			Island Trees, NY	9, 10	See entry for *Best Short Stories by Negro Writers*

continued

Title, author, publication date	Objector	Objection	Results	Place	Source, date of objection	Legal Case (if any)
	Concerned Citizens	Against pornography and filth	—	LA	7	—
	Parents, English Dept. Chairman		Restricted to upper grades only	—	2	—
	Principal	Too critical of whites and the language stirs up trouble with lots of blacks against whites	Placed on closed shelf	OH	1	—
	—	—	—	CT	1	—
	—	—	—	NY	10	—
The Sound and the Fury, W. Faulkner, 1929	Superintendent	Certain implications of sex that our students shouldn't have to read	Use halted	NE	2	—
Soup, R.N. Peck, 1974	Another teacher	Boys went skinny dipping	Denied	IA	1	—
	—	—	—	IA	1	—
Speaking For Ourselves, L. Faderman and B. Bradshaw, 1969	Parent	"Foul" language	Denied	IL	1	—
Special Olympics, J.S. Young, 1978	Principal	Objected to word "damn"	—	VA	1	—
*Speculations	Gablers	—	—		9	—
Spencer's Mountain, E. Hamner, 1961	Superintendent	Sex, language	—	AZ	8	—

Title	Initiator	Grounds	Action	State	District	Notes
Starting From San Francisco, L. Ferlinghetti, 1960	Board of Education	See entry for A Coney Island of the Mind for Aurora, CO			9, 10	See Coney Island entry
The Stepford Wives, I. Levin, 1972	School board	See The Bell Jar entry		Warsaw, IN	9, 10	See The Bell Jar entry
The Sterile Cuckoo, J. Nichols, 1945	Parent	Explicit sex	Book removed from library	KS	2	—
Sticks and Stones, L. Hall, 1972	Parent	Language	Still in circulation	KS	1	—
*The Sting	Parent	Teaching witchcraft and black magic	Book removed from classroom use	OH	6	—
Story of a Hypnotist, F. Polgar, 1951	Parent	Destroy faith in Christ's healing power	Removed	AZ	8	—
The Story of Mankind, H. Van Loon, 1959	Teacher	Shouldn't force theory of evolution on students	Denied	—	4	—
The Stranger, A. Camus, 1946	Parent, Librarian, Teacher	"Trash," cause incorrect thinking, too mature for students	Closed shelf	—	4	—
—	Parent	Concerned a passage where the word "fondled" in reference to the breasts was made	Student had the option to select another book	—	3	—
Stranger In a Strange Land, R. Heinlein, 1961	Teacher	Objected to nudity and inferences which can be drawn from the word "grok," objections also made to most of book from page 270 on	Book removed from classroom use	PA	2	—

continued

335

Title, author, publication date	Objector	Objection	Results	Place	Source, date of objection	Legal Case (if any)
The Strawberry Statement, J. Kunen, 1969	Teacher	Language was too vulgar, too radical	Denied	Northeast	3	—
	Parent	Language	Placed on closed shelf	OH	1	—
Street Kids, L. Cole, R. Romero, and others, 1970	Library supervisor	Use of foul language	—	Southwest	3	—
	Parent	Language	Material placed on closed shelf	TX	1	—
	Parent	"I don't want my kid reading that kind of language"	Material removed from library	WA	1	—
A Streetcar Named Desire, T. Williams, 1947	Student	Religious	Students were given other books to read	South	3	—
	Parent	"Author's life style"	Material removed from classroom	IL	1	—
Streetcorner Research, R. Schwitzgebel, 1964	Superintendent	—	Removal	—	4	—
The Student Critic, R.D. Cox, 1974	—	—	—	IN	10	—
Studs Lonigan, J. Farrell, 1935	Parent, Clergyman, Superintendent	Kids shouldn't be subjected to "filth"	Removal	—	4	—
Summer of '42, H. Raucher, 1971	Parent	Language, too vulgar	Book placed on closed shelf	Middle West	3	—
	Parent, Principal	Immoral, sex was too explicit, "too much" for high school students	Book removed and reinstated	NY	2	—

Title/Author	Initiator	Objection	Action Taken	State	No.	
—	Parent	Corrupted morals of her child	Material placed on closed shelf	IN	1	—
—	Parent, Member of Board of Education	Explicit language, "This should not be available in a school library"	Material placed on closed shelf	LA	1	—
The Sun Also Rises, E. Hemingway, 1926	—	—	—	San Jose, CA	17	—
—	Principal	—	Removal	—	4	—
—	Parent	Characters too flagrant in behavior—language too explicit	Book removed from recommended list	VA	2	—
—	Parent	Language	Material removed from classroom use	IN	1	—
Sunshine, N. Klein, 1974	Concerned Citizens	Against pornography and filth	—	LA	7	—
—	Principal	—	Removed	East Baton Rouge, LA	9	—
Sybil, F. Schreiber, 1973	Parent	Parent didn't like sexual implications	Removed from classroom use and library	OH	2	—
A Tale of Two Cities, C. Dickens, 1896	Teacher	Too difficult for low groups	Denied	—	4	—
—	Parent	Vocabulary too difficult	Remained	AZ	8	—
Tales From the Cloud Walking Country, M. Campbell, 1958	Parent	Confused 9th grader about sex	Temporarily closed shelf	—	4	—
Tales of the Supernatural, A. Blackwood, 1983	—	—	—	OH	6	—

continued

Title, author, publication date	Objector	Objection	Results	Place	Source, date of objection	Legal Case (if any)
Talks to Teenagers, A. Landers, 1963	Superintendent	Homosexuality discussed	—	AZ	8	—
The Tamarack Tree, H. Breslin, 1947	Teacher	Obscene	Closed shelf	—	4	—
Tap Roots, J. Street, 1942	Principal	Unsuitable for school library	Removal	—	4	—
Tea and Sympathy, R.W. Anderson, 1955	Parent	Homosexuality as a theme	Student was assigned other work	West	3	—
Teen Angel, S. Pilcer, 1978	Parent, Superintendent	The language was obscene, in poor taste, objectionable	Material removed from library	AR	1	—
Teen Days; a Book for Boys and Girls, F. Strain, 1946	Teachers	Caused students to become sexually aroused, explained reproductive system too frankly	Closed shelf	—	4	—
Tell Me How Long The Train's Been Gone, J. Baldwin, 1968	Parent, Principal	Inappropriate language	Book removed from classroom use	NH	2	—
Tell Me That You Love Me, Junie Moon, M. Kellogg, 1968	Parent	—	Student allowed another book selection	IL	2	—
—	—	—	—	MD	9	—
—	Parent	Sections of book inappropriate reading for children in 6th and 7th grade	Parent requested no further action after talking with the principal	MN	1	—
Ten Modern Chronological Short Stories	Parent	Certain selections dealt with death	Permitted to read alternate book	West	3	—

Title	Initiator	Reason	Action	State		No.		Notes
Ten North Frederick, J. O'Hara, 1955	Superintendent	—	Removal	—		4		—
The Terminal Man, M. Crichton, 1972	Teacher	Sexual overtones—computer and man	Denied	WA		1		—
**Test*, T. Thomas	Concerned Citizens	Against pornography and filth	—	LA		7		—
Testament, D. Morrell, 1975	Parent	Obscene language, profanity	Denied	OR		1		—
That Was Then, This Is Now, S. Hinton, 1971	Director of Instruction	The book lacked "literary merit," it demeaned policeman and advocated juvenile delinquency	Denied	CA		2		—
Them, J.C. Oates, 1969	Parent	Objected to opening scenes of violence and sex	Substitute reading	IL		1		—
Themes in Science Fiction; a Journey into Wonder, L. Kelley, 1972	Concerned Citizens	Against pornography and filth	—	LA		7		—
Themes in the One-Act Play, S. Cox, and R. Cox, 1971	Concerned Citizens	Against pornography and filth	—	LA		7		—
Then Again, Maybe I Won't; a Novel, J. Blume, 1971	Parent	Did not approve of some incidents described in the book	Material removed from library	TX		1		—
—	See *Deenie* entry					10		See *Deenie* entry
—	Principal	Explicit description of biological actions, not appropriate for students (7–9)	Removed from library	—		1		

continued

Title, author, publication date	Objector	Objection	Results	Place	Source, date of objection	Legal Case (if any)
—	Another teacher	References to "wet dreams" considered offensive	Denied	FL	1	—
—	Superintendent, School officials	They are "pervasively vulgar"	Removed from library shelves for 3 months, then reinstated	LA	11	—
And Then We Heard the Thunder, J. Killens, 1962	Parent	Language, situations	Remained	—	8	—
The Thin Red Line, J. Jones, 1962	Parent	Language used	—	WI	5	—
—	—		Not ordered	—	4	—
This Crowded Planet, M. Hyde, 1961	Teacher	Objected to title	Denied	—	4	—
This Perfect Day, I. Levin, 1970	Student, Library supervisor	Sex and foul language	—	Northeast	3	—
—	Parent	"Vulgar and obscene descriptions of sexual activities"	No disposition reached as yet	NY	2	—
The Three Billy Goats Gruff	Parents	It was "too violent for children"	Book retained	OR	11	—
365 Days, R. Glasser, 1971	Parent, school board	Obscene language	Removed by board, returned by federal district court; court ordered strict procedures for future challenges, forbade restricted shelves	ME	10	Sheek v. Baileyville School Committee 530 F Supp 679 (D. Maine 1982)

Title		Initiator	Reason	Action	State	No.
The Time Machine, an Invention, H.G. Wells, 1895	—	Clergyman	Religious—against Mormon belief	—	WA	1
Time to Love and A Time to Die, E. Remarque, 1954	—	Policeman	Passages concerning sex	Removed	WI	5
Tisha: the Story of a Young Teacher in the Alaska Wilderness, A. Purdy	—	Parent	The language (swearing) was offensive—religious reasons	Child didn't need to read the required story/book in class	WI	1
To Kill a Mockingbird, H. Lee	—	Teacher	—	—	WI	5
	—	Parent, Student, Teacher	Immoral, obscene trash, unsuitable, objected to rape scene, indecent, vulgar	—	—	4
	—	Parent	Racial situation and reference to rape	Remained	AZ	8
	—	Parent	Language and theme	Alternate selection	West	3
	—	School board	—	Censored	MN	9
	—	Parent	Objection to rapes	Denied	Il	1
	—	Parent	Used "damn"	Denied	AL	1
	—	Parent	Words used, "piss" was the objectionable word	Removed from library	PA	1
	—	Parent, Another teacher	Racial language, volatile, rape	Denied	OH	6
	—	Alderman	Racism and language	—	IL	11

continued

341

Title, author, publication date	Objector	Objection	Results	Place	Source, date of objection	Legal Case (if any)
To Sir, With Love, E. Braithwaite, 1959	Student	"What a superior bitch"—this language was objected to	Denied	PA	2	—
To Turn A Stone, T. Clymer, 1969	—			—	9	—
Tobacco Road, E. Caldwell, 1932	Principal	Language, situations	Removed	AZ	8	—
Too Late the Phalarope, A. Paton, 1953	Clergyman	For adults only		WI	5	—
	Superintendent		Removal	—	4	—
Tortilla Flat, J. Steinbeck, 1935	Principal, Parent	Not suitable	Removed	AZ	8	—
The Town, C. Richter, 1950	Librarian		Available	WI	5	—
	Librarian		Closed shelf		4	—
Track of the Cat, W. Clark, 1949	Parent	Word "whore" used several times, this in addition to paperback format assured parents that book is trash	Book still read	—	3	—
A Tree Grows in Brooklyn, B. Smith, 1947	—			WI	5	—
	Parent	Sexual relations, contained "trash and nasty words"	Denied	South	3	—

Title	Initiator	Objection	Action	Location	No.	Note
The Tribe That Lost Its Head, N. Monsarrat, 1959	Parent	—	Remained	WI	5	—
Trinity, L. Uris, 1976	Parent	Objectionable language	Denied	TX	1	—
Trout Fishing in America, R. Brautigan, 1967	See *The Abortion* entry	—	Censored	Anderson, CA	9, 10	See *The Abortion*
True, False, Or In Between, D. Hiatt, 1975	Board of Eucation	—	—	PA	9	—
Truth About Ghosts, Holzer	Parent	Language and description in witchcraft ceremony	—	South	3	—
Turkey Legs Thompson, J. McCord	Parent	Not appropriate for grade level—bad language	Material removed from library	WA	1	—
20 Best European Plays on the American Stage, J. Gassner, 1957	Parent, Church	—	—	WI	5	—
Two and the Town, H. Felsen, 1952	Teacher, Librarian	—	Removed	WI	5	—
	Board of Education	Children don't need to know about this subject	Removal	—	4	—
Two and Twenty; a Collection of Short Stories, R. Singleton, 1962	Parent	Objectionable reference to Negro race	Denied	—	4	—
Two Gentlemen of Verona, W. Shakespeare	Administrative assistant	Language	Removed from library	MD	1	—

continued

Title, author, publication date	Objector	Objection	Results	Place	Source, date of objection	Legal Case (if any)
The Ugly American, W. Lederer and E. Burdick, 1958	Teacher, Parents	Critical pictures of Americans abroad, immoral, obscene	—	WI	5	—
—	Parent	Filthy language and references to sex, profane and vile language	Denied	—	4	—
Ulysses, J. Joyce, 1968	Parent	"Use of obscenity"	Book removed from recommended list	NJ	2	—
The Uncle, M. Abrams, 1962	Parent, Librarian, Principal	Incidents and ideas relating to sex	Removal	—	4	—
Uncle, J. Markus, 1978	Parent	Explicit sex	Material removed from library	—	1	—
Uncle Tom's Cabin, H. Stowe, 1879	Students, Parents, Alderman	Because of "racism" and "language"	Removed from required reading list	Waukegan, IL	11	—
*Understanding Health	Parents, Church groups	It was "anti-Christian" and "pro-abortion"	Adopted the book	OH	11	—
—	Citizens for Decency in Public Schools	Because of "sex education applications of materials" and "lack of morality"	Retained book	KY	11	—
Understanding Sex; a Young Person's Guide, A. Guttmacher, 1970	Concerned Citizens	Against pornography and filth	Denied	LA	7	—
—	Former Teacher	Promotes sexual activity between adolescents	Denied	IA	1	—
Up in Seth's Room: A Love Story,	School librarian	Events not true to life—could be mis-	Placed on closed shelf	TN	1	—

Title/Author	Initiated by	Reason	Action	State	Incident no.	Notes
N. Mazer, 1979	—	leading and possibly damaging to a young girl	Book kept	NH	11	—
Up, Into the Singing Mountain, R. Llewellyn, 1960	Parents	Because of "sexual content"	Removed	AZ	8	—
Up the Down Staircase, B. Kaufman, 1964	Superintendent	Sex language	Denied	—	4	—
—	Principal	Team used by student	Removed from library	OK	2	—
The Upstairs Room, J. Reiss, 1972	Parent	—	Denied	PA	1	—
—	Parent	Language used felt to be offensive	Denied	—	1	—
U.S.A., J. Dos Passos, 1937	English Dept. Chairman	Unsuitable language and subject for juniors	Denied	—	4	—
Values Clarification, S. Simon, 1972	School board	See The Bell Jar entry		Warsaw, IN	9, 10	See The Bell Jar entry
Vanity Fair, W. Thackeray, 1847	Parent	Immoral behavior of character	Removed from classroom use	—	4	—
Venereal Disease: The Hidden Epidemic, Encyclopaedia Britannica, Ed. Corp, 1972	Parent	Part of the content was objectionable to a 7th-grade student's parent	—	IN	1	—
The View from Pompey's Head, H. Basso, 1954	Teacher	Ugliness, loose morals, etc.	Removal	—	4	—
Vision Quest, T. Davis, 1981	Parent	Because of language and sexual content	Book has not yet been returned	WI	11	—

continued

Title, author, publication date	Objector	Objection	Results	Place	Source, date of objection	Legal Case (if any)
Voices in Literature, I through IV, Cline, Mahoney, and Dzuik	—	—	Denied	South	2	—
The Vulgarians, R. Osborn, 1960	Teacher	—	Denied	CA	1	—
The Wall, J. Hersey, 1950	—	Adults only	—	WI	5	—
Walls, J. Daly	Student	Language and incidents	Removed from library	—	1	—
The Walls Came Tumbling Down, M. Ovington, 1969	Concerned Citizens	Against pornography and filth	—	LA	7	—
The Wanderers, R. Price, 1974	School board	Vulgar and obscene	Book removed from library; removal upheld by the courts	VT	10	Bicknell v. Vergennes Union High School Bd. of Directors, 475 F. Supp 615 (D. Vt. 1979), aff'd, 638 F.2d 438 (2nd Cir. 1980).
The Wanting Seed, A. Burgess, 1962	—	—	—	NY	12	—
The War on Villa Street; a Novel, H. Mazer, 1978	Parent	Language	Denied	NY	1	—
The Warriors, J. Jakes, 1977	Parent	Language and violence	Removed from classroom use	IL	1	—
War Year, J. Haldeman, 1972	Parent	Obscene language	Denied	MI	1	—

Title	Initiator	Objection	Action	State	No.
The Wasteland, T.S. Eliot, 1971	—	Adults only	Removal	WI	5
The Way It Spozed To Be, J. Herndon, 1965	Principal	"Dirty words"	Book placed on closed shelf	West	3
*A Way of Love, A Way of Life.	Media clerk	"Students would want to try what was described"	Material placed on closed shelf	FL	1
	School librarian	Didn't feel materials on homosexuality were necessary	Denied	CT	1
	Teacher, Parents	Homosexual content; book described as "filthy, rotten stuff"	Retained book but restricted to Sr. high students	AK	11
Way to Womanhood, W. Bauer and F.M. Bauer, 1965	Teacher	Outdated or misleading material	Material removed from library	MD	1
The Wayward Bus, J. Steinbeck, 1947	—	Adults only	Removal	WI	5
The Way West, A. Guthrie, Jr., 1949	—	Charges of obscenity and political ideas	Withdrawn from libraries	Amarillo, TX	17
Webster's New World Dictionary of the American Language—College Edition, 1959	Commissioner of Education	—	Removed from his list of recommendations	TX	9
Webster's Seventh New Collegiate Dictionary, 1972	Commissioner of Education	—	Removed from his list of recommendations	TX	9
Welcome to The Monkey House, K. Vonnegut, 1968	Parent	Sexual activity in the title story	Denied	—	2

continued

Title, author, publication date	Objector	Objection	Results	Place	Source, date of objection	Legal Case (if any)
—	—	—	—	MN	9	—
—	Principal, Assoc. Superintendent, parents, students	Literary garbage; condones killing off elderly people and free sex	Teacher dismissed; dismissal constituted an unwarranted invasion of her First Amendment right to academic freedom—court decision	AL	16	Parducci v. Rutland, 316 F. Supp. 352 (M.D. Ala. 1970).
West Side Story, L. Bernstein, 1958	Parent	Language	Denied	Northeast	3	—
—	Parent	Offensive language	Student allowed to leave classroom while material being studied	TX	1	—
—	Parent	Not suitable reading for her 9th grade son			1	—
What Is a Girl? What Is a Boy?, S. Waxman, 1976	See Deenie entry				10	See Deenie entry
What It's All About, N. Klein, 1975	Parent	Because of "profanity, nudity, and an excessive number of divorced people"	Book was kept	IA	11	—
What Made Me?, E. Hamilton, 1970	Concerned Citizens	Against pornography and filth		LA	7	—
What The Negro Can Do About Crime, J. Parker and A. Brownfeld, 1974	Concerned Citizens	Against pornography and filth		LA	7	—
When You Marry, E. Duvall and R. Hill, 1945	—	—	Reserved		4	—

Title	Complainant	Objection	Action	State		
Where Are the Children?, M. Clark, 1975	English Resource Teacher	Too much violence	Book removed from classroom use	OH	2	—
Where The Bright Lights Shine, A. Stallworth, 1977	Parent	Offensive language	Denied	AL	1	—
White Dog, R. Gary, 1970	Library	Obscene language	Book removed from library	TN	2	—
Who's Afraid of Virginia Woolf?, E. Albee, 1962	Parent, Principal	Language	Book removed from classroom use	Middle West	3	—
Who Shall Survive?, J. Moreno, 1931	Concerned Citizens	Against pornography and filth	—	LA	7	—
Why I Am Not a Christian, B. Russell, 1957	Concerned Citizens	Against pornography and filth	—	LA	7	—
Why Wait Until Marriage?, E. Duvall, 1965	Principal	"Somebody might think this title suggests premarital sex, I want to avoid controversy"	Book placed on closed shelf	IN	2	—
The Wild Boys, W. Burroughs, 1971	Concerned Citizens	Against pornography and filth	—	LA	7	—
Winesburg, Ohio, S. Anderson, 1919	Parent	Vulgarity	Remained	—	8	—
Wings of the Dove, H. James, 1902	Parent	Immorality	Removed	AZ	8	—
Winning, R. Brancato, 1977	Parent	Objectionable language—sexual innuendo	Material placed on closed shelf	IN	1	—

continued

Title, author, publication date	Objector	Objection	Results	Place	Source, date of objection	Legal Case (if any)
—	Parent	—	Material removed from recommended list	NY	1	—
—	Parent	Curse words in text when boy is in hospital, something about a "damn nurse"	Denied	NJ	1	—
Witchcraft: the Story of Man's Search for Supernatural Power, E. Maple, 1973	Parent	Witchcraft book—"was teaching her son to be a devil worshipper"	Denied	OH	1	—
Witchcraft and occult: any book on.	Clergyman, Student	Material was satanistic	Material placed on closed shelf	NY	1	—
Without Magnolias, B. Moon, 1949	Concerned Citizens	Against pornography and filth	—	LA	7	—
The Woman Who Was Poor, L. Bloy, 1939	—	Risk to student's morality	—	WI	5	—
*Women Are Fatal	Librarian	"Cheap"—not good for students	Removal	—	4	—
The Wonderful Story of How You Were Born, S. Gruenberg, 1952	Parent	Sex too vividly portrayed	Removal	—	4	—
The Wonderful Story of You, B. and S. Gruenberg, 1960	Parent	Sex too vividly portrayed	Removal	—	4	—
The Word, I. Wallace, 1972	Clergyman, Parent, Librarian	Explicit sex, filthy terms and implications	Removed from library	AR	2	—
Work Hard and You Shall Be Rewarded:	Parents	Obscene language and cartoons	Material placed on closed shelf	PA	1	—

Title	Complainant	Reason	Action	State		
Urban Folklore from the Paperwork Empire, A. Dundes, C. Pagter, 1975						
Working, S. Terkel, 1974	Parent	Too negative, objectionable language	Denied	CA	2	—
	—			WI	9	—
	Parent	Obscenities	Complainant did not follow through	MI	1	—
	School board members	Too "profane" for use in 7th- and 8th-grade classrooms	Book removed	AZ	11	—
The World According to Garp, J. Irving, 1978	Teacher	Sex, its obscenities and its use of explicit sex, high school students will miss the satire and dwell on the sex	Book removed from library	OH	6	—
The World of Delacroix, T. Prideaux, 1966	Clergyman	Pictures were obscene	Denied	AR	2	—
Worlds in the Making; Probes for Students of the Future, M. Dunstan, P. Garlan, 1970	Member of Board of Education	—	—	ND	1	—
World Geography Today, L. Durand and others, 1966	Patriotic group	Too little nationalism	—	WI	5	—
The World's Number One, Flat-Out, All Time Great Stock Car Racing Book, D. Bledsoe, 1974	Another teacher	Subject matter	Material removed from library	—	1	—

continued

Title, author, publication date	Objector	Objection	Results	Place	Source, date of objection	Legal Case (if any)
The Yage Letters, W. Burroughs & A. Ginsberg, 1964	See entry for *A Coney Island of the Mind* for Aurora, CO				9, 10	See *Coney Island* entry
Yearbook: a Novel, D. Marlow, 1977	Parent	Sexual content	Material removed from library	NY	1	—
The Yearling, M. Rawlings, 1938	Teacher	Unsuitable language	Denied	—	4	—
You!, S. Gordon, 1975	—	—	—	—	1	—
—	Parent	This is pornography	Material placed on closed shelf	TX	1	—
You and the Law, J. Archer, 1978	Parent	Material not suitable for this age group	Denied	—	1	—
You and Your Child, K.E. Moyer, 1974	—	—	—	—	1	—
You Never Knew Her As I Did, M. Hunter	—	—	—	NC	1	—
Young and Black in America, R.P. Alexander & J. Lester, eds. 1972	School board, parent	Vulgar and obscene language, sexually explicit, anti-religious sentiment	Book removed; after lawsuit was filed, book returned	MN	10	Antoinnette R. Maris v. Independent School District #728 Elk River, MN
The Young in Love, D. Brookman, 1962	Student, Teacher	Objectionable descriptions of scene	Removal	—	4	—
Youngblood Hawke, H. Wouk, 1962	Librarian	Too much sex in too plain terms	Not recommended	—	4	—

352

SELECTED BIBLIOGRAPHY

Baker, Robert K. and Ball, Sandra J. *Mass Media and Violence: A Staff Report to the National Commission on the Causes and Prevention of Violence.* Washington D.C.: National Commission on the Causes and Prevention of Violence, 1969.

Bamber, Chrissie. *Student and Teacher Absenteeism.* Bloomington, Indiana: Phi Delta Kappa Educational Foundation, 1979.

Barnes, Clive, intro. *The Report of the Commission on Obscenity and Pornography.* New York: Bantam Books, 1970.

Bartlett, Jonathan. *The First Amendment in a Free Society.* New York: Wilson, 1978.

Baugh, Albert C., *et al.*, eds. *A Literary History of England.* New York: Appleton-Century-Crofts, 1958.

Berninghausen, David K. *The Flight From Reason: Essays on Intellectual Freedom in the Academy, the Press, and the Library.* Chicago: American Library Association, 1975.

Blanshard, Paul. *The Right to Read; the Battle Against Censorship.* Boston: Beacon Press, 1956.

Blotner, Joseph. *Faulkner: A Biography.* New York: Random, 1979.

Bosmajian, Haig A. *The Language of Oppression.* Washington: Public Affairs Press, 1974.

Bradbury, Ray. *Fahrenheit 451.* New York: Ballantine, 1953; New York: Ballantine, Special Book Club Edition, March, 1976; Author's Afterword. New York: Ballantine, 1979.

Brown, E. F. *Library Services To The Disadvantaged.* Metuchen, NJ: Scarecrow Press, 1971.

Brucker, Herbert. *Freedom of Information.* New York: Macmillan, 1949.

Bryson, Joseph E., and Elizabeth W. Detty. *Censorship of Public School Library and Instructional Material.* Charlottesville, VA: The Michie Company, 1982.

Burress, Lee and Karolides, N., eds. *Celebrating Censored Books.* Wisconsin: Wisconsin Council of Teachers of English, 1985.

_____. *How Censorship Affects the School and Other Essays.* Racine, Wisconsin: Wisconsin Council of Teacher of English, 1984.

_____, and Jenkinson, Edward. *The Students' Right to Know.* Urbana, IL: National Council of Teachers of English, 1982.

353

354   SELECTED BIBLIOGRAPHY

Cambron, Nelda H. and McCarthy, Martha M. *Public School Law, Teachers'
   and Students' Rights.* Boston, Toronto: Allyn and Bacon, 1981.
Caravaglia, Jody. "The City to a Young Girl." From *Male and Female Under
   Eighteen.* New York: Avon Books, 1973.
Carlsen, G. Robert. *Books and the Teen-age Reader: A Guide for teachers,
   librarians, and parents.* New York: Bantam Books, 1967.
Cash, W. J. *The Mind of the South.* New York: Knopf, 1941.
Castagna, Edwin. "Censorship, Intellectual Freedom, and Libraries," in *Ad-
   vances in Librarianship,* ed. Melvin J. Voigt. Vol. II New York: Seminar
   Press, 1971.
Chambers, E. K. *The Elizabethan Stage.* London: Oxford, 1923.
Chandos, John. *To Deprave and Corrupt . . . Original Studies in the Nature
   and Definition of Obscenity.* New York: Association Press, 1962.
Cline, Victor B. *Where do You Draw the Line?* Provo, UT: Brigham Young
   University Press, 1974.
Clor, Harry M. *Obscenity and Public Morality; Censorship in a Liberal Society.*
   Chicago: University of Chicago Press, 1969.
Commager, Henry Steele. *The American Mind: An Interpretation of American
   Thought and Character Since the 1880's.* New Haven: Yale University
   Press, 1950.
Craig, Alec. *Suppressed Books.* Cleveland: World, 1963.
Daily, Jay Elwood. *The Anatomy of Censorship.* New York: M. Dekker, 1973.
Daniels, Walter M. *The Censorship of Books.* New York: Wilson, 1954.
Davis, James E., ed. *Dealing With Censorship.* Urbana, IL: National Council
   of Teachers of English, 1979.
DeGrazia, Edward. *Censorship Landmarks.* New York: Bowker, 1969.
Demac, Donna A. *Keeping America Un-Informed: Government Secrecy in the
   1980's.* New York: Pilgrim Press, 1984.
Donelson, Kenneth, ed. *The Students' Right to Read.* Urbana, IL: National
   Council of Teachers of English, 1972.
Downs, Robert B. *The First Freedom; Liberty and Justice in the World of Books
   and Reading.* Chicago: American Library Association, 1960.
Drury, Robert, and Ray, Kenneth D. *Principles of School Law.* New York:
   Appleton-Century-Crofts, 1965.
Duscha, Julius, and Fischer, Thomas. *The Campus Press: Freedom and Re-
   sponsibility.* Washington, D.C.: American Association of State Colleges
   and Universities, 1973.
Edwards, Newton. *The Courts and the Public Schools, the Legal Basis of School
   Organization and Administration.* Chicago: The University of Chicago
   Press, 1956.
*The Effects of Reading Huckleberry Finn on the Racial Attitudes of Ninth Grade
   Students.* A cooperative study of the State College, Pa. Area School
   District and The Forum on Black Affairs of the Pennsylvania State Uni-
   versity, Fall, 1983.
Ennis, James J. *Views on Censorship, Racine, Wisconsin.* Racine, WI: Racine
   Education Association, 1984.
Ernst, Morris L. and Schwartz, Alan U. *Censorship: The Search for the
   Obscene.* New York: Macmillan, 1964.

_____. *The First Freedom*. New York: Macmillan, 1946.

Estrin, Herman A. and Sanderson, Arthur M. *Freedom and Censorship of the College Press*. Dubuque, IA: W.C. Brown, 1966.

Fader, Daniel N. and Morton H. Shaevitz, *Hooked on Books*, New York: Berkley Medallion Books, 1966.

Fellman, David. *The Censorship of Books*. Madison: University of Wisconsin Press, 1957.

Fiske, Marjorie. *Book Selection and Censorship*. Berkeley and Los Angeles: University of California Press, 1959.

Frank, Jerome, and others. *Censorship and Freedom of Expression: Essays on Obscenity and the Law*. Chicago: Rand McNally, 1971.

Frank, John P. *Obscenity, the Law and the English Teacher*. Champaign, IL: National Council of Teachers of English, 1966.

Freedom of Information in the Market Place. The Freedom of Information Center. Fulton, MO: Ovid Bell, 1967.

Fryer, Peter. *Mrs. Grundy: Studies in English Prudery*. New York: London House and Maxwell, 1963.

Giacoma, Peter. "When Librarians Fight, The Media Responds." A mimeographed report, n.d.

Gillet, Charles R. *Burned Books; Neglected Chapters in British History and Literature*. New York: Columbia University Press, 1932.

Goldstein, Michael J. and Kant, Harold S. with Hartman, John J. *Pornography and Sexual Deviance*. Berkeley: University of California Press, 1973.

Goodman, Michael B. *Contemporary Literary Censorship: The Case History of Burrough's Naked Lunch*. Metuchen, NJ: Scarecrow Press, 1981.

Goodman, William R. Jr., and Price, James J.H. *Jerry Falwell, an Unauthorized Profile*. Virginia: Paris and Associates, 1981.

Graves, William B. *Readings in Public Opinion; Its Formation and Control*. New York: D. Appleton, 1928.

Gwynn, Minor J. *Curriculum Principles and Social Trends*. New York: Macmillan, 1960.

Haiman, Franklyn S. *Speech and Law in a Free Society*. Chicago: University of Chicago Press, 1981.

Haney, Robert W. *Comstockery in America, Patterns of Censorship and Control*. Boston: Beacon Press, 1960.

Hart, Harold H., intro. *Censorship For and Against*. New York: Hart Publishing Co., 1971.

Hatfield, Wilbur. *An Experience Curriculum in English*. Urbana, Illinois, NCTE, 1935.

Hentoff, Nat. *The First Freedom: The Tumultuous History of Free Speech in America*. New York: Delacorte Press, 1980.

Hocking, William E. *Freedom of the Press, A Framework of Principle*. Chicago: University of Chicago Press, 1947.

Hollingshead, August B. *Elmtown's Youth: The Impact of Social Class on Adolescence*. New York: Wiley, 1949.

Hoyt, Olga and Edwin. *Censorship in America*. New York: Seabury Press, 1970.

Hudon, Edward G. *Freedom of Speech and Press in America.* Washington, D.C.: Public Affairs Press, 1963.

Hutchinson, E. R. *Tropic of Cancer on Trial; A Case History of Censorship.* New York: Grove Press, 1968.

Hyde, H. Montgomery. *A History of Pornography.* New York: Farrar, Straus, and Giroux, 1965.

Iabedz, Leopold. *Solzhenitsyn: A Documentary Record.* New York: Harper and Row, 1971.

Jenkinson, Edward B. *Censors in the Classroom, The Mind Benders.* Carbondale: University of Southern Illinois Press, 1979.

Johnsen, Julia E. *Freedom of Speech.* New York: Wilson, 1936.

Kanawha County, West Virginia, A Textbook Study in Cultural Conflict. Washington, D.C.: National Education Association Teacher Rights Division, 1975.

Konvitz, Milton R. *First Amendment Freedoms, Selected Cases on Freedom of Religion, Speech, Press, Assembly.* New York: Cornell University Press, 1963.

Krieghbaum, Hillier. *Pressures on the Press.* New York: Crowell, 1972.

Kronhausen, Eberhard and Phyllis. *Pornography and the Law.* New York: Ballantine Books, 1959.

Krug, Judith F. *The Librarian as a One Man Band: Intellectual Freedom in a World of Censors.* Wisconsin: Wisconsin Public Library Video Program, 1975.

Kuh, Richard H. *Foolish Figleaves? Pornography In and Out of Court.* New York: Macmillan, 1967.

LaBrant, Lou. "The Use of the Communication Media." From *The Guinea Pigs After Twenty Years,* ed. Margaret Willis. Columbus: Ohio State University Press, 1961.

Lancourt, J.E. *Confront or Concede: The Alinsky Citizen-Action Organization.* tion. Lexington, Mass.: Lexington Books, 1979.

Lawrence, David H. and Miller, Henry. *Pornography and Obscenity, Handbook for Censors.* Michigan City, IN: Fridtjof-Karla Publications, 1958.

Levine, Alan H. and Cary, Eve. *Rights of Students.* New York: Avon Books, 1977.

Lynch, James J. and Evans, Bertrand. *High School English Textbooks: A Critical Examination.* Boston: Little, Brown, 1963.

McClellan, Grant S., ed. *Censorship in the United States.* New York: Wilson, 1967.

McCormick, John and MacInnes, Mairi. *Versions of Censorship.* New York: Doubleday, 1962.

McKeon, Richard; Merton, Robert and Gellhorn, Walter. *The Freedom to Read: Perspective and Program.* New York: Bowker, 1957.

McShean, Gordon. *Running a Message Parlor: A Librarian's Medium-rare Memoir About Censorship.* Palo Alto, CA: Ramparts Press, 1977.

Marnell, William H. *The Right to Know; Media and the Common Good.* New York: Seabury Press, 1973.

Marshall, Robert A. *The History of Our Schools.* Washington, D.C.: National Council For The Social Studies, 1962.

Martindale, Joanna, ed. *English Humanism: Wyatt to Cowley*. London: Croom Helm, 1985.

Medvedev, Zhores A. *Ten Years After Ivan Denisovich*. New York: Knopf, 1973.

Miller, Perry, ed. *The American Puritans: Their Prose and Poetry*. New York: Doubleday, 1956.

Miller, Perry and Johnson, Thomas H., eds. *The Puritans*. New York, American Book Co., 1938.

Moon, Eric. *Book Selection and Censorship in the Sixties*. New York: Bowker, 1969.

Moscato, Michael, and Leslie LeBlanc. *The United States of America v. one Book Entitled Ulysses by James Joyce*. Frederick, MD, University Publications of America, 1984.

Mosier, R. *Profile of the Freshman Class of the University of Wisconsin, Stevens Point*. Unpublished report, UWSP, 1981.

Moyer, Wayne A. and Mayer, William V. *A Consumer's Guide to Biology Textbooks, 1985*. Washington, D.C.: People For The American Way, 1985.

Nelson, Jack and Roberts, Gene Jr. *The Censors and the Schools*. Boston: Little, Brown, 1963.

Nikitenko, Aleksandr. *The Diary of a Russian Censor*. Amherst: University of Massachusetts Press, 1975.

Norwick, Kenneth P. *Lobbying for Freedom: A Citizen's Guide to Fighting Censorship at the State Level*. New York: St. Martin's Press, 1975.

Oboler, Eli M. *The Fear of the Word: Censorship and Sex*. Metuchen, NJ: Scarecrow Press, 1974.

Official Censorship in the Polish People's Republic. Ann Arbor, MI: North American Study Center for Polish Affairs, 1978.

O'Neil, Robert M. *Classrooms in the Crossfire*. Bloomington: Indiana University Press, 1981.

Parker, Barbara and Weiss, Stefanie. *Protecting the Freedom to Learn: A Citizen's Guide*. Washington, D.C.: People for the American Way, 1983.

Paul, James and Schwartz, Murray. *Federal Censorship; Obscenity in the Mail*. New York: Free Press of Glencoe, 1961.

Pell, Eve. *Big Chill: How the Reagan Administration, Corporate America and Religious Conservatives are Subverting Free Speech and the Public's Right to Know*. Boston: Beacon Press, 1984.

Perrin, Noel. *Dr. Bowdler's Legacy*. New York: Atheneum Press, 1969.

Perry, Stuart. *The Indecent Publications Tribunal, A Social Experiment*. Christchurch: Whitecombe and Tombs, 1965.

Phelps, Edith M. *Civil Liberty*. New York: H. W. Wilson, 1927.

Pooley, Robert C. and Williams, R. D. *The Teaching of English in Wisconsin*. Madison: University of Wisconsin Press, 1948.

Rationales for Commonly Challenged Taught Books. Connecticut Council of Teachers of English, *Connecticut English Journal*, 15:1 (1983): Entire issue.

Reading Explosion, New York: International Paper, 1962.

Rembar, Charles. *The End of Obscenity, The Trials of Lady Chatterley, Tropic of Cancer, and Fanny Hill*. New York: Random House, 1968.

Remmlein, Madaline Kinter. *School Law*. New York: McGraw-Hill, 1950.

Report of the Select Committee on Pornographic Materials. House of Representatives, 82nd Congress, Union Calendar No. 797, House Report No. 2010. Hereafter referred to as the Gathings Committee Report, United States Government Printing Office, 1952.

Riegel, Oscar W. *Mobilizing for Chaos; The Story of the New Propaganda*. New York: Arno Press, 1934.

Rubin, David. *The Rights of Teachers*. New York: Discus Books, 1972.

Schroeder, T. A. *Free Speech Bibliography*. New York: B. Franklin, 1969.

Simmel, Ernest, ed. *Anti-Semitism*. New York: International Universities Press, 1946.

Slate Report. Urbana, IL. NCTE, (2, No. 8 November, 1977), pp. 1–3.

Smith, Dora. *Evaluating Instruction in Secondary School English*. Chicago: NCTE, 1941.

Stahlschmidt, Agnes D. "The Iowa Plan Revisited: Ten Years Later." A presentation at the 71st Annual Convention, NCTE, Boston, November 20, 1981.

Strauss, Leo. *Persecution and the Art of Writing*. Glencoe, IL: Free Press, 1952.

Summers, Robert E. *Wartime Censorship of Press and Radio*. New York: Wilson, 1942.

Sussman, Alan and Guggenheim, Martin. *The Rights of Parents*. New York: Avon, 1980.

Swayze, Harold. *Political Control of Literature in the USSR, 1946–1959*. Cambridge: Harvard University Press, 1962.

Thomas, Donald. *A Long Time Burning; The History of Literary Censorship in England*. New York: Praeger, 1969.

Trager, Robert. *Student Press Rights*. Urbana, IL: Journalism Education Association, 1976.

Warner, William Lloyd, with Wilfred C. Bailey and others, *Democracy in Jonesville*. New York: Harpers, 1964.

Widmer, Kingsley and Eleanor. *Literary Censorship: Principles, Cases, Problems*. San Francisco: Wadsworth, 1961.

Wittenberg, Philip. *The Protection of Literary Property*. Boston: Writer, Inc., 1968.

Woods, L.B. *A Decade of Censorship in America: The Threat to Classrooms and Libraries, 1966–1975*. Metuchen, NJ: Scarecrow Press, 1979.

Woodworth, Mary L. *The Young Adult and Intellectual Freedom*. Madison: Publications Committee, Library School, University of Wisc., 1977.

Whorfian Thesis or Linguistic Relativity

Alexander, Hubert G. *Language and Thinking*. Princeton, NJ: Van Nostrand, 1967.

Bourne, L. E., Jr., Elkstrand, B. R. and Dominowski, R. *The Psychology of Thinking*. Englewood Cliffs, NJ: Prentice-Hall, 1971.

Brown, Roger. *Psycholinguistics*. New York: Free Press, 1970.

Devito, Joseph. *The Psychology of Speech and Language*. New York: Random House, 1970.

Eisenson, Jon J., Auer, Jeffery and Irwin, John. *The Psychology of Communication*. New York: Appleton-Century Crofts, 1963.

Foss, Donald J., and Hakes, David T. *Psycholinguistics, an Introduction to the Psychology of Language*. Englewood Cliffs, NJ: Prentice-Hall, 1978.

Fromkin, Victoria, and Rodman, Robert. *An Introduction to Language*. New York: Holt, Rinehart and Winston, 1974.

Hayes, Curtis W., Ornstein, Jacob and Gage, William W. *ABC's of Language and Linguistics*. Silver Spring, MD: Institute of Modern Language, Inc., 1977.

Hormann, Hans. *Psycholinguistics, An Introduction to Research and Theory*. New York: Springer-Verlag, 1971.

Houston, Susan H. *A Survey of Psycholinguistics*. The Hague: Morton, 1972.

Johnson, Donald M. *A Systematic Introduction to the Psychology of Thinking*. New York: Harper and Row, 1972.

————. *The Psychology of Thought and Judgement*. New York: Harper and Brothers, 1955.

Johnson, Wendell. *People in Quandaries*. New York: Harper and Row, 1946.

Kess, Joseph F. *Psycholinguistics, Introductory Perspectives*. New York: Academic Press, 1976.

Laffal, Julius. *Pathological and Normal Language*. New York: Atherton Press, 1965.

Lambert, Wallace E. *Language, Psychology, and Culture*. Stanford, CA: Stanford University Press, 1972.

Lyons, John. *Language and Linguistics*. Cambridge, MA: Cambridge University Press, 1981.

Marchomara, John. *Names for Things*. Cambridge, MA: M.I.T. Press, 1982.

Markel, Norman N. *Psycholinguistics: An Introduction to the Study of Speech and Personality*. Homewood, IL: The Dorsey Press, 1969.

Miller, Casey and Swift, Kate. *The Handbook of Nonsexist Writing*. New York: Barnes and Noble, 1981.

Miller, George A. and Johnson-Laird, Philip N. *Language and Perception*. Cambridge, MA: Belknap Press, 1976.

Poole, Millicent E. *Social Class and Language Utilization at the Tertiary Level*. St. Lucia, Queensland: University of Queensland Press, 1976.

Potter, Simeon. *Language in the Modern World*. Baltimore: Penguin, 1960.

Rieber, R. W., ed. *Psychology of Language and Thought*. New York: Plenum Press, 1980.

Sapir, Edward. *Language*. New York: Harcourt, Brace and World, 1949.

Taylor, Insup. *Introduction to Psycholinguistics*. New York: Holt, Rinehart, and Winston, 1976.

Terwilliger, Robert F. *Meaning and Mind, A Study in the Psychology of Language*. New York: Oxford, 1968.

Whatmough, Joshua. *Language, A Modern Synthesis*. New York: St. Martin's Press, 1956.

Whitehurst, Grover J. and Zimmerman, Barry, ed., *The Functions of Language and Cognition*. New York: Academic Press, Inc. 1979.

Whorf, Benjamin Lee. *Language, Thought, and Reality.* Cambridge, MA: M.I.T. Press, 1966.

Dissertations

Ahrens, Nyla H. *Censorship and the Teacher of English: A Questionnaire Survey of a Selected Sample of Secondary School Teachers of English.* Ph.D. dissertation, Columbia University, 1965.
Ball, Catherine. *Language and Censorship.* M.A., University of Wisconsin Stevens Point, 1979.
Baxter, James Edward. *Selection and Censorship of Public School Textbooks: A Descriptive Study.* Ed.D. dissertation, University of Southern Mississippi, 1964.
Douma, Rollin. *Book Selection Policies, Book Complaint Policies, and Censorship in Selected Michigan Public High Schools.* Ph.D., dissertation, University of Michigan, 1973.
Eakin, Mary Lida. *Censorship in Public High School Libraries.* M.A., Columbia University, 1948.
Farley, John J. *Book Censorship in the Senior High School Libraries of Nassau County, New York.* Ph.D., dissertation, New York University, 1964.
Goode, Don J. *A Study of Values and Attitudes in a Textbook Controversy in Kanawha County, West Virginia: An Overt Act of Opposition to Schools. Schools.* Ph.D. dissertation, Michigan State University, 1984.
Katz, John Stuart. *Controversial Novels and Censorship in the Schools.* Ph.D. dissertation, Harvard University, 1967.
Knudson, Rozanne R. *Censorship in English Programs of California's Junior Colleges.* Ph.D. dissertation, Stanford University, 1967.
Last, Ellen. *Textbook Selection or Censorship: An Analysis of The Complaints Filed in Relation to Three Major Literature Series Proposed for Adoption in Texas in 1978.* Ph.D. dissertation, University of Texas, 1984.
Peterson, Carolyn McCannon. *A Study of Censorship Affecting the Secondary School English Literature Teachers.* Ed.D. dissertation, Temple University, 1975.
Piasecki, Frank. *Norma and Mel Gabler: The Development and Causes of Their Involvement Concerning the Curriculum Appropriateness of School Textbook Content.* Ph.D. dissertation, North Texas State University, 1983.
Stephens, Ronald W. *A Study of U.S. Supreme Court Decisions from 1970 to 1977.* Ph.D. dissertation, University of Nebraska, 1978.
Symula, James F. *Censorship of High School Literature.* Ed.D. dissertation, State University of New York, 1969.
Thaxton, Carlton J. *An Analysis of the 24 Novels Published Between 1947 and 1957 Which Were Reported in Either the 'Censorship Bulletin' or the 'Newsletter on Intellectual Freedom' as Having Been Banned or Blacklisted in the U.S. in the Years 1956 or 1957.* M.A., Florida State University, 1958.
Torke, Keith. *Sex Education Books, Censorship, and Colorado High School*

Libraries: A Survey. Ed.D. dissertation, University of Northern Colorado, 1975.

Weathersby, Dorothy T. *Censorship of Literature Textbooks in Tennessee; A Study of the Commission, Publishers, Teachers, and Textbooks.* Ed.D. dissertation, University of Tennessee, 1975.

Woods, L. B. *Censorship Involving Educational Institutions in the United States, 1966–1975.* Ph.D. dissertation, University of Texas. 1977.

Vandertie, Susan Ann Frisque. *Censorship in the Elementary Schools of the CESA Nine District of Wisconsin.* A Seminar Paper Submitted in Partial Fulfillment of the Requirements for the Degree of Master of Arts Library Science at University of Wisconsin–Oshkosh, June, 1980.

Publications by the School Critics

Carle, Erica. *The Hate Factory.* Elm Grove, WI: Education Service Council, 1978.

———. *Give Us the Young.* Elm Grove, WI: Echoes and Shadows, 1981.

Duncan, Homer. *The Religion of Secular Humanism and the Public Schools.* Lubbock, TX: MC International Publications, n.d.

Duncan, Homer. *Secular Humanism: The Most Dangerous Religion in America.* Lubbock, TX: Christian Focus on Government, 1979.

Gabler, Mel and Norma with James C. Hefley. *What Are They Teaching Our Children?* Wheaton, IL: Victor Books, 1985.

Hefley, James C. *Textbooks on Trial.* Wheaton, IL: Victor Books, 1976.

LaHaye, Tim. *The Battle for the Mind.* Old Tappan, NJ: Fleming H. Revell, 1980.

McGraw, Onalee. *Secular Humanism and the Schools: The Issue Whose Time Has Come.* Washington, D.C.: The Heritage Foundation, 1976.

Morris, Barbara M. *Change Agents in the Schools.* Upland, CA: Barbara M. Morris, 1979.

———. *Why Are You Losing Your Children?* Upland, CA: Barbara M. Morris, 1976.

Morris, Henry M. *What is Creation Science?* San Diego, CA: Creation Life Publishers, 1982.

Thomas, Cal. *Book Burning.* Westchester, IL: Crossway Books, 1983.

Periodical Articles

Arons, S. "Book Burning in the Heartland," *Educational Digest,* 45 (September 1979) 11–14.

Asheim, Lester. "Not Censorship but Selection," *Wilson Library Bulletin* 28 (September 1953) 63–67.

———. "Selection and Censorship: A Reappraisal," *Wilson Library Bulletin,* 58 (November 1983) 180–184.

Booth, W. C. "Censorship and the Values of Fiction," *English Journal,* 53 (March 1964) 155–64.

Bradley, Julia T. "Censoring The School Library: Do Students have the Right to Read?" *Connecticut Law Review*, 10 (Spring 1978) 747–771.

Bullough, Vern L. "Myths About Teenage Pregnancy," *Free Inquiry*, 1 (Summer 1981) 12–13.

Campbell, Patricia B. and Wirtenberg, Jeana. "How Books Influence Children: What the Research Shows," CIBC *Bulletin*, 11:6 (1980) 3.

Carlsen, G. Robert, "The Magic of Bringing Young People to Books," *Wilson Library Bulletin*, 33 (October 1958) 134–137.

Davidow, Robert P. Commentary: "Secular Humanism as an Established Religion, A Response to Whitehead and Conlon," *Texas Tech Law Review*, 11 (1979) 51ff.

Donelson, Kenneth, "Censorship in the 1970's: Some Ways to Handle it When It Comes (and It Will)," *English Journal* 63 (Feb. 1974) 47–51.

Donelson, Kenneth L. "What To Do When the Censor Comes," *Elementary English*, 51 (March 1974) 403.

Egerton, J. "Can We Save Our Schools? Yes, But There Isn't Much Time," *The Progressive*, 46 (March 1982) 26.

Fitzgerald, Frances. "A Disagreement in Baileyville." *New Yorker*, 59 (January 16, 1984) 47–90.

Gray, D. "Books: A Review Essay, The 1978 Consumer Research Study on Reading and Book Purchasing," *College English*, 42 (November 1980) 283–292.

Howells, W.D., "What Should Girls Read?" *Harpers Bazaar*, 36 (November 1902) 956–60.

Jenkinson, Edward B. "Tell City Rejects The Secular Humanism Charge," *Focus: Teaching English Language Arts*, 11 (Fall 1984) 35–42.

Kamhi, Michelle M., "Building Bridges Instead of Walls: An Anti-censorship Effort That Worked," *Education Week*, 2, No. 4 (Sept. 29, 1982), pp. 20,ff.

Kemble, Eugenia, "The Test Score Decline: Much More Than Meets The Eye," *American Education*, 1 (October 1977) 26–27.

Kreitlow, B.W., Martin, C. and Gustrom, M.A. "Adults without Diplomas," *The Wisconsin Vocational Educator*, 5 (Summer 1981) 12–13.

Lettis, R., "Book is Not for Burning," *Journal of Reading*, 21 (November 1977) 106–8.

Logan, Maureen F., "Star-Crossed Platonic Lovers or Bowdler Redux," *English Journal*, 74 (Jan. 1985) 53–55.

McNearney, C.L., "Kanawha County Textbook Controversy," *Religious Education*, 70 (September 1975) 519–40.

Meyer, Howard, "Neutralism Isn't Neutral," CIBC, *Bulletin*, 11 (1980) 12–13.

Moore, Robert V., "From Rags to Witches: Stereotypes, Distortions and Anti-Humanism In Fairy Tales," CIBC *Bulletin*, 6 (1975) 1.

Moyer, Wayne A., "How Texas Rewrote Your Textbooks," *The Science Teacher*, 52, no. 1 (Jan. 1985), 23–27.

Niccolai, Frances R., "The Right to Read and School Library Censorship," *Journal of Law & Education*, 10 (January 1981) 23–36.

O'Neil, Robert M., "Libraries and the First Amendment," *Cincinnati Law Review*, 42 (No. 2, 1973) 209–52.

Orleans, Jeffrey H., "What Johnny Can't Read: 'First Amendment Rights' in the Classroom," *Journal of Law & Education*, 10, No. 1 (January 1981) 1–15.

Pahringer, Herald Price and Brown, Michael J., "The Rise and Fall of Roth—A Critique of the Recent Supreme Court Obscenity Decisions," *Kentucky Law Journal* 62 (No. 3, 1973–74) 731–768.

Parker, Barbara. "The Gablers of Longview, Texas," *The American School Board Journal*, 166 (June 1979) 21.

Seitz, William J., "Recent Cases," *Cincinnati Law Review*, 45 (1976) 701–709.

Smith, W., "Book Burning: Drake, N.D.," *Progressive*, 38 (July 1974) 11–12.

Taylor, Kenneth, "Are School Censorship Cases Really Increasing?" *School Library Media Quarterly*, 14 (Fall, 1982) 351ff.

"U.S. Journal: Kanawha County, West Virginia," *New Yorker*, 50 (September 30, 1974) 119–127.

Wise, H. D., "Book Burning and Bannings," *Intellect*, 102 (April 1974) 417.

INDEX

Bell, William B. 146
Bell for Adano, A 55
Bellevue Is a State of Mind 66
Berkley, June 170
Best Short Stories of Negro Writers 46
Bettelheim, Bruno 132
Beyond the Horizon 95
Bible, The 17, 55, 90, 105, 138, 152, 153, 160, 162, 163, 183
Big Sky, The 44, 55
Bill of Rights of the American Library Association 176
"Birthmark, The" 117
Births per thousand 84
Black, Justice Hugo 37
Black Boy 46
Black Elk Speaks 178
Black Like Me 12, 39, 44, 45, 55, 66, 124, 180
Black literature 133, 134
Black Literature for High School Students 8
Black Voices 133
Black writers 102, 103
Blacks 112
Bless the Beasts and Children 45
Bloody Tenent of Persecution, The 136
Blume, Judy 8, 65
Bok, Judge Curtis 2, 187
Book Burning 32, 62, 83, 176
Book burning 10, 11
Books as food 181
Books as poison 179, 181
Books for You: A Booklist for Senior High Students 8
Books Our Children Read 109
Born Free 55
Bosone, Reva Beck 1
Bourne, L.E., Jr. 129
Bowdler, Harriet 89
Bowdler, Dr. Thomas 89
Bowdlerization 108
Bradbury, Ray 104
Bradford, William 102
Bradley, Julia T. 14
Brave New World 40, 55, 66, 180
Bridge of San Luis Rey 55
British and Western Literature 108
Brooklyn Public Library 40
Brown, Roger 130
Bryson, Joseph 51
Bryson and Detty report 4, 49
Buck, Pearl 111